H

DATE DUE

vos to

all His

Jan. 2001

History, Design AND THE End OF TIME

GOD'S PLAN FOR THE WORLD

BRENT KINMAN

BROADMAN
&HOLMAN
PUBLISHERS

NASHVILLE, TENNESSEE

0–8054–2138–6

Published by Broadman & Holman Publishers, Nashville, Tennessee

Dewey Decimal Classification: 236
Subject Heading: ESCHATOLOGY

Library of Congress Cataloging-in-Publication Data

Kinman, Brent.
    History, design, and the end of time : God's plan for the world / Brent Kinman.
        p.   cm.
    Includes bibliographical references and indexes.
    ISBN 0–8054–2138–6 (pbk.)
    1. End of the world. I. Title.

BT876.K49 2000
236'.9—dc21

00–21681

1 2 3 4 5 04 03 02 01 00

CONTENTS

✧

✧

Acknowledgments

✧

✧ *Chapter Nine* ✧

✧

✧

✧

✧

✧

✧

Acknowledgments

This book would not have seen the light of day without the editors' willingness to publish a book dealing with a controversial topic. I am grateful to them, and especially to Len Goss, for making it possible to reach a wider audience with my ideas than would otherwise have been the case.

S. Craig Glickman and Davey Naugle have been especially influential in shaping my thinking about eschatology and worldview. I am grateful for their friendship and tutelage. Though neither will endorse all I've written here, each has had a profound and positive effect on me.

To my mentors at Dallas Theological Seminary and Cambridge University I offer warm thanks for the training I received—a training from which I continue to profit in preaching, writing, and living.

Several esteemed friends and colleagues read and offered valuable criticism on portions of the manuscript: the Reverend Dr. Anthony Bash, vicar of All Saints in North Ferriby, England, and originator of the Cambridge New Testament Seminar's (unofficial) handkerchief award; Captain James Roy, USAF; David E. Sheely of i2; Craig Smith, of Castle Rock, Colorado; and Professor Frank Thielman, Beeson Divinity School, Birmingham, Alabama. I have benefited from several conversations with my good friend, Dr. Stephen Meyer of Whitworth College in Spokane, Washington, who stimulated my thinking about design in creation. The elders at my church have graciously allowed me to write while carrying on the duties of a pastor. Though many people have assisted in various ways with the preparation of this book, I am responsible for the final product, mistakes and all.

My "girls"—my wife Sharon and my daughter Michele—are a constant source of love, entertainment, and blessing. "All my love, forever."

Finally, this book is dedicated to my parents, Leroy and Shirley Kinman. Each was raised during the Depression—Mom in rural Montana and Dad in rural Kentucky. They possess a depth of character that has blessed their family, friends, and many, many others over the years. Their confidence and affirmation of me has been a constant and unique source of inspiration. My debt to them, who taught me about compassion and honesty and second chances, is vast and unrepayable.

INTRODUCTION

From the first century A.D. until now, Christians have looked forward to the return of Jesus—his "second coming." Indeed, this expectation originated with Jesus himself (Mark 13:26; Luke 17:24; John 14:3). By the fourth century it was viewed as so basic to the fabric of Christian doctrine that it was incorporated into the first creed agreed upon by the church as a whole, the Nicene Creed.[1] In spite of this, modern Christians who entertain a lively hope of Jesus' return have often been regarded with suspicion, and some have been thought downright kooky. Some of the criticism has been justified, especially when people set a date for the return—something Jesus himself warned against (Mark 13:32–33). In other instances the criticism stems not from a proper understanding of the Scriptures or from a cautious approach to them, but rather from a disbelief of them. People simply do not believe Jesus will return; hence, any talk of it is misguided.

This book is written from the perspective of faith: I believe Jesus died for sins, rose bodily from the grave, and will come again. Furthermore, I do not think it misguided to contemplate and look forward to his second coming. After all, it is worth remembering that Christians throughout the ages have looked for Jesus' return because *he* urged us to do so. Not only is he the major source of teaching about the end (Mark 13; Matt. 24–25; Luke 17:20–37; 21:5–36), but in these passages and elsewhere he identifies for his followers some signs of the end to look for.

In principle, we should expect Jesus to have spoken reliably about his return. Why? Because he spoke reliably on other matters. For example, he warned that his followers would suffer for their allegiance to him (Mark 13:11–13). In various places throughout the centuries, Christians have suffered terribly. Similarly, his observations about the inherent depravity of human nature have been confirmed in human experience (Matt. 15:19). He predicted his own death and resurrection (Matt. 20:17–19), and they came to pass.[2] There is a reason therefore, to take seriously Jesus' teaching about the last days. On the topic of the "end times," Jesus' words, concentrated in Matthew 24, Mark 13, and Luke 21, imply that readers can recognize the phenomena—the "signs of the times"—he refers to. The goal for us, obviously, is to understand what Jesus and the Scriptures meant and not to supplant their meaning with our own plausible but errant speculations. But this, of course, is the task and responsibility of the interpreter in dealing with every passage in Scripture.

The Theory

It is the contention of this book that there is a detectable design to history, one imposed by God, the Lord of history and maker of the universe. History is directed toward the realization of a purpose or goal set by God. In this book I will examine what that goal might be according to Scripture. Further, I will argue it is possible to have an idea of how near it is to being met by knowing what the Scriptures say about the end times and comparing that with what has or is happening in the modern world.

From one point of view, it is hardly new for me or any other Christian to think the last days are upon us. After all, according to the Scriptures the "last days" commenced with the advent, ministry, death, and Resurrection of Jesus (Heb. 1:2). In that respect, every Christian from Jesus' day to the present could justifiably say, "I'm living in the last days." Moreover, it is obvious that by definition we are nearer the return of Jesus now than we were twenty or two hundred years ago (every second that ticks by brings us another second closer to his coming). But the thesis of the book implies that not only can we say Jesus' return is near by definition, but that it is both possible and biblically warranted to think there are certain recognizable preconditions that must be met before he returns. It is the aim of this book to spell out for the reader *what* those conditions are and the extent to which they already have been met.

Certain people, perhaps even some of my friends, will by now have begun to roll their eyes. Many who eagerly look forward to Jesus' return are disquieted by any talk of his coming soon or of the signs of the times. They have heard it all before (and often from people with strange theological axes to grind). On this point their caution is warranted. Looking back over the history of the Christian church, we observe that Christians from virtually every generation have felt as though they were living in the last days. History has proved them wrong, or at least wrong in the sense of equating last days with the soon coming of Jesus. And if Christians of this generation repeat the earlier claim, what is to prevent thoughtful people from being skeptical? On the other hand, if Jesus will come again, it is obvious that one generation will be vindicated when it says, "Jesus is coming soon."

Talk of the end times is also disquieting to some people because they think Scripture does not speak specifically enough for us to know when the end is near. For them, the Bible simply does not give information about the end time with sufficient precision for anyone to claim with confidence that it is near. In their minds such talk actually distracts believers from the larger and clearer concerns of day-to-day living (e.g., "seek first God's kingdom and his righteousness"). As for this, it seems to me that Scripture speaks more clearly than some imagine, yet it is for the reader to judge how convincing the arguments in the following pages are.

Why This Book?

There are several reasons for this book, but two are most important. The first has to do with what is *missing* from most popularly written books on the end times: a presentation of major end-times themes set in the context of the larger message of Scripture as a whole. Popular books on the subject tend to have a "dispensational"[3] point of view, one that emphasizes things such as the timing of the rapture, the role of Russia and Europe in the end times, and the dangers of a one-world government. These are interesting topics, but Scripture says little about them. On the other hand, the Scripture has quite a lot to say about the second coming and the judgment of God. This is not to say I won't address some of these popular issues, but I hope to do so while maintaining a sense of proportion—stressing what Scripture stresses and noting the distinction between what Scripture says or implies and personal conjecture.

A second reason for this book has to do with its theological perspective. If we were to survey Christianity as a whole, we would find that the theological perspective known as "dispensationalism" is a minority position. Yet most popular books about eschatology are written by dispensationalists. One could say that dispensationalists sell books like there is no tomorrow, a view that some of them come near to advancing! On the other hand, those who are not dispensationalists tend not to write books on eschatology for popular audiences. While one cannot question the fact that God has used dispensationalists powerfully to advance the cause of the gospel, some features of their view of the end times are worth calling into question. It seemed to me that the time might be right to address a popular audience from something other than a dispensational perspective, while affirming the integrity of Scripture and, where appropriate, offering criticism in an irenic tone.

The Audiences for This Book

I write this book with different audiences in mind, and in doing so I realize that at points each audience will suffer.

I write first of all for Christians who are interested in what the Bible says about the last days. Included in this group—and it is large—are various subgroups. Among them are Christians who are relatively uninformed about the topic but interested in it, given their belief that the Bible is a reliable guide to truth. Their curiosity about the end may have been further aroused by the hoopla surrounding the end of the millennium.

I also write to a second group of Christians, a group predisposed to agree with my conclusions (if not my means of arriving at them). These are people who think it highly plausible, if not likely, that we are living in the last days and that the Bible speaks specifically to our generation. My hope is to bolster their faith, both by affirming the view that the last days are upon us and by challenging some aspects of current thought and teaching on the subject.

A third group of Christians addressed is those who are evangelical in orientation but have thus far steered clear of what they regard as merely sensationalistic talk about the end times. This avoidance might be based on the way "the last days" has been presented to them or because they simply have a different theological background, one that tends not to speak much of "the end times." They might never have seen a plausible argument in favor of the idea that the last days are near. Many presentations of popular eschatology are clearly sensationalistic and can be criticized for using the Bible unfairly or wrongly. Some emphasize minor points while losing the big picture. I hope to provoke this third group to fresh and thoughtful contemplation of the subject.

Finally, the book is written to others who are curious about what, if anything, the Bible says about modern-day events. In a world where people look to everything from crystals to the stars in hopes of knowing the future and understanding the meaning of life, it is not surprising that some will wonder what the Bible teaches. I hope this presentation will be sufficiently clear and interesting to encourage them to grapple not only with the biblical teaching about the future but also with the larger issues of the existence of God and the claims of Jesus of Nazareth.

This is not a book for scholars. It is not exhaustive in scope or detail. Endnotes are kept to a minimum: this might annoy those who want a more thorough discussion of various issues; it will be a great relief to those who want to read an uncluttered book. The endnotes typically contain references and detail certain arguments best omitted from the body of the work. The reader can read the book without pausing to look up every note. Throughout the work I will, on occasion, cite the Hebrew or Greek of a particular biblical passage; in the body of the text, I will transliterate the original words; in the endnotes the original words will be cited.

Popular Thinking about "the End Times"[4]

Hal Lindsey's best-selling book *The Late, Great Planet Earth* appeared in 1969, at the height of the Cold War. Since then almost thirty million copies have been sold, and the dispensational view of eschatology promoted in the book has carried the day in popular thinking about "the end times." Before Lindsey, study of end times had focused on those themes most emphasized in the Bible: the return of Jesus, the resurrection of the dead, the judgment of God, and the appearance of a new heaven and earth.[5] With Lindsey, the timing of the rapture and the identification of the signs of the times came to occupy center stage.

It is hard to gauge the extent to which the Cold War influenced thinking about the end times. Certainly the proliferation of thermonuclear weapons and belligerence between the United States and the Soviet Union gave rise to concerns about a world-ending conflagration, even among nonreligious people. The division of world powers into two camps fostered an "us versus them" mentality—even a "good versus evil" mentality. However, as the Cold War and the threat of nuclear obliteration waned in the late 1980s and early 1990s, so did the frenzied popular interest in eschatology.

The Gulf War in early 1991 reawakened interest in the themes. The War captured popular attention for several reasons: it was broadcast almost continually on the major television news networks; it provided the public a glimpse of the sophisticated technologies involved in today's warfare; it involved the Middle East—a source of precious oil for Europe, Japan, and the United States; it threatened to involve Israel, a fact that aroused the passions of Jews worldwide and those Christians who think Israel is the key to biblical prophecy; and it involved the sinister figure of Saddam Hussein—to some minds the incarnation of evil.

The coming of the new millennium has increased speculation about the end of the world, or at least the end of the world as we know it. This speculation is likely to continue. One has only to visit a local bookstore or surf the Internet to discover dozens upon dozens of books, websites, and the like devoted to the topic.[6] This book is added to the mix in hopes of encouraging the faith of those who believe. It is also offered in hopes of challenging those who do not yet believe to consider thoughtfully what the Bible has to say about the future—and about *their* future.

Part 1
Background

That Which Lies Behind

✦ Chapter One ✦

HISTORY
BY DESIGN

✦

A s I was writing this book, two high school students in Littleton, Colorado, a town about twenty miles from my home, walked into their school and savagely attacked classmates and teachers before turning their guns on themselves, leaving fifteen people dead. The nation was stunned by this profoundly sad, but unfortunately not unique, turn of events. No satisfactory explanation emerged to account for these senseless and wicked acts.

The modern person who spends a few minutes reading a daily newspaper may well conclude that history is happenstance: a series of events—some interesting, some banal, some interconnected (but more often disconnected)—which in the end give no evidence of thought or design. History appears to involve madness rather than method. It could be regarded as a long and dismal tale of competing peoples and individuals, some known and many more anonymous; as Shakespeare's Macbeth put it, "A tale told by an idiot, full of sound and fury, signifying nothing." As understandable and widespread as this conclusion might be, there are reasons to doubt it.

This book, though limited in scope, is at once a work of theology and apologetics, with emphasis on the former. As theology, it deals primarily with the Bible and its teaching about God's acts in history—both history past and, if I may take some liberty with the word, history yet to come. While Christians over the years have generally agreed on the most important aspects of their faith, they have disagreed on many details concerning "the last days." I hope to shed new light on the topic and to do so by presenting the biblical hope for the future in the context of its larger message and themes. As apologetic (the word refers to a reasoned defense of a particular point of view), the book seeks to argue that the theology presented is not merely biblical but also *true*. Christians who think the Bible is revelation from God already believe this, but others may wonder why or how Christians can respond to the apparent chaos of history with faith. I wish to argue that history is *teleological*; that is, it is goal-oriented; it is designed. This in turn presupposes a goal-setter, a planner, a designer.

Detecting Design

There is something of a revolution afoot in the physical sciences, particularly biology. For over a century Darwinism (evolutionism), with its stress on time and chance as essential ingredients for advantageous mutations and the evolution of new species, has dominated scientific thought. Over the years various objections have been raised against the philosophical-theological presuppositions of the theory; profound and well-articulated scientific objections have also emerged, most recently in Michael Behe's *Darwin's Black Box.*[1] Behe concludes his work with the observation that even the simplest cell life is, in fact, incredibly complex; and this complexity, in turn, suggests design.

One of the most important elements of Behe's book is the concept of "irreducible complexity." Behe defines irreducible complexity as "a single system composed of several well-matched, interacting parts that contribute to the basic function, wherein the removal of any one of the parts causes the system to effectively cease functioning."[2] He illustrates irreducible complexity with the example of a common mousetrap. It has five parts (platform, spring, hammer, catch and holding bar), all of which must be present, properly sized, organized, and working for the trap to achieve its aim: catching a mouse. If any of the parts is missing or malfunctioning or out of place, the trap will not work. Since these parts must not only be present but also present in the right size, shape, and order, it is reasonable to infer that the trap is a product of design. According to Behe, a cell is like a mousetrap, though far more intricate.

For Behe a living cell is composed of several irreducibly complex parts, such as the mitochondria, the nucleus, and the plasma membrane, each of which must be in place and operate smoothly for the cell to function properly—for there to be life. If one of the parts is missing or malfunctioning, life cannot continue. Furthermore, he concludes that these cell parts could not have organized themselves to perform their roles. They could not have "pulled themselves up by their own bootstraps"; rather, they had to have been acted upon by something outside themselves. The irreducible complexity of cell life points to an Organizer, a Designer.

For Christians, the Designer responsible for the right size, shape, and order of the parts in the smallest cells is God. But if the smallest cells point to a Designer, what about history and the universe as a whole? How might Behe's theory about the design and irreducible complexity of cells—things invisible to the naked eye—have any relevance and validity for our evaluation of history? Can we say that history consists of well-designed events that ultimately achieve a purpose? How would we test such a theory?

The philosopher of science William Dembski has convincingly argued that to infer design "we must establish two things—complexity and specification."[3] He adds, "Complexity ensures that the object in question is not so simple that it can readily be explained by chance. Specification ensures that this object exhibits the type of pattern that is the trademark of intelligence."[4]

To say that history has a design, we would need to demonstrate that it possesses the same two traits. Dembski notes that detecting design often occurs not in advance of events but subsequent to them. We could infer design in history were we to detect complexity and specification in it *after* the fact. We might infer design if, for example, we noticed that the last names of American presidents have proceeded in alphabetical order the past two hundred years, along with the names of their wives. Such a phenomenon would demand our attention, because we know from experience that such an ordering of names could hardly be coincidental. During the preparation of this book, my young daughter Michele would occasionally seek to emulate me by typing on a home computer. She would hunch over the keyboard, ponder it for a moment, then type furiously. Her line of text would typically look like this:

kjfiuf8uwiknmekyithgtbjklsida8rhmtrtrhgtgjksks

It was complex—to be sure—but it was not sufficiently specific to qualify as the product of intelligent design. She did not really know how to type. Despite her studious gaze and enthusiasm for the work, she was not typing. If, on the other hand, her text had read, "Dear Mom and Dad, Because I'm interested in attending college, may I suggest that you begin to set aside massive amounts of money in a specially designated account for the purpose of future tuition payments?," I would conclude that she either possessed or had access to someone with intelligence enough to produce a sensible line of typed text. The presence of complexity and specification allows us to infer design. Dembski employs the example of the code-breaking utilized by intelligence agencies. They collect raw data, then analyze them to discover whether or not a discernible code is present. Could a "code" be present in history? Would its presence enable us to infer design in history?

The Bible claims to be the Word of God (Deut. 4:1–2; Ps. 119; 2 Tim. 3:16–17). In it the Creator and Master of the universe reveals his character, his acts in history, and his plans for the world. The Bible reveals something of the design of history and the character of the Designer. Contrary to the modern mentality that produces bumper stickers to the effect that "stuff happens," Christians affirm that a loving God is responsible for the orchestration of history. This does not mean that life and history are simple or easily explained in all their particulars. Far from it. But it does mean that mankind is neither alone nor in complete control—control belongs, ultimately, to God.

One of the ways his sovereignty over history is displayed is through the phenomenon of prophecy-fulfillment. An important question for this study is: How might prophecy-fulfillment be related to the notion of irreducible complexity and design in history? Part 1 of this book deals with the past. In it I hope to show that God's control over history is revealed through creation, the history of Israel, and the life of Jesus. Many features of Israel's history and Jesus' life are related to the concept of prophecy-fulfillment, so that God's control over the life of a nation and the life of an individual are strongly asserted and his design for history as a whole is implied.

In Part 2 we consider the present and the future. We ask whether or not Scripture gives any clear indication of how God will act in the future and if we can discover more specifically when he will do so. The presumption here is that if in the past God spoke about future events which have already come to pass, it is reasonable to believe that his other pronouncements about the more distant future are equally reliable.

During the preparation of this book, my wife and I contracted to build a house. It was nicely designed—hence it involved complexity and specification. After signing a contract, we waited as the earth was excavated, piers were drilled, a foundation poured. This was followed by the delivery of various building materials. Next came the framing of the house. Before the project began, I was rather ignorant of all it involved. Without knowing better, I thought, *We'll be in the house soon.* After all, we had the land, the materials, the workmen, and a blueprint. What I failed to appreciate was the extent to which a prescribed order of construction had to be followed. Certain things could be built only after certain other things were already in place. Inevitably, there were delays between steps. Obviously, a house is not built when enough lumber for three bedrooms and a garage is dumped on a construction site. Similarly, the framing of a house only means that it is on the way to completion—but it's far from being ready for occupation. It's not enough for the raw materials to be present; there must be a design; and the design itself might involve many complex steps before it is completed.

The biblical picture of the end likewise involves complexity and specification. The "last days" involve many different elements—some of which occur only at the end; others of which are almost commonplace. For events in our world to be recognized as part of a biblically predicted end-times scenario, they must appear in conjunction with other predicted events. For example, if "earthquakes and famines" are part of the end-times scenario, the mere fact that we are experiencing "earthquakes and famines" does not necessarily mean that we are living in the end times because in the biblical end-times scenario these things take place in the context of other, related events. Without a proper context for the events, we cannot say whether they belong to the Bible's picture of the last days.

One purpose of this book is to understand clearly what God's design for history is, then—to the extent possible—relate these findings to contemporary events and developments. In chapters 5 to 7 I will identify what these events (or "parts") are and indicate the extent to which they are, or are not, present in the modern world. It is (or will be) obvious that not all the parts are in place; it will be equally obvious, I think, that many of them are and that those not present could fall into place on relatively short notice.

Prophecy and Fulfillment

The labels *prophecy* and *prophetic* apply to certain individuals, biblical passages, and whole books from the Bible. *Prophecy* is the term given to inspired utterances from God that seem typically to contain affirmations of God's love, warnings to individuals and nations to change behavior lest God's judgment fall, and, on occasion, predictions of destruction and/or restoration. Many people, however, assume that if a biblical book or text is prophecy or prophetic, it is also *predictive*. Indeed, when we speak of prophecy we normally think of "prophetic foretelling." Strictly speaking, the terms *prophecy* and *prediction* are not always interchangeable. For example, Old Testament prophets often predicted, but it was just as common for them simply to *preach* without forecasting the future. Nevertheless, for the purposes of this book, these terms will be used as synonyms unless noted otherwise.

It has been observed that much of the Old Testament was predictive at the time of its composition. The prophecies of Scripture are used to warn God's people and others of God's displeasure and the need to repent (lest judgment come). They are also used to comfort God's people by offering a message of hope or consolation, often to people in the midst of great suffering. But either use would be in vain if God were not the Lord of history and thus able to effect judgment or salvation. It's easy enough to forecast the future—a visit to the supermarket newsstand will unearth books and tabloids in which psychics and the like claim to do just that. But it's another thing to forecast accurately, to get it right. Being able to foretell the future was an important dimension of Old Testament prophecy. Indeed, a crucial test for the trustworthiness of prophets in the Old Testament was whether their predictions came to pass. Moses wrote to the Israelites:

> You may say in your heart, "How shall we know the word which the LORD has not spoken?" When a prophet speaks in the name of the LORD, if the thing does not come about or come true, that is the thing which the LORD has not spoken. The prophet has spoken it presumptuously; you shall not be afraid of him (Deut. 18:21–22).

Old Testament prophets spoke about the future with authority and certainty because the Designer of history had revealed it to them. The Bible is the story of God's acts in history—a story that speaks with equal certainty of events in the past and events in the future.

But it's not enough simply to read the Bible and assume that its prophecies apply directly to modern events—they might or might not. Effort is required on the part of the reader not merely to read, but to interpret correctly. I will not attempt to lay out an entire method of interpretation. There are good books by reputable scholars for that.[5] But because the vexing issue of interpreting prophecy is so relevant to this study, it does require further explanation here.

In reading the Old and New Testaments, it is relatively easy to determine when a prophet is predicting. His words are typically introduced with a formula like "behold, the days are coming . . .," or he employs a future-tense grammatical construction to convey his thoughts (e.g., Jer. 23:5; Amos 4:2; Acts 13:11).

What is not always so easy to determine is when and how a prophecy has been fulfilled. Prophetic fulfillments do not all happen the same way. There is not always a neat, one-to-one correspondence between a prophecy and its fulfillment. Biblical scholars use various labels to describe the relationship between a prophecy (or foretelling) and its fulfillment(s). We can classify most instances of prophetic fulfillment in the following three ways: patterned fulfillment, plenary fulfillment, and partial fulfillment.[6]

PATTERNED FULFILLMENT

The names da Vinci, van Gogh, and Picasso are as famous as the art they produced. But for any given piece of their artwork to be valuable, other terms must apply: genuine, authentic. A painting is valuable if it is authentic, and it is authentic if it is identifiable. But how are fakes distinguished from the real? Typically, painters identify their work in two ways: first, by the signature of the artist and, second, by the pattern of the brush stroke on the canvas. For obvious reasons the latter is regarded as more reliable than the former.

If we think of history as a canvas, and the Old Testament as a landscape depicting the work of God, we note that there are patterns in the way God works. He is the Creator and Lord of history. He promises something, and he does it. He works according to divine plan, not human expectation (for example, he chooses the humble but rejects the proud). He is Lord over history, and he works through history.

From earliest days Christians have viewed themselves and their faith as the ultimate fulfillment of Old Testament promises. But how do we know that the same God is at work in both Old and New Testaments? One way to know is to recognize how the Old Testament patterns of God's work are repeated in the New. These patterns show God's unmistakable signature and stroke on the canvas of history.

Jesus' miraculous conception and birth are not isolated events in history; rather, they are part of the ongoing story of salvation, and they take place in accordance with a divinely revealed pattern. The Gospel of Matthew connects Jesus' birth with a prophecy from Isaiah, "the virgin will be with child and will give birth to a son, and they will call him Immanuel—which means, 'God with us' " (Isa. 7:14 = Matt. 1:23 NIV). Did the prophet Isaiah, writing about seven hundred years before the events of Matthew 1, predict Jesus' virgin birth? If not, why does Matthew apply Isaiah's words to Jesus' birth and what does this say about the way Matthew quotes the Old Testament?

Some interpreters believe the words of Isaiah are a prediction of Jesus' birth and had little or no relevance to Isaiah and the people of his day. Is this likely? What did the words of Isaiah mean in their original setting?

According to Isaiah, two kings went up to wage war against Jerusalem and its king, Ahaz, but they were stymied in their attempt to conquer them (v. 1). Through Isaiah the prophet, God told Ahaz not to be alarmed by the assault against the city because it would not succeed (vv. 3–7). God then announced a sign to confirm the prophecy to the king: a child, whose mother would call him "Immanuel," would be born, and before he reached the age of knowing good and evil, the land of the two Aramaean kings would be deserted (vv. 7:10–16). Further, even though Jerusalem would be spared assault by two relatively minor kings, it would not escape the wrath of the Assyrians (vv. 17–25). The child, in other words, is God's sign that he is in control of the nations and will act both to spare and to judge Jerusalem.

The Hebrew word translated "virgin" in 7:14 (*alma*) is found just a handful of times in the Old Testament and is translated elsewhere as "maiden" (Gen. 24:43; Ps. 68:25; Prov. 30:19; Song of Sol. 1:3) and "girl" (Exod. 2:8). In Song of Solomon 6:8 the "virgins" (*almoth*) are set apart from the queens and concubines, strengthening the notion that the term relates not only to age but also to sexual inexperience. In general, the term *alma* denotes a young woman who, to be sure, according to the morality of the day, was presumed to be a virgin. The most important thing for Isaiah, however, is not the sexual status of the young woman involved but the fact that the birth of her son would be a sign to Ahaz and those near him (the "you" in verse 14 is plural, and explained further in verse 17 as "you and . . . your people and . . . the house of your father").

In other words, for the prophet's words about the young woman to be fulfilled, the child's birth would have to be *known to Ahaz*. To consider the words of Isaiah as related only to the virgin birth of Jesus, then, is improbable, for Ahaz never would have gotten the sign promised him by God. It is likely, on the other hand, that the words of Isaiah were fulfilled in Isaiah's day either through the birth of a son to the prophetess mentioned in Isaiah 8:3 or to an unnamed virgin known to Isaiah and the king.[7]

Ultimately, however, Matthew took the words of Isaiah and applied them to Jesus. There is, in other words, more than one fulfillment of the prophecy.[8] For Matthew there was no question about the sexual status of Jesus' mother, Mary: she was a virgin whose child was miraculously conceived through the Holy Spirit (this is mentioned twice, Matt. 1:18, 20).

When viewed against the background of Isaiah's prophecy, Matthew's birth story indicates two things: (1) Jesus' birth is miraculous, for Mary is a virgin, and Jesus is conceived by the Holy Spirit; (2) the virgin birth is a sign that the God of Isaiah and the rest of the prophets is once again at work in the story of Jesus.

How, then, did Matthew use the Old Testament? Did he cite a well-known prediction about a coming virgin-born Messiah? No. Rather, he applied the prophecy of Isaiah's day to Jesus: just as the birth of a child named Immanuel in Isaiah's day was a sign that God was in control of the nations and would deliver Israel from its oppressors, so for Matthew, Jesus' miraculous virgin birth was a sign that God remained in control of the nations and would deliver his people from their oppressors; in particular, he would deliver them from the greatest burden of all—their sins.[9]

There are other examples of New Testament writers indicating that Old Testament prophecies were "fulfilled" by Jesus, even when these prophecies had apparently been fulfilled prior to Jesus. The thrust of these "patterned fulfillments" is that the God who had acted and revealed himself in the life and history of Israel was now, in a familiar way, at work in Jesus. This "patterned fulfillment" is commonplace in the New Testament. But it is only one kind of prophecy-fulfillment motif.

PLENARY FULFILLMENT

We have already seen how Matthew depicted Jesus as fulfilling a Scripture by replicating in his life the pattern of God's working in the Old Testament. It is interesting to discover that alongside the "patterned fulfillment" previously noted in Matthew 1 we see a "plenary fulfillment" in Matthew 2. By "plenary fulfillment" I mean a fulfillment that is complete, entire, and unqualified. There is a direct correspondence between what was predicted and what happened.

In Matthew 2 the magi from the east traveled to Jerusalem to locate the newly born king of the Jews. It was only natural for them to assume the king would be in Jerusalem, the historic capital of Israel (they were unaware that Jesus and his parents were in Bethlehem, about seven miles outside Jerusalem). Upon arrival they made inquiry about the new king's whereabouts (Matt. 2:1–2). Although King Herod seemed unaware of Jesus' birth, he turned to the Jewish experts in Scripture to ask where the king would be born. They recalled the ancient prophecy of Micah 5:2 (Matt. 2:4–7). In

Bethlehem, they said, the king would be born. Directed by the prophetic Scriptures, the magi went to Bethlehem to honor Jesus.

The gospel of Matthew describes how the magi came to visit Jesus in Bethlehem. The Gospel of Luke, however, narrates the story of how Jesus and his parents ended up in Bethlehem. According to Luke 1:26–27 and 2:4, Joseph and Mary were residents of Galilee, the northern territory (Bethlehem was in the southern territory, Judea). At some point in Mary's pregnancy, Joseph was required to return to his ancestral city, Bethlehem, by a decree of Caesar (Luke 2:1). In other words, his journey southward to Bethlehem is initiated by imperial decree. He dutifully obeys the decree and takes Mary along with him. There is no hint or suggestion that the young couple went to Bethlehem of their own accord in order to (self)fulfill Micah's prophecy. Indeed, the hardship of travel, particularly for a woman who was nearly full-term in her pregnancy, would argue otherwise. Furthermore, God did not direct them to Bethlehem by a dream, an angel, or some other form of special revelation. Rather, we see God orchestrating history and using a decree by the polytheistic Roman emperor Augustus to achieve his own ends.

From these few verses in Matthew and Luke two general observations can be made. First, Matthew gives the impression that "the chief priests and scribes" pointed to Micah's prediction without hesitation. That is to say, among those familiar with the Scriptures it was understood that the birthplace of a coming king had been foretold and, importantly, that it awaited fulfillment.[10] God had revealed his plans through this prophetic Scripture, and the promise was uniquely fulfilled by Jesus.

Second, as was true for our example of "patterned fulfillment" (noted above), the prophecy of Micah and its fulfillment by Jesus demonstrate that the God who revealed his will and power so frequently in the Old Testament was also at work in Jesus—and had impressed on him the stamp of divine authenticity.[11]

PARTIAL FULFILLMENT

Some biblical prophecies that get applied to Jesus are fulfilled once ("plenary" fulfillment), others more than once ("patterned" fulfillment). There obviously remain those that have yet to be fulfilled at all (the second coming of Jesus, for example). But alongside "patterned" and "plenary" fulfillments stand another type: prophecies that have been *partially* fulfilled. A particularly striking example of this is found in the book of Zechariah, written in the sixth century B.C.

Zechariah 9 promised God's judgment on the nations around Israel (vv. 1–8), God's salvation for Jerusalem (vv. 9–10) and God's further blessing of the nation (vv. 11–17). At the outset of the second section, verses 9 and 10, we find the famous prophecy regarding the coming of Israel's king to Jerusalem and the promise that his coming will be accompanied by God's intervention to bring peace to Jerusalem and the nations and his rule to the earth.

In the New Testament both Matthew and John cite Zechariah's prophecy in describing Jesus' coming to Jerusalem on a colt at his so-called "triumphal entry" (Matt. 21:5; John 12:15). In each Gospel the action described is introduced by a comment to the effect that Jesus' entry to the city was in accordance with Scripture. However, it is clear that in the case of Jesus' coming only part of Zechariah's prophecy finds fulfillment: the king comes as foretold, but rather than inaugurating peace for Jerusalem and the nations, his advent spells doom for Jerusalem because the city does not receive him properly (see especially Luke 19:41–44). With respect to Jesus' life, Zechariah's prophecy is only partially fulfilled; the time of God's bringing peace to Jerusalem and the nations awaits complete fulfillment. Nevertheless, to the extent the prophecy is fulfilled by Jesus, it suggests that his life unfolds according to the divine plan; hence, God's control over history is once again affirmed.

The phenomenon of prophecy-fulfillment—whether it be patterned, plenary, or partial—points to God's control over history. Beyond this, however, we can also look to the Scriptures to learn more about the character of God and his original intention for the world.

In the Beginning . . .

Virtually every facet of human existence is affected by our answer to the question, "Where did I, we, and the universe come from?"[12] Are we the by-product of matter plus time plus chance, or are we the handiwork of a Creator? This is not the place to offer an extended defense of theism or of Christianity; there are plenty of good books for that.[13] But it is worth noting that no self-respecting atheist could speak in one breath the words *history* and *design*. Design implies intelligence, and as applied to the universe, super-intelligence. The atheist or materialist must view creation as accidental and mankind as the most complex accident of all. Far-reaching consequences emerge from this view of the world.

If the materialists are correct and there is no God, there is no absolute source of truth and morality; there can be no virtue. We don't praise the character and virtue of a person for winning the lottery (he/she simply won by chance); neither, if the materialists are correct, should we praise or dignify mankind which just happens to be at the top of the evolutionary heap. The atheist is "ethically challenged," not because he or she is an inherently unethical person, but because there is no authoritative foundation for his or her ethics. And while there is no lack of moral indignation among atheists, particularly those in the fields of education, law, and politics when the causes they treasure are criticized or threatened, they seem not to recognize that they have no coherent rational basis for their pronouncements on what is good, valuable, and worthwhile.[14]

I saw this firsthand in a conversation with a fellow student in England. He was interesting: a Jew, a rabbi, and an atheist. One evening he was speaking out in favor of moral relativism. I objected. He insisted. I asked whether he supported the embargo against South Africa in protest of its racial policy of apartheid, whether he thought it was "right." He clearly understood where the conversation was headed and quickly said, "I don't say it's *right*— but I support it because it achieves an outcome I desire." I was put off, then decided to be as rude as he was outrageous. I commented, "A few years ago what I call a wicked man killed almost six million of your people. Was he morally wrong, or do you simply wish he had done otherwise? Mind you, you can't really express moral outrage at his actions if you don't regard them as fundamentally and absolutely wrong."

His face flushed with anger as he commented on my dirty little argument—while steadfastly refusing to label Hitler's atrocities "evil." It was interesting to note that he left our conversation to play Ping-Pong (he was an accomplished player), and during the course of one game insisted that he had won a point by appealing to the rules of the game. While unwilling to admit the existence of any moral absolutes in conversation, he was quick to appeal to the rules of the game as absolute when it came to Ping-Pong. His philosophical commitments wrecked his morality—at least some of it! The thoroughgoing New Ager fares no better than the materialist when it comes to ethics, for if everything that exists is a manifestation or embodiment of god, who's to say that mankind is more divine, dignified, and valuable than the platypus?[15]

Nevertheless, this book is mainly concerned with God's design in history and, as a consequence, with presenting a biblical view of the world. Because the biblical view of the end of the world is fundamentally connected to its beginning, it is necessary to look briefly at the Genesis creation story. The biblical picture of the origin of the world and mankind stands in stark contrast to the one painted by naturalistic evolutionary scientists and New Age religions. In the biblical account we learn how the omnipotent Lord of the universe weds himself to the earth and mankind via creation; we see the royal dignity he bestows on mankind and the lofty purpose for which mankind was created.

The book of Genesis was originally compiled by Moses and was addressed first of all to those Israelites whom God had led out of Egypt in order to establish them in the promised land.[16] Genesis is not the only book from antiquity to deal with the question of beginnings. Most ancient cultures had legends that described how the world came to be. In Egyptian legend there were several gods who exercised authority in a particular local sphere of the universe. A nightly conflict was waged between the serpentine forces of darkness and chaos and the forces of light and order; creation was sustained by the repeated, hard-won victories of the sun god. The Canaanites (those people who inhabited the "promised land" [= Canaan] before Moses led the Jews there) also had many gods. For them the founding and establishment of the cosmos was the result of brutal conflict between the gods.[17]

The creation account of Genesis 1 through 3 painted a very different picture of the origin of the world than the one the descendants of Abraham, Isaac, and Jacob would have heard in Egypt or among the peoples living in the promised land before the Jews' return from Egypt. The biblical account emphasizes the power of the true God not simply over one small aspect of the world but over all creation! Like some other ancient creation accounts, the primeval world of Genesis 1:2 is shrouded in darkness and chaos. Yet in what follows, rather than wrestling with a serpent or fighting in hand-to-hand combat with an enemy, God merely speaks a word, and the world is made (Gen. 1:3, 6, 9, 11, 14, 20, 24). The contrast with other creation narratives is striking, for in Genesis God's control is absolute; his will is exercised without challenge; his speaking is responsible for all creation. His command that something be done—be it the creation of the earth or the appearance of plant life—is matched with the refrain "and it was so" (Gen. 1:7, 9, 11, 15, 24). Additionally, the acts of creation are infused with moral dignity, for God repeatedly calls them "good" (Gen. 1:4, 10, 12, 18, 21, 25). As described in Genesis, the process of God creating not only highlights his power, it also displays his wisdom, for there is order to the creation. On the first three days the universe is "prepared," on the next three it is "populated":

Preparation (days 1–3)	Population (days 4–6)
light made, light and darkness separated (day 1; vv. 3–5)	lights fill heaven; sun, moon, and stars made (day 4; vv. 14–19)
heavens and skies separated from waters (day 2; vv. 6–8)	life emerges to fill the skies and the waters (day 5; vv. 20–23)
dry land separated from the waters, vegetation appears (day 3; vv. 9–13)	living creatures of every kind appear on dry land (day 6; vv. 24–31)

The climax of this beautiful account is the story of mankind's creation (Gen. 1:26–28). It is clearly the most extraordinary feature of this already extraordinary account. It says:

> Then God said, "Let Us make man in Our image, according to Our likeness; and let them rule over the fish of the sea and over the birds of the sky and over the cattle and over all the earth, and over every creeping thing that creeps on the earth." And God created man in His own image, in the image of God He created him; male and female He created them. And God blessed them; and God said to them, "Be fruitful and multiply, and fill the earth, and subdue it; and rule over the fish of the sea and over the birds of the sky, and over every living thing that moves on the earth."

In the context of Genesis 1, several items in the story of man's creation alert the reader that something special is happening. For example, whereas the creation of most things simply involved God saying "Let there be . . . ," the creation of man is preceded by slightly different wording. The phrase "Let Us make . . ." (v. 26) indicates deliberation or contemplation: it's as if God pauses to consider more carefully what he is about to do. Nowhere else in the creation account do we find this kind of pause.[18] In addition, mankind is uniquely created to have a special and direct relationship to God: they (male and female) are made in the "image" and "likeness" of God (v. 27). These concepts are basic to a biblical view of what it is to be a human being. What do they mean?

The Hebrew word translated "image" in Genesis 1 (*tselem*) is found sixteen times in the Old Testament. It frequently refers to the images or idols of pagan gods (Num. 33:52; 1 Sam. 6:5, 11; 2 Kings 11:18; Ezek. 7:20; 16:17; Amos 5:26). A similar term is found in extrabiblical literature from the ancient Near East, and there it also typically refers to concrete, three-dimensional representations of gods or kings.[19] So what are we to make of mankind's identification as the "image" of God?

There seem to be three essential aspects to the identification. First, there is the concept of *relationship*. It is clear in context that mankind was to have a personal relationship with God and one another. God "walks and talks" with them, and the rest of the Bible is the story of this loving God taking active measures to re-establish the relationship so horribly broken by sin. Second, there is the notion of *representation*. In the ancient Near East the images of gods or kings were not the gods or kings themselves, but they represented them. For example, the image situated in a temple did not mean the god was literally there but that he was present by virtue of his image. Similarly, a king might erect a statue or image in a conquered land "to signify his real, though not his physical, presence there."[20] This notion of representation was taken so seriously that insulting the image was tantamount to insulting the divine or human person it represented. Interestingly, in the literature of Egypt it was the king who was said to be God's image. This is worth noting since Moses, who compiled Genesis, was originally from Egypt. In contrast to Egypt, where only the king had such dignity, in the Bible there is a democratization of the concept in that *all* people, both men and women, are made in God's image.

Mankind is created to represent God. How might they do that? We are given a hint in Genesis 1:26—mankind is to represent God by "ruling" over the earth and all that is in it (the mandate is restated in verse 28). In other words, mankind is to carry on the work of "ruling" the earth that God has begun. God molded the creation to make it usable, beautiful, and good. Mankind was to represent God on earth, we may surmise, by engaging in similar activities.

Our human instincts to create and achieve are God-given and abiding ones. In Genesis 2 man is given the responsibility of tending the garden and naming the animals. From agriculture to art, mankind has created. Mankind has propagated, as well, increasing its number and, as a result, its rule. As image-bearers, mankind was to stand as a testament to the power, wisdom, and goodness of the God who created it. The greatness and wisdom and power of God were to be reflected through the work of his "image" and "likeness"—mankind.

History stands as testament to the God-given human impulse to relate, to create, and to achieve. God had a relationship with Adam and Eve in the beginning, and they in turn had a relationship with one another. Once their relationship with God was broken, mankind continued to seek religious experiences—though typically not with the true God but with a host of false ones.

A third essential ingredient to the concept of "image" is that of *substance.* Images were three-dimensional, concrete *things.* They were material; they were substantial. How does that fact relate to mankind as God's image? Human beings have bodies—and our bodies are not a secondary feature of our existence—they are basic to our role as image-bearers! As the Old Testament scholar David Clines says, "The body cannot be left out of the meaning of the image; man is a totality, and his 'solid flesh' is as much the image of God as his spiritual capacity, creativeness, or personality, since none of these 'higher' aspects of the human being can exist in isolation from the body."[21] This is not to say that human beings look like God (we are told that "God is Spirit" [John 4:24] and that no one has seen his form [Deut. 4:12, 15–18]), but it is to insist that our bodies are a basic ingredient of what it means for mankind to be made "in the image" of God. The implications of this are far-reaching indeed!

To take but one example, from a biblical perspective death is not merely a step toward the unknown world or a spiritual transition—it is a fundamental disruption of what we are as human beings, as image-bearers. This is true because at death body and soul are separated and we become less than we were intended to be. We might also observe that the commandments to love God and neighbor are related by virtue of the fact that one's neighbor is made in the image of God. To love God is to love his image; conversely, to love his image is to love him (as the apostle John once exhorted, "If someone says, 'I love God,' and hates his brother, he is a liar; for the one who does not love his brother whom he has seen, cannot love God whom he has not seen. And this commandment we have from Him, that the one who loves God should love his brother;" 1 John 4:20–21). Likewise, murder can be viewed as the ultimate sin because it both extinguishes the life of a neighbor and cuts down one who bears the image of God. As we shall see in subsequent chapters, the notion of man as God's substantial image also bears on the Jewish and Christian doctrine concerning resurrection. To understand "image" as involving these features does not mean we are not God's image when, for example, we fail to have a relationship with Him. We are God's image by His decree (see also Gen. 9:6, where fallen mankind is said still to be God's image).

To return to the creation account, at the end of the sixth day (the day on which man was made), God surveyed his handiwork and made a unique pronouncement. Not only was it good (as was noted earlier in vv. 4, 10, 12, 18, 21); it was "very good" (v. 31)—a further indication of the special place mankind occupies in the creation account.

The book of Genesis provides glimpses of the creation and earliest days of the human race. These early days are characterized by wholeness, harmony, and peace between God and mankind. Man and woman are made in God's image and set in a garden. They have a clear purpose in life—to rule and subdue the earth—and experience a personal relationship with the Creator who walks in their midst (Gen. 1:26–28). In fact, there is only one limitation—they must obey God and not eat from one of the trees lest disaster (death!) befall them (Gen. 2:16–17).

We don't get too far along in the story, however, before we encounter the serpent who entices man and woman to disregard God's word in hopes of becoming "like God" (Gen. 3:5). The subsequent deception of the woman and the disobedience of the man have immediate, tragic, and far-reaching consequences for mankind. In general, we may speak of a series of fractures or separations that occur.

First, mankind is separated from God by sin, and in the place of a personal relationship with God come fear, guilt, and shame (Gen. 3:7–10). Ultimately the sin results in expulsion from the garden and the promise of physical death (Gen. 3:22–24). Man and woman are destined to return via death to the earth from which they were formed, just as God had warned (Gen. 3:18; 2:17).[22]

Second, man is separated from woman by sin and by the subsequent emergence of guilt and blame (Gen. 3:10–12). When God confronts Adam with evidence of wrongdoing, his first reaction is to set blame on the woman (and God!), pointing out that God had sent her (Gen. 3:9–12). As for the woman, as part of God's curse, she will long to dominate the man although she will not be able to do so (Gen. 3:16).[23] Instead, he will rule over her.

Finally, mankind is separated from the earth—so to speak—by God's curse on the land, a curse that promises to make life more difficult (Gen. 3:17–19). The garden that at the beginning only required tending gives way to a land cursed by thorns and thistles. Not only will getting life from the earth be harder (i.e., "by the sweat of your face")—so will giving life. For the woman, childbearing will henceforth involve severe pain (3:16).

The curses anticipate the difficult life that mankind, both ancient and modern, experiences. Death comes to us all. Childbearing is difficult. Work is toilsome. And yet in the midst of this gloomy picture, we see a flicker of hope. In Genesis 3:15 God addresses the serpent, "And I will put enmity between you and the woman, And between your seed and her seed; He shall bruise you on the head, And you shall bruise him on the heel." A "bruise on the heel" refers to a hurtful, but not ultimately destructive wound; the "bruise on the head" speaks of a more serious wound. The enigmatic statement suggests that someday God will work (particularly through the woman) to destroy the serpent (whom later Scripture identifies as the devil; 2 Cor. 11:3; Rev. 12:9). The passage implies that God will someday undo the disastrous consequences of the Fall.

In the next several chapters of Genesis, we see two themes emerge. The first of these is the repeated and ever-increasing wickedness of mankind. The rebellion against God continues and results in two great acts of judgment: the Flood (Gen. 6–8) and the scattering of the nations (Gen. 11). The second theme is God's preservation of a line of righteous people. Though few in number and seemingly on the brink of annihilation, some people are preserved by God in order to fulfill the ancient promises of redemption.

This is the beginning of our story, a beautiful and elegantly told description of what human life was originally created to be, and of what it has become through mankind's disobedience to God and the influence of the forces of spiritual darkness. There was design, order, and symmetry to human life from the beginning—all disrupted through the pernicious influence of Satan and the willful disobedience of mankind.

Conclusion

Biblical teaching about the design of history and the creation and purpose of mankind infuses the world and human experience with *gravitas* and purpose. It is unbiblical to ignore the fundamental link between God's goal for history and the material world in which we live.[24] Unlike certain religions that downplay the significance of the material world and our bodily existence and seek to reach God-consciousness by escaping this world, Christianity has as its *foundation* the acts of God in history and as its *goal* the further acts of God and his people in a redeemed and transformed earth (more on this in chapters 3 through 9). Accordingly, we must recognize that

Christianity is firmly rooted in this world—not in the sense of being a part of its corruption—but as offering a remedy to it.

Rather than seeing history as a random hodgepodge of events, the Bible says history is the unfolding of God's great design. From the creation onward God has had a plan for humanity, a purpose for mankind. This plan is revealed in the Bible and experienced in history—it is His-story. In the following chapters we shall survey God's involvement in creation, in the life of Israel, and in the life of Jesus as prelude to our study of the end times. This prelude will turn out to be highly significant in understanding various elements of end-time prophecy and of the biblical view of the goal of history.

✧ Chapter Two ✧

ISRAEL:
ELECTION, FAILURE,
AND PROMISE

✧

Based on their understanding of the New Testament, many Christians think they know the point of the Old Testament prophetic Scriptures: God promised to send his Son to die for the sins of the world. It is easy to understand why people might think this; after all, Jesus' death for sinners is one of the major themes of the New Testament, and New Testament writers sometimes quote or allude to the Old Testament to make this very point (e.g., 1 Pet. 2:22–24 citing Isa. 53; also Rom. 3:25; John 1:29; 1 Pet. 1:19; 1 Cor. 15:3).[1] But is this the central theme to emerge when we read the Old Testament on its own terms? Is it fair to read back into the Old Testament the theology (or part of the theology) of the New?[2]

As it turns out, Jesus' death for sinners is not the central theme of the Old Testament. Instead, we find other ideas emphasized. Among them, God's choice of and various dealings with Israel and the themes associated with a prophesied "new age." These will be traced briefly in this chapter. A glimpse at what Jewish people writing between the Old and New Testaments anticipated in the way of God's future for Israel will also be offered. These backgrounds are important for the modern reader to understand, not only for the insight they provide regarding Jesus' role as the prophesied Messiah, but also because they prepare us to see the extent to which many Old Testament prophecies are fulfilled in the New.

The Choice of Israel

As I write, there are nearly two hundred member states of the United Nations. We are all aware of the vast ethnic, racial, and cultural diversity that is present in our world. There are thousands of people groups. It seems a little strange—particularly in an era that emphasizes the equivalence of cultures—to speak of one group as "chosen." The idea runs counter to our cultural sensibilities. This is especially true if we equate being "chosen" with being "better." Why are the Jews called "the chosen people"? Why would God choose them? Were the Jews "better"?

As observed in the previous chapter, before Eve's expulsion from the Garden of Eden, God promised that one of her offspring would crush the head of the serpent—that is, one of her posterity would come along and help undo the devastating effects of mankind's fall into sin (Gen. 3:15). But a deliverer does not appear immediately; if anything, the more people there were, the more sins there were. The human condition does not improve, but markedly worsens.

Mankind's sin increases so that God must intervene—through the destruction brought by Noah's flood—to stop its spread (Gen. 6–8). And still the promised deliverer does not appear. After the Flood, God begins afresh with Noah. Like Adam and Eve, Noah is told to be fruitful and multiply (Gen. 9:1). Unfortunately, sin enters the picture again when Noah gets drunk and his son Canaan "sees his [Noah's] nakedness" and is cursed for it (Gen. 9:22–26). This is hardly an auspicious restart! Like Adam and Eve, Noah died. After his death, mankind's rebellion against God increased, culminating in the Tower of Babel episode and God's scattering of the nations (Gen. 11). And still the promised deliverer is nowhere to be found. The alert reader of Genesis reads on in anticipation of a "seed of Eve" whom God will use to rescue mankind. In the early chapters of Genesis, we find a collection of narratives which emphasizes, on the one hand, mankind's unwillingness and inability to be faithful to God and, on the other, God's repeated efforts to give mankind another chance and to provide the promised deliverer.

After the scattering of the nations from the Tower of Babel in Genesis 11, we are introduced to Abram, a man from the city of Ur of the Chaldees (Gen. 11:27; Ur was located somewhere near modern-day Iraq). He was invited by God to leave his pagan homeland and journey to the land of Palestine. God then promised him:

> I will make you a great nation, And I will bless you, And make your name great; And so you shall be a blessing; And I will bless those who bless you, And the one who curses you I will curse. And in you all the families of the earth shall be blessed (Gen. 12:2–3).

The language of blessing and cursing reminds the reader of comments made to Adam and Eve in the creation account. One wonders if at last the deliverer promised to Eve is about to appear. The passage contains a clear command: Abram is told to leave his family and homeland. As reward for his obedience, several promises are made. First, Abram will become a "great nation" (v. 2; the phrase is repeated in Gen. 46:3 where Jacob = Israel is consoled that, though he must travel to Egypt, God will make him a great nation).[3] Hence, the promise clearly looks forward to the day when Abram's descendants will multiply and become the nation of Israel. Second, Abram will be blessed by God (v. 2). The idea of "blessing" is associated with physical or spiritual enrichment, and in the course of the Genesis narrative, Abram gets both (although not without difficulty).[4] Third, God promises to make Abram's name great (v. 2). This comment probably has to do with the great status and reputation that Abram will get throughout the course of history on account of his faith in God (e.g., Heb. 11:17–19). In addition, God promised protection for Abram in that he would bless those who blessed Abram and curse those who cursed him (v. 3). The same promise of protection was applied to Jacob by his father Isaac in Genesis 27:29 and by the prophet Balaam to the nation of Israel in general at Numbers 24:9. God thus set a protective hedge around Abram to ensure that he would be preserved and that God's intention to bring a deliverer through him would be realized. Lastly, God promised that Abram would become a source of blessing for all the families of the earth (v. 3). There is, in other words, an international dimension to Abram's blessing.

It is hard to overstate the importance of this last observation. God's choice of Abram was related to his intention to bless all the families of the earth (as hinted at in his words to Eve regarding a future deliverer). Abraham and his descendants (beginning with Isaac, then Jacob and his sons) were to be the conduits of God's blessing to the world. Without a doubt his (and their) obedience would involve a measure of personal benefit, but the larger picture is that of God choosing one man, and through him, one nation, as a means of blessing all others. The choice of Abram is related to the promise made to Eve that her posterity (her "seed") would have an important role in undoing the damage caused by sin. This role for Abraham is hinted at in Genesis, expanded in the Old Testament (where Israel is the place to which all nations will come to learn about God; Isa. 2:2; Mic. 4:1–2), and made more specific in the New Testament.

The apostle Paul hearkened back to the promises to Abraham and observed that in Jesus of Nazareth, a descendant of Abraham, God had made good his promise to bless all the nations of the earth: "And the Scripture, foreseeing that God would justify the Gentiles by faith, preached the gospel beforehand to Abraham, saying, ALL THE NATIONS SHALL BE BLESSED IN YOU" (Gal. 3:8). The same theme is present in the introduction to Matthew's Gospel where we read, "A record of the genealogy of Jesus Christ the son of David, the son of Abraham" (Matt. 1:1 NIV). At first glance the mention of Abraham seems unnecessary—after all, if Jesus is a descendant of David, he must of necessity be a descendant of Abraham, since *all* Jews are descended from Abraham. But Matthew probably mentioned Abraham in connection with Jesus to remind his readers of God's promise to "bless all the nations" through Abraham—something that would happen, according to Matthew, when believers obeyed Jesus' word to preach the gospel to and "make disciples of *all the nations*" (Matt. 28:18–20).

But what sort of agreement did God make with Abraham? Was it like a contract between parties where each agrees to uphold one end of the bargain, or was it something else? Genesis 15 records a solemn ceremony in which God swore to fulfill the previously made promises. This was done in response to Abraham's question, "How may I know that I shall possess it [the promised land]?" (v. 8). In the covenant ceremony described in Genesis 15, the promises to Abram (whose name by now has been changed to Abraham) were formally ratified. This form of covenant ceremony was well-known in the ancient world. It was employed by kings to convey grants of land to loyal vassals.[5] In the covenant ceremony, God acted while Abraham watched. This anticipates the fact that God has chosen Abraham and his offspring without regard to their behavior (though it is clear that Abraham is a righteous man whose faith moves him to obey God).

The call of Abraham is unconditional. God and Abraham do not have a contract that is valid only if each person lives up to his obligations; rather, God unilaterally obliges himself to do for Abraham what he has sworn. This is important to remember in the light of the history of Israel that unfolds in the remainder of the Old Testament—a history littered with accounts of Israel's unfaithfulness and God's repeated attempts to secure their loyalty.

As unpalatable as it might be to those living in modern democratic societies, Scripture says the descendants of Abraham through his son Isaac (the Jews) were chosen for the simple reason that God was pleased to choose them; no poll was taken, no election held. God unilaterally took the initiative to choose and use Abraham and his offspring. Was this arrangement fair? The answer depends on how one understands God to have chosen. If the basis for God's choice was national beauty, wealth, or righteousness,

then other people may well have had a claim to be better than Abraham and
his offspring. But this is not how the selection was made. The notion of
unfairness necessarily involves the idea of merit. But God's choice of the
Jews was not based on any idea of merit, that they deserved to be chosen;
rather, it was based on his sovereign will and desire.

We moderns are familiar with this kind of selection. Benefactors, for
example, regularly choose to give money to one college rather than another.
Someone might give millions to Cambridge. Is this unfair to Oxford? Someone may donate land for a university or hospital to one group. Is this unfair
to others? Of course not. In the book of Deuteronomy, Moses commented
on God's choice of the Jews:

> The LORD your God has chosen you to be a people for His
> own possession out of all the peoples who are on the face of the
> earth. The LORD did not set his love on you nor choose you be-
> cause you were more in number than any of the peoples, for
> you were the fewest of all peoples, but because the LORD loved
> you and kept the oath which He swore to your forefathers
> (Deut. 7:6–8).

Elsewhere God (through Moses) connected the choice of the Jews of
Moses' era to the original choice of the patriarchs (e.g., Abraham, Isaac,
and Jacob): "Because He [God] loved your fathers, therefore He chose
their descendants after them. And He personally brought you from Egypt
by His great power, driving out from before you nations greater and might-
ier than you, to bring you in and to give you their land for an inheritance"
(Deut. 4:37–38).

If God's choice of Israel was unconditional, why does so much of the Old
Testament focus on Israel's obligation to obey God? Further, might Israel be
"un-chosen" if they were to disobey God? How do these concepts—unconditional election and the requirement of obedience—fit together?

God chose Israel as a means to an end. The goal was to reveal himself to
the other nations and peoples of the world so they might know him. As his
chosen people, Israel was to depict to the nations—through their obedience
to God's laws—the character of the one true God and the benefits of obeying
him. In this way Abraham's offspring would be a "blessing to the nations."

Even though God's choice of Israel was unconditional, the nation would
experience God's blessing based on their obedience.[6] Israel was to be a holy
nation; they were to distinguish themselves by conforming their lives to
God's will as revealed in the Scriptures. The Law, also known as the Torah

(originally including the books of Genesis, Exodus, Leviticus, Numbers, and Deuteronomy), was given to Moses and the people so they might know how to please the only true God, who brought them out of Egypt in an unprecedented act of deliverance. The Law was not given so people might know how to follow rules and thus "get to heaven"; rather, it was given so God's people might know how they ought to live in order to please God, live in fellowship with him, and reflect his character in the midst of nations that did not know him.

Corresponding to God's demands of obedience were promises of blessing. These are spelled out in Deuteronomy 28:1–15, where Moses gave a charge to the nation before they entered the promised land. Verses 11–13 summarize the message:

> The LORD will make you abound in prosperity, in the off-spring of your body and in the offspring of your beast and in the produce of your ground, in the land which the LORD swore to your fathers to give you. The LORD will open for you his good storehouse, the heavens, to give rain to your land in its season and to bless all the work of your hand; and you shall lend to many nations, but you shall not borrow. And the Lord shall make you the head and not the tail, and you only shall be above, and you shall not be underneath, if you will listen to the commandments of the LORD your God, which I charge you to-day, to observe them carefully.

The passage echoes many of the promises made to Abraham: security in the land, protection from enemies, material blessing, and a posterity. Greatness, the passage says, would accrue to the nation if it obeyed God.

Conversely, failure to obey God would have tragic consequences. These are listed in the remainder of Deuteronomy 28 (vv. 16–68). The ultimate sting of God's judgment on the nation, should it stray from God, would involve defeat at the hand of foreign armies and exile from the promised land (esp. vv. 63–64). This long passage makes clear that the nation could expect a very difficult time if it failed to obey God—the God who had delivered its people from Egypt. For Israel, and for believers throughout the ages, the experience of God's deliverance brought with it obligations to obey.

How did the nation respond to its deliverance from Egypt and the promise of God's blessing? Did it live up to its end of the bargain? And what about God? Did he prove to be faithful?

Failure, Promise, and Exile

The Old Testament is the story of God's dealings with Israel. Unfortunately, the faith of Abraham was often not duplicated by his descendants. After the heady days of the Exodus, the people soon reverted to the idolatrous practices they had learned in Egypt. As a result, the generation of people whom God led out of Egypt did not get to settle in the promised land; instead, that privilege was granted to their children.

Once the Israelites were in the promised land, it was only a matter of time until they reneged on their covenant obligations. Over the next several hundred years (from about 1200 B.C. until around 600 B.C.) we see a pattern in the nation's behavior.[7] Time and again Israel

✧ spurned obedience to the law;

✧ got involved in idolatry and other forbidden practices;

✧ got warnings from God's spokesmen and prophets that judgment would come unless it repented;

✧ experienced the judgment of God—to one extent or another—and then repented, leading to deliverance and blessing after which it

✧ spurned obedience to the law.

For Israel the gravest consequence of disobedience involved the possibility of destruction at the hands of foreign enemies and expulsion from the promised land. Although its people often went astray spiritually, for many generations the nation avoided the devastating experience of exile. However, toward the middle of the eighth century B.C., things began to change. The greatest world power in the ancient Near East in the eighth century B.C. was Assyria (located in modern Syria, Iraq, and Turkey); toward the middle of the seventh century B.C., Assyria's power was eclipsed by that of the neo-Babylonian dynasty. During these centuries, Jews in both the northern part of the country (then called Israel) and in the south (then called Judah) repeatedly engaged in idolatry to the extent that exile from the promised land was threatened by God's prophets (Isa. 2:8; 10:10–11; Jer. 16:18; Ezek. 5:11; 6:4–6; Hos. 4:12, 17).

The prophets warned time and again that Israel's unfaithfulness to God would have grave consequences. The nation was told of God's displeasure and warned to repent lest judgment come. The words of the prophets frequently echoed the warnings first given by Moses in Deuteronomy 28. The prophets' language is striking and graphic. Isaiah, for example, wrote:

> Hear, O heavens! Listen, O earth! For the LORD has spoken: "I reared children and brought them up, but they have rebelled against me. The ox knows his master, the donkey his owner's manger, but Israel does not know, my people do not understand." Ah, sinful nation, a people loaded with guilt, a brood of evildoers, children given to corruption! They have forsaken the LORD; they have spurned the Holy One of Israel and turned their backs on him. Why should you be beaten anymore? Why do you persist in rebellion? Your whole head is injured, your whole heart afflicted (Isa. 1:2–5 NIV).

Along the same lines, Hosea lamented:

> Hear the word of the LORD, you Israelites, because the LORD has a charge to bring against you who live in the land: "There is no faithfulness, no love, no acknowledgment of God in the land. There is only cursing, lying and murder, stealing and adultery; they break all bounds, and bloodshed follows bloodshed" (Hos. 4:1–2 NIV).

The prophets' warnings went on and on, and we might be tempted to think that the ugly picture of Israel's unfaithfulness would provoke not only God's judgment but also his rejection. After all, he judged and rejected a sinful world through the flood in Noah's time (Gen. 6–8). But true to his promises in Deuteronomy 28–30, though Jewish unfaithfulness might result in his anger and judgment, it would not lead to the revocation of his promises. Instead, the Old Testament prophets looked beyond the threats of destruction to a new age, a most blessed epoch, when God would come to establish his reign on earth and thus inaugurate an era of peace, righteousness, and prosperity. Indeed, if we take into account the Old Testament as a whole, we may safely regard this promised new age as the central hope of the Old Testament. One Old Testament scholar says, "The religious core of the whole salvation-hope . . . is to be found in the coming of Yahweh to set up his dominion over the world."[8]

These prophecies of the new age are set against the backdrop of serious threats against the nation from foreign enemies. Although the language of the prophets has primary reference to particular historical situations, it often goes beyond them to portray the new age in cosmic and universal terms. We may sketch out certain features of the promised new age that appear time and again in the prophets.

THE COMING OF THE LORD

The new age was first of all to begin with the coming of the Lord himself. His coming would signal that the present evil age, characterized as it was by the oppression of Israel, the apparent victories of sinners, and the widespread domination of sin and death, was ended.

The coming of God is frequently mentioned in the Old Testament as a future hope. Isaiah looked to a future day ("that day") and warned the people, "Behold, the LORD is about to come out from His place [to earth]" (Isa. 26:21). Later Isaiah was commanded to encourage the brokenhearted and oppressed, "Take courage, fear not. Behold, your God will come" (Isa. 35:4). Micah warned, "The LORD is coming forth from His place. He will come down and tread on the high places of the earth" (Mic. 1:3). In a long passage dealing with the last days, the prophet Zechariah promised, "Then the LORD my God will come, and all the holy ones with him" (Zech. 14:5 NIV). He later added, "And the LORD will be king over all the earth; in that day the LORD will be the only one" (Zech. 14:9 NIV).

As one scholar put it, "The faith of the Old Testament rests on two certainties, equally profound and indissolubly bound together. The first is that God has come in the past, and that he has intervened in favour of his people. The other . . . is the hope that God will come anew in the future."[9] Another scholar concludes, "There could never have been a stage in Israel's history when the kingdom of God was looked for apart from the coming of Yahweh."[10]

JUDGMENT AND SALVATION

This second feature of the new era is related to the first: the arrival of the Lord was to involve judgment against the wicked and salvation for the righteous who were oppressed. This was so because God is holy and almighty. Psalms 145:17 says, "The LORD is righteous in all His ways." The prophet Isaiah recorded, "The LORD is a God of justice" (30:18).

We find the principle stated often in the Old Testament that the wicked and sinners cannot remain in the presence of the Lord. For example, the very first Psalm observes:

> The wicked are not so [i.e., they do not prosper], but are like chaff which the wind drives away. Therefore the wicked will not stand in the judgment, Nor sinners in the assembly of the righteous; For the LORD knows the way of the righteous, But the way of the wicked will perish. (Ps. 1:4–6).

A psalmist also said:

> "You are not a God who takes pleasure in evil; with you the
> wicked cannot dwell. The arrogant cannot stand in your pres-
> ence; you hate all who do wrong. You destroy those who tell
> lies; bloodthirsty and deceitful men the LORD abhors"
> (Ps. 5:4–6 NIV).

Through the prophet Isaiah God advised that the Lord was coming "to
punish the inhabitants of the earth for their iniquity" (26:21). Micah 4:13
NIV says that in the future the nations who have gloated over the hardship
of Jerusalem will be broken into pieces. Similarly, Isaiah spoke of the coming judgment against all the proud people, especially the foreigners (Isa.
2:12–21). Obadiah said, "The day of the LORD is near for all nations" who
will face retribution for their treatment of Israel (vv. 15–21 NIV). The Lord
instructed Ezekiel, "Son of man, prophesy and say, 'Thus says the LORD
God, "Wail, 'Alas for the day!' For the day is near, Even the day of the LORD
is near; It will be a day of clouds, A time of doom for the nations" ' " (Ezek.
30:2–3). According to Zechariah, those nations of the earth which gathered
to make war on Jerusalem would be destroyed in the day of the Lord (Zech.
12:3–4). The prophets agreed that the nations that had oppressed Israel
would fare poorly when God came to visit them. Moreover, their idols (the
false gods) would vanish (Isa. 2:18; Zech. 13:2). This concept may be connected to the idea found in Micah that before God takes his seat to reign on
Mount Zion he will punish "the host of heaven . . . and the kings of the
earth" (Isa. 24:21).[11] God's very character, then, demands that when the
LORD comes to the earth he must deal with the wicked, especially those who
have oppressed Israel.

God's coming will bring destruction to those nations and people who
have oppressed Israel.

But God's righteous anger at sinners is not confined to those outside
Israel. Indeed, the prophets also warned that God's coming would have serious implications for the unrighteous people of Israel. For example, Joel
spoke of the coming "dark day," and after describing it exhorted:

> Blow the trumpet in Zion, declare a holy fast, call a sacred
> assembly. Gather the people, consecrate the assembly; bring
> together the elders, gather the children, those nursing at the
> breast. Let the bridegroom leave his room and the bride her
> chamber. Let the priests, who minister before the LORD, weep
> between the temple porch and the altar. Let them say, "Spare

your people, O LORD. Do not make your inheritance an object of scorn, a byword among the nations. Why should they say among the peoples, 'Where is their God?' " (Joel 2:15–17 NIV).

Joel suggested that the coming day of the Lord would be anything but pleasant for those in Israel who needed to repent. In a similar way, the prophet Amos warned his countrymen, "Woe to you who long for the day of the LORD! Why do you long for the day of the LORD? That day will be darkness, not light" (Amos 5:18 NIV). In an even more pointed comment, Amos continued, "All the sinners of My people will die by the sword, Those who say 'the calamity will not overtake or confront us' " (Amos 9:10; Mal. 2:17–3:2 made much the same point). It is easy to understand how Israel, oppressed by their neighbors, would have longed for the day of the Lord's visitation so they might be freed from and, indeed, exalted over, their enemies. It is surely a natural tendency to point out the vices of one's national enemies while preserving a dignified silence about one's own national shortcomings. But the prophets would not be silent. They taught that just as the Lord is the Lord of all the earth and cannot be confined to one locale, so his indignation over sin could not be confined to Israel's enemies. His coming brings judgment for sin on those outside and within the nation.

Nevertheless, the Lord's coming new age is also marked by deliverance for the righteous. This deliverance was to involve not only rescue from enemies but exaltation over them. Like the inevitable coming of judgment, deliverance for the righteous is connected to God's impeccable character. It naturally follows that when he comes he will rescue and vindicate his people. Joel 2:18–19 says:

> Then the LORD will be zealous for His land, And will have pity on His people. And the LORD will answer and say to His people, "Behold, I am going to send you grain, new wine, And oil, and you will be satisfied in full with them; And I will never again make you a reproach among the nations."

Isaiah 2 paints a similar picture of Israel's exaltation in the last days:

> Now it will come about that in the last days, the mountain of the house of the LORD will be established as the chief of the mountains, and will be raised above the hills; and all the nations will stream to it. And many peoples will come and say, "Come, let us go up to the mountain of the LORD, to the house of the God of Jacob; that He may teach us concerning His ways, and that we

may walk in His paths." For the law will go forth from Zion, and
the word of the LORD from Jerusalem (Isa. 2:2–3).

These passages (and many others that could be cited) indicate that the
promised new age would be a particularly blessed one for Israel. It is easy to
understand why the nation, oppressed over the years as it was by various
foreign powers, was so eager to experience the coming of God.

THE RULE OF MESSIAH

A third element in the Old Testament picture of God's new age is that it
will be presided over by a Davidic Messiah. The word *Messiah* is built off the
Hebrew verbal *mashach*, which means "to anoint." The verb is often used in
reference to the Old Testament practice of anointing or smearing certain
people and things with oil to signify they were set aside for sacred use
(Exod. 28:41; 1 Kings 19:16; Ps. 105:15; Num. 7:1). The anointing ceremony is best known in connection with kingship. Beginning with Saul, Jewish kings were anointed with oil to mark them as God-ordained (1 Sam.
10:1; 16:1, 3, 13; 1 Kings 1:34; 2 Kings 9:3). The word *Messiah* means
"anointed one," and thus became a way of referring to Israel's king (because
of the promises made to David in 2 Samuel 7, it was also possible to refer to
the king of Israel as David's son or as the offspring of Jesse, David's father).

A particularly full description of the link between the new age and a
Davidic Messiah is found in Isaiah 11:1–9:

> There shall come forth a Rod from the stem of Jesse, and a
> Branch shall grow out of his roots. The Spirit of the LORD shall
> rest upon Him, the Spirit of wisdom and understanding, the
> Spirit of counsel and might, the Spirit of knowledge and of the
> fear of the LORD. . . . The wolf also shall dwell with the lamb,
> the leopard shall lie down with the young goat, the calf and the
> young lion and the fatling together; and a little child shall lead
> them. The cow and the bear shall graze; their young ones shall
> lie down together; and the lion shall eat straw like the ox. The
> nursing child shall play by the cobra's hole, and the weaned
> child shall put his hand in the viper's den. They shall not hurt
> nor destroy in all My holy mountain, for the earth shall be full
> of the knowledge of the LORD as the waters cover the sea.
> (NKJV)

In much the same vein Jeremiah wrote:

> "Behold, the days are coming," declares the LORD, "When I
> shall raise up for David a righteous Branch; and He will reign

as king and act wisely and do justice and righteousness in the land. In His days Judah will be saved, and Israel will dwell securely; and this is His name by which He will be called, 'The LORD our righteousness' " (Jer. 23:5–6; see also Ps. 2; Isa. 9:1–7; Jer. 30:8–11; 33:14–18; Ezek. 34:23–24; 37:21–25).

The connection between a Davidic Messiah and the new age was frequently made by the prophets. But this fact must not cloud the realization that in the Old Testament there was "a much greater interest in the Messianic Age itself and the activity of God during the Age than in the person of persons whom God would use to bring it about and to accomplish his purposes."[12] The Messiah was but one feature of the Old Testament hope for the future.

OTHER FEATURES OF THE KINGDOM

There are other important but less prominent features of the new era. Among them are the expectations that the new era would be characterized by peace and the transformation of nature. It would also involve the unprecedented giving of the Holy Spirit and the phenomenon of resurrection.

Transformations. Professor Donald Gowan observed:

> The O[ld] T[estament] has made the bold theological move of introducing an ethical cause for what is . . . wrong with nature. Human sin, it says, has inflicted a curse on the natural world so that it suffers because of our misdeeds, and because of our dependence on nature that curse rebounds upon us, making life in its divinely intended fullness impossible until the curse is removed. The eschatology of the OT says it is God's intention also to make things right in nature.[13]

The prophets sometimes spoke of a future blessing of the land of Israel in association with the Lord's coming in the last days. For example, Joel wrote:

> Then the LORD will be zealous for His land, and will have pity on His people. And the LORD will answer and say to His people, "Behold, I am going to send you grain, new wine, and oil, and you will be satisfied in full with them; and I will never again make you a reproach among the nations." . . . So rejoice, O sons of Zion, and be glad in the LORD your God; for He has given you the early rain for your vindication. And he has poured down for you the rain, the early and latter rain as before. And the threshing floors will be full of grain, and the vats will overflow with the new wine and oil. (Joel 2:18–19, 23–24).

Put another way, God will graciously grant to his people the blessings promised in Deuteronomy 28:1–15. In the idealized future, even the specters of war and death are removed. Micah promised that in the last days,

> They will hammer their swords into plowshares and their spears into pruning hooks; nation will not lift up sword against nation, and never again will they train for war. And each of them will sit under his vine and under his fig tree, with no one to make them afraid, for the mouth of the LORD of hosts has spoken (Mic. 4:3–4).

Hosea said, "In that day . . . I (God) will abolish the bow, the sword, and war from the land" (Hos. 2:18). Isaiah wrote, "Then the eyes of the blind will be opened, and the ears of the deaf will be unstopped. Then the lame will leap like a deer, and the tongue of the dumb will shout for joy. For waters will break forth in the wilderness and streams in the Arabah" (Isa. 35:5–6). In an extended passage dealing with "that day," Isaiah wrote, in part, that "on this mountain He [God] will swallow up the covering which is over all peoples, even the veil which is stretched over all nations. He will swallow up death for all time" (Isa. 25:7–8).

We could summarize these descriptions of the new age by observing that the presence of the Lord seems to have the effect of reversing the catastrophic and cosmic consequences of mankind's original sin and the curses that flowed from it.

The Spirit. In the Old Testament the Holy Spirit is frequently mentioned as the source of special enablement given to certain leaders to equip them for their tasks (e.g., Exod. 28:41; 1 Kings 19:16). The Spirit is not often mentioned in connection with the coming new age, but when it is, the texts are particularly noteworthy because they point to a remarkable difference between God's dealing with people in the Old Testament era and in the age to come.

Certain prophetic texts indicate that the new age will be marked by God giving the Spirit not only to political and religious leaders, but to all sorts of people. This is most clearly mentioned by Joel, through whom God said:

> It will come about after this that I will pour out My Spirit on all mankind; and your sons and daughters will prophesy, your old men will dream dreams, your young men will see visions. And even on the male and female servants I will pour out My Spirit in those days (Joel 2:28–29).

The Spirit is first mentioned in Genesis 1:2, where it plays a role in God's creation of the world. It is thus perhaps not surprising that the Spirit was also mentioned by certain prophets in passages that speak of God's giving new life to Israel in the last days (Ezek. 36–37; Zech. 12:10).

Resurrection. Finally, we observe that another feature of the new age is the phenomenon of resurrection. In one respect we can view resurrection as an extension of the idea that God's presence transforms nature—the abolition of death being perhaps the most striking transformation of all. In another respect, because we are all personally affected by death, the hope of resurrection is a far more striking and individually relevant event than the mere concept of nature being transformed.

The linkage between resurrection and the last days is most clearly presented in Daniel 12:1–2, where we learn that "many of those who sleep in the dust of the ground will awake, these to everlasting life, but the others to disgrace *and* everlasting contempt." It is also hinted at in Isaiah 26:19, where the prophet said that in that day, "your dead will live; their corpses will rise. You who lie in the dust, awake and shout for joy." The doctrine of resurrection is not much elaborated on in the Old Testament, yet it was sufficiently present to emerge as one of the major points of disagreement between the Pharisees and Sadducees in New Testament times (Matt. 22:23; Acts 23:6–8).

The picture of the new age just sketched is a composite one, yet even if different prophets used various images to describe it, in the end the picture is remarkably consistent. God will personally intervene to set right all wrongs, to fulfill the ancient promises, to give his people a hope and a future. This is the prophetic hope and warning.

EXILE

But Israel did not heed the prophets' warnings to repent. The northern kingdom was scattered by the Assyrians in 722 B.C. In the south, Judah experienced the promised exile and destruction at the hands of the Babylonians. A deportation of Jews from Jerusalem to Babylon began in about 605 B.C., and in 586 B.C. the Babylonian armies laid siege to Jerusalem, tore down its walls and temple, and killed many of its inhabitants. The terrifying specter of squalor and devastation described in the prophetic writings became a reality, and for many Jews the future of the nation must have been an open question.

Nevertheless, the Exile was not the end of the story. Alongside several of the prophetic warnings of destruction were also consoling promises of restoration. These promises spoke grandly of better days to come so that even while threatening to chastise them severely, God reassured his people that despite what they were about to experience, he would forget neither them nor the covenant he had made with them. Jeremiah 30:3 says, "'Behold, days are coming,' declares the LORD, 'when I will restore the fortunes of My people Israel and Judah.' The LORD says, 'I will also bring them back to the land that I gave to their forefathers, and they shall possess it'" (also Jer. 23:3–4; Ezek. 28:25–26).

To sum up: prophetic warnings were not heeded by Israel, and the nation's sin resulted in God's judgment. Nonetheless, the prophets anticipated God dealing with Israel in the future.

After the Exile

The prophet Jeremiah predicted an exile of seventy years duration (Jer. 25:12; 29:10; also Dan. 9:2). Indeed, seventy years after the Exile began, King Cyrus of Persia allowed certain Jews to return to their homeland to restore the temple (ca. 538 B.C.; Ezra 1:1–3; 2 Chron. 36:22–23). Many years later (ca. 444 B.C.) King Artaxerxes permitted Nehemiah to conduct a mission to Jerusalem that resulted in the rebuilding of the city.

A crucial question for those who read the promises of restoration listed earlier is this: Did the return to the land under Ezra, Zerubbabel, Nehemiah, and others fulfill the predictions of glorious restoration made by the prophets who prophesied before the Exile? Did God's new age begin with Jewish restoration to the land in the sixth century B.C.?

This period of restoration, beginning about 538 B.C., *cannot* be regarded as fulfilling completely the ancient promises. True enough, the Exile did seem largely to achieve success in eradicating idolatry from Israel. But after the return from Exile, no Davidic king occupied the throne of Israel (contrary to the hope of Jeremiah 23). Far from being exalted among the nations or free of foreign entanglement, Israel was often engaged in serious disputes with her neighbors. She was dominated by the Persians from 539 to 331 B.C., by the Greeks from 331 to 323 B.C., by the Ptolemies (of Egypt) from 323 to 198 B.C., and by the Seleucids (of Syria) from 198 to 143 B.C. There followed a brief interlude of Jewish independence under the Maccabees (143–63 B.C.), but this was soon followed by an extended period of Roman domination (63 B.C. to the fall of the Roman Empire).[14]

Malachi was the last Old Testament prophet to speak.[15] But this does not mean that the pens of Jewish writers were stilled in the years between the Testaments (i.e., from the fifth century B.C. to the first century A.D.). Many examples of nonbiblical religious literature composed in this era have come to us. These books were not inspired in the way that books in our Old and New Testaments were, but they are valuable nonetheless because they enable us to learn how writers between the Testaments interpreted and commented on important Old Testament texts. For the most part, these writings built on themes found in the Old Testament. In this respect they bridge the gap between the Testaments, but they do so not merely by echoing the prophets (though this often happens) but by amplifying certain of their themes and, on occasion, by muting others. It is important to recognize the existence of this material and to be aware of its contribution to the background of the New Testament.

The prophets wrote openly and often about a coming new age. It is evident that Jewish writers living between the Testaments did not regard these promises as fulfilled. Instead, like the prophets of old they looked forward to the day when God would come to save his people, judge the wicked, and reign in peace and righteousness. The hopes of these nonbiblical writers for the future may be summarized as follows.

We have already seen that the coming of God was an important feature in Old Testament eschatology. Indeed, it was the fundamental element of the promised new era. As for literature that appeared between the Testaments, the scholar D. S. Russell observed that among intertestamental apocalyptic writers, "there was an air of eager, even desperate, expectancy that soon, very soon, God's rule would suddenly and devastatingly break in and God himself, either in person or through his Messiah, would right all wrongs and reward the patience and long-suffering of the righteous."[16]

On the destruction of the wicked, the Testament of Moses 10:7 (second century B.C.) reads, "For the Most High will arise, the Eternal God alone; and he will appear to punish the Gentiles, and he will destroy all their idols." On a related note, even though the nations—the enemies of Israel—continued to be spoken of as objects of God's wrath, for many of these writers an important new development was evident. Namely, "these evil powers are no longer the great empires and kings of which the prophets had spoken; they are the 'principalities and powers in high places,' demonic beings under the control of the leader Satan."[17] The destruction of the wicked was to be accompanied by the vindication of the righteous. As Jubilees 23:30 (second century B.C.) says, "At that time the Lord will heal his servants, and they will rise up and see great peace and drive out their adversaries. And the righteous will see and be thankful." Part of this vindication involves resurrection from the dead. As the writer of 2 Maccabees put it, "The king of the universe will raise us up to an everlasting renewal of life, because we have died for his laws" (2 Macc. 7:9).

As was true in the Old Testament, the coming Davidic Messiah is not the central feature of God's new era among intertestamental writers; in fact, in many of these writings he is not mentioned at all. But in other places he does occupy a central role, and as Russell points out, "No longer was he thought of simply as coming after God had established his kingdom; rather he was God's instrument in the establishment of it, and his foremost task was the destruction of God's enemies from the face of the earth."[18] For example, the 17th Psalm of Solomon (ca. first century B.C.) says, "See, O Lord, and raise up for them their king, the son of David, to rule over your servant Israel in the time known to you, O God. Undergird him with the strength to destroy the unrighteous rulers, to purge Jerusalem from gentiles who trample her" (vv. 21–22).[19]

Many elements of the Old Testament framework of the last days are reiterated by Jewish writers from the intertestamental era. Furthermore, many of the expectations found in the intertestamental writings are echoed in the New Testament. In chapter 3 we'll look more closely at what the New Testament has to say about God's new era.

Israel and History by Design

It should be clear by now that the history of Israel affords us opportunity to see design in two ways. First, in the prophetic predictions of subsequently fulfilled events, the prophets warned of an Assyrian invasion—and it happened; they warned of a Babylonian dispersion—and it occurred; they foretold the number of years their people would be in exile—and it came to pass. Second, we can recognize design in Israel's history by detecting a pattern in the events described. These events took place according to a pattern first set forth by Moses, hundreds of years before their fulfillment.[20] Hence, by reading the Old Testament we begin to see the history of Israel unfold in accordance with a plan—God's plan.

Conclusion

The Old Testament chronicles the story of God's relationship to Israel. It is a story filled with dramatic acts of salvation and equally dramatic pictures of judgment. Through it all, God remained loyal to his people. In fact, despite the faithlessness of the people, God promised to bless them in a new era—an era characterized by peace, righteousness, and prosperity. The promises were clearly expressed in the prophets and restated in other Jewish writings from between the Testaments. Against these backgrounds the events of the New Testament took place, and it is to the New Testament that we now turn our attention.

✧ Chapter Three ✧

JESUS AND
THE BEGINNING
OF THE END

✧

New Testament writers often quote or allude to the Old Testament when talking about Jesus. They do so in order to establish that his coming fulfilled Old Testament expectations and that he possessed the proper credentials to be regarded as "Messiah." Implied in all this is an understanding that Jesus' birth, death, and resurrection were foretold and therefore part of God's design for history.

Many popular books on eschatology do an admirable job of noting the Old Testament expectations regarding the promised new era of salvation. Unfortunately, these same books often fail to discuss the extent to which these expectations were met in the preaching of Jesus and the early church.

As noted in the previous chapter, an important feature of Old Testament eschatology is the coming of Messiah. It stands to reason, then, that the presence of Messiah can be regarded as an eschatological or end-times event. There are various reasons for the failure of certain popular books to discuss this, but two figure most prominently. First, many of these writers apparently think of eschatology or "last things" almost exclusively as related to events that occur near the time of Jesus' return. Since they understand eschatology in this rather limited way, by definition they have little interest in Jesus' first advent as eschatology. But a second reason that the possibility of Jesus having already fulfilled many Old Testament expectations is not discussed is that for many writers the era of salvation—the kingdom of God—did not begin in any meaningful way with Jesus' first coming. For them, though Jesus may have preached that the kingdom was near, it never actually arrived because he was rejected. Although this view is a minority position in biblical scholarship, it has tended to dominate popular discussions of eschatology.

In this chapter we will consider whether this notion of a postponed kingdom is the best interpretation of the New Testament evidence. We will also investigate how Jewish rejection of Jesus affects our understanding of the kingdom of God and of eschatology.

Jesus and the Kingdom of God

The New Testament era is set against the background of widespread recognition among Jewish people that the ancient promises of God's salvation had not been fulfilled. The long years between the composition of the last Old Testament book and the appearance of John the Baptist witnessed the rise of various political factions and religious movements among the Jewish people, but none appears to have believed that the ancient promises had been fulfilled. Many people continued to hope that fulfillment would come.

Several hundred years after Malachi was written, John the Baptist, then Jesus of Nazareth appeared to Israel. John warned the people to repent so they might be ready for the coming of the Lord and the era of salvation which was about to dawn (Luke 3:1–14). He also told his audiences to expect an even greater messenger from God to appear after him (Luke 3:15–17). Jesus of Nazareth was the "greater one" to whom John bore witness.

The central message of Jesus' preaching concerned the kingdom of God. Indeed, this message was the motivation for his preaching. This is perhaps most clearly expressed in Luke 4. After he was asked to remain in a particular village, Jesus replied, "I must preach the kingdom of God to the other cities also, for I was sent *for this purpose*" (Luke 4:43, italics added). It is worth noting that Jesus nowhere defined precisely what he meant by "the kingdom of God." The phrase appears to have been readily understood by his audiences, who never asked him to define it (although they did, on occasion, have questions about it). It is not a phrase, however, so easily understood by the modern reader.

There are several interpretations of the phrase. For some it is equivalent to "heaven," so that when Jesus describes the kingdom he is, in effect, describing heaven. For others, the phrase refers to the reign of Jesus upon the earth after he returns. For still others, "kingdom of God" designates a relationship with God, so that when Jesus speaks of the kingdom of God being "within you" he means that peace with God, a relationship with God, is an internal matter, a disposition of the heart. For some the kingdom is a present reality; for others it is exclusively future.

Before we can sort though the various options, before we can discuss whether the kingdom has begun or has been postponed, we need to know what it is. Accordingly, we will examine the meaning of the term "kingdom"; the meaning of the phrase "kingdom of God"; and evidence for the presence of God's kingdom in the ministry of Jesus and the early church. After that we will consider two related themes: the future element of the kingdom of God in Jesus' preaching and the "mystery" of the kingdom.

The Meaning of the Kingdom

One basic difficulty we face in understanding what Jesus meant by "the kingdom of God" has to do with our understanding of the Greek word translated "kingdom" (*basileia*). In English we normally think of "kingdom" as a noun that refers to a place. Hence, "The kingdom of Queen Elizabeth II is otherwise known as Great Britain." Here "kingdom" refers to the place ruled by a sovereign. "Kingdom" (*basileia*) sometimes has this meaning in the New Testament. For example, Jesus compared Satan's kingdom to a house or territory in Mark 3:24–25: "If a kingdom (*basileia*) is divided against itself, that kingdom cannot stand. And if a house is divided against itself, that house will not be able to stand."

But in many New Testament passages this is probably not the connotation of *basileia* (kingdom). For instance, if we think of "kingdom" as a place, what are we to make of the following verse: "But if I cast out demons by the finger of God, then the kingdom of God has come upon you" (Luke 11:20). Is Jesus suggesting that the *place* where God rules has now come to earth? In this verse, and in many others, taking "kingdom" as referring to a "place" seems not to yield a clear meaning.

But this apparent difficulty need not deter us. If we look at the literature from the New Testament era, including the New Testament itself, we find that the fundamental meaning for the Greek word *basileia* is "rule" or "reign." In other words, *basileia* (or "kingdom") refers primarily not to a place but to royal power or kingly authority. In English, of course, the concepts of "kingdom" (as a *place*) and "reign" (as a *power*) are related. To return to our previous example, we could say, "Great Britain is the place where Queen Elizabeth II *reigns*." The same is also true in Greek where a "reign" (*basileia*) takes place in a locale, in a "kingdom" (also *basileia*). Put another way, the same Greek word *basileia* can refer both to "royal authority" (the inherent power of a king to rule) and to the place where that authority is exercised. In these two nuances of the term *basileia*, the notion of "royal authority" is the most basic component. Obviously, before there is a *place* that is reigned (a "kingdom"), there must be the power to reign (also "kingdom").

We find the Greek word *basileia* used to denote "reign" in the Greek version of the Old Testament.[1] Its use there may illuminate its meaning in the New Testament.[2] For example, in the Greek Old Testament, after King Saul flagrantly disobeyed God, he was told, "Now your reign [*basileia*] will not be established" (1 Sam. 13:14). In other words, Saul's royal authority, his rule, would not continue. The term *basileia* is similarly used in 1 Kings 2:12, where we read that "Solomon sat on the throne of his father David, and his rule [*basileia*] was firmly established" (NIV). We learn from the subsequent narrative that Solomon did serve out his days as king. His right to rule, his *basileia*, was established, then exercised, throughout his years as king. Finally, in Jeremiah 52:4 we learn that the Babylonian King Nebuchadnezzar came to Jerusalem "in the ninth year of his [the Jewish King Zedekiah's] reign [*basileia*]." Here, and in each of the preceding examples, *basileia* denotes not a place, but royal authority. Importantly, because these "reigns" occurred in history—that is, at a particular point in time—the term *basileia* also means, by extension, the era in which kingly authority is exercised.

In the New Testament, an especially clear example of *basileia* meaning "royal authority" is found in the parable Jesus told in Luke 19:12. There we read, "A certain nobleman went to a distant country to receive a kingdom [*basileia*] . . . and then return." What did the nobleman journey to receive? The nobleman went to a far country to receive the power or authority to rule as king. Once he had been granted this authority, his reign began. According to the parable, he eventually returned to his country where he put his reign, his *basileia*, to work (Luke 19:15).

If the Greek word translated "kingdom" in most English Bibles refers primarily to "royal authority" and, by extension, the era in which that authority is exercised, how might this shape our understanding of the phrase "kingdom of God"?

THE MEANING OF THE KINGDOM OF GOD

If we take the word *kingdom* as denoting "reign" or "royal authority," then the words "of God" signify who it is that reigns. God reigns. The phrase "kingdom of God" then refers to the rule of God and, by implication, the era in which he exercises that rule. But if this is the meaning of the phrase, are we saying that God did not reign before Jesus came preaching that the kingdom was at hand?

The Scriptures teach that God is and always has been the sovereign Lord of the universe. Psalm 103:19 says, "The LORD has established His throne in the heavens; and His sovereignty rules over all." Psalm 47:2–8 asserts, "The LORD most high is to be feared, a great King over all the earth . . . God is the King of all the earth . . . God reigns over the nations, God sits on His holy throne."

But while affirming the maxim that God rules the universe, the Scriptures also look forward to a time when God's power, his sovereign rule, will intervene in the history of this world in a special way. Much of chapter 2 explored the Old Testament promises concerning this new era. In the prophetic books it is often introduced by phrases like "in that day" or "in those days" (e.g., Isa. 11:10; Jer. 33:15; Joel 3:1). In the Old Testament this era is not given the specific label "the kingdom of God," but it could nevertheless be aptly characterized as such. It is undoubtedly the case that Jesus and his audiences made the connection between these Old Testament promises and his phrase "kingdom of God."

If we are right to connect the New Testament phrase "kingdom of God" with the Old Testament promises about the future new era, then it is clear that the phrase means more than simply "God reigns"; it is infused with a host of prophetic expectations. There is a specific content to and clearly understood expectations of what that era will look like. To anticipate our conclusion, we can say *the kingdom is the era in which God reveals and imposes his promised salvation and judgment through his son Jesus.* It will be worth exploring how these expectations were fulfilled in the ministry of Jesus and the experiences of the early church.

THE PRESENCE OF THE KINGDOM

From the earliest days of the Christian church, believers have looked forward to the day when the kingdom of God would fully come. In Scripture, this fullness is associated with the return of Jesus. Yet some Christians think the blessings of the kingdom are to be realized *only* in the future. They do *not* see the kingdom of God as beginning with the ministry of Jesus; rather, they believe Jesus' rejection by the Jews meant the postponement of the kingdom. Are they correct? Does this view of the kingdom correspond to New Testament passages that deal with the issue?

In what follows I will argue that the kingdom of God began to intrude into the history of this world through the ministry of Jesus, and that its presence has expanded since then. There are two lines of evidence to point us in this direction: direct statements to the effect that the kingdom has begun and actions that make the same point.

Explicit teaching. One of the clearest direct statements to support the idea that the kingdom began with the coming of Jesus is found in Luke 11:17–20. Here Jesus' authority to cast out demons was challenged by his opponents, who suggested that his power to exorcise derived from Beelzebub (a particularly potent demonic prince). He responded to their charge: "If I cast out demons by the finger of God, then the kingdom of God has come upon you." If we examine Jesus' words a little more closely, we see that he put his answer into an "if-then" proposition. As to the "if " portion, it is clear from Luke's Gospel and from the rest of the New Testament that Jesus did indeed exorcise demons "by the Spirit of God." As a result ("then"), we also conclude that the kingdom has come. The verb here translated "has come upon" (*ephthasen*) does not imply mere proximity, but actual arrival. The same verb was used by Paul in Romans 9:31, where Paul noted that although Jews pursued a law of righteousness they did not attain (*ephthasen*) it (9:31). Paul wasn't arguing that the Jews hadn't come close to attaining righteousness; he meant they hadn't reached their destination. When Jesus said the kingdom had come, he did *not* mean it had merely come near; he meant it had arrived.

Other New Testament writers reiterated Jesus' teaching about the presence of the kingdom. Paul cited the example of Israel's wandering in the desert and God's dealings with them there to warn the church at Corinth not to repeat the sin of Israel. He then observed that Old Testament stories serve as examples for us (believers) "upon whom the ends of the ages have come" (1 Cor. 10:11). The last phrase must mean that the longed-for era of savation has begun. The verb employed by Paul, *katantao*, is used thirteen times in the New Testament. It normally refers to the attainment of a goal or reaching a destination.[3] The fact that it is in the perfect tense here (*katenteken*) suggests that from Paul's point of view the arrival of the kingdom was a accomplished fact, and its arrival had an ongoing effect.[4] Although the apostle John rarely used the phrase "kingdom of God," he did indicate its arrival by statements from Jesus like these: "Yet a time is coming and *has now come* when the true worshipers will worship the Father in spirit and truth, for they are the kind of worshipers the Father seeks" (John 4:23 NIV, italics added). "I tell you the truth, a time is coming and *has now come* when the dead will hear the voice of the Son of God and those who hear will live" (John 5:25 NIV, italics added). These words from Jesus suggest the time of fulfillment had come.

Something like this is also found in the book of Hebrews. Although his identity is unknown to us, the writer of Hebrews displayed both a profound and nuanced understanding of the Old Testament. It can scarcely be a coincidence, therefore, that he employed the catchphrase "in these last days" in referring to the advent and ministry of Jesus (Heb. 1:2; also 1 Pet. 1:20). As we have seen, the phrase "in these days" or its equivalent is often used in the Old Testament to refer to the era of God's salvation. Time and again Old Testament expectations concerning the kingdom are met—if not fully, then initially—in the person of Jesus, in his ministry, and in that of his followers.

The coming of the Lord and Messiah. In our survey of Old Testament expectations regarding the new era, we observed that it would begin with the coming of God and be ruled by his Messiah. In the New Testament we find the joining of these two ideas in the person of Jesus: he is at once the Lord who comes, and the Davidic Messiah who will rule.

Several Old Testament texts that refer to God or the Lord, i.e., Yahweh, are quoted by New Testament writers who see Jesus as the "Lord" in view. For example, under the influence of the Holy Spirit Zechariah, the father of John the Baptist, predicted that John would fulfill Malachi's prophecy and go "before the Lord to prepare his ways." Malachi must have been thinking of the Lord (Yahweh), but in context the Lord before whom John goes is Jesus of Nazareth. Elsewhere, in his first recorded public sermon, the apostle Peter quoted an extended passage from the prophetic book of Joel which includes the comment, "Everyone who calls on *the name of the Lord* shall be saved" (Acts 2:21). Moments later, after he was asked by the gathered crowd what they should do, Peter declared, "Repent, and let each of you be baptized *in the name of Jesus Christ*" (Acts 2:38). In other words, Peter affirmed the Old Testament truism that those who call on the name of the Lord will be saved, but he gave further amplification to the identity of that Lord: it is Jesus.

Similarly, the apostle Paul quoted the prophet Joel: "Whoever will call upon the name of the LORD will be saved" (Joel 2:32 in Rom. 10:13); yet for Paul the Lord whom people must call on is Jesus Christ (Rom. 10:9). Admittedly there are places in the Gospels where Jesus is called "Lord" wherein the person or persons doing the calling probably did not view him as a divine person. Yet one cannot fail to be impressed by the passages just dis-cussed and the fact that writers of the New Testament—all either Jews or those deeply influenced by the Old Testament—would have applied the term "Lord" to Jesus, when in the Old Testament the word was most com-monly applied to God. Moreover, the deity of Jesus is implied in several other passages where he is said to be the agent of creation (John 1:1–3; Col. 1:16) and the object of worship (Heb. 1:6; Phil. 2:10).

As we saw in chapter 2, the label "Messiah" typically referred to a descen-dant of David who would rule as king in the era of salvation. As New Testa-ment writers indicate, Jesus of Nazareth was not only "Lord"; he was "Messiah." Among Gospel writers Matthew and Luke emphasized that Jesus was of Davidic ancestry (Matt. 1; Luke 1). In other words, from an Old Tes-tament point of view, he had the right pedigree to be God's Messiah. Every Gospel writer either alludes to or explicitly affirms Jesus as "from David," as do other New Testament writers (Mark 10:47–48; John 1:41, 49; Rom. 1:3–4; Acts 2:30; Rev. 5:5). Jesus of Nazareth thus fulfilled the Old Testa-ment expectation that a Davidic Messiah would have a significant role in God's new era of salvation.

The giving of the Holy Spirit. Another important feature of the promised era was the unprecedented outpouring of the Holy Spirit. In the Old Testa-ment the Spirit is often mentioned in connection with the ministries given to special leaders, particularly kings, prophets, and priests (1 Sam. 16:13; 19:20; 1 Kings 19:16; Exod. 28:41). But the Scriptures also looked forward to a time when the Spirit would be more widely distributed. We see this most clearly in passages such as Joel 2:28–3:21, Ezekiel 36–37 and Zecha-riah 12:10, which depict the Spirit as coming to old and young, male and female.[5] The scope of those who get the Spirit was to be significantly wid-ened in the new era.

After Jesus' death and resurrection, the Spirit was poured out on the dis-ciples on the Day of Pentecost (Acts 2). At that time the leader of the apostles, Peter, cited the prophecy of Joel to say—in effect—that the prom-ised era of the Spirit's outpouring had begun (Acts 2:16–21). Not only in this passage, but in other narratives in Acts, we see various groups of people getting God's salvation and the anointing by the Spirit. In the letters of Paul, we learn that all believers have been "Spirit-baptized" without regard to eth-nicity, social status, or sex (e.g., Gal. 3:26–27) and that all believers have received a spiritual gift from God (1 Cor. 12:4–11).

Judgment and salvation. According to the prophets, the new era of salvation was to result in the destruction of Israel's enemies. Many of Jesus' contemporaries viewed with contempt the Roman army that controlled their land. From a Jewish point of view, subjection to their heathen enemies was another indication of how wrong things had gone in the present age. As noted in chapter 2, it was widely expected that the coming of the Lord and his Messiah would signal the end of foreign domination of Israel. Jesus did not engage the Romans, and this undoubtedly proved to be a disappointment for many people. But to observe that Jesus did not challenge *these* "enemies" of Israel is not to say that he utterly failed to engage the enemies of his people.

Again in chapter 2, we saw the idea had developed in the intertestamental era that Israel's real oppressors were the spiritual forces, the demons, who energized the hostile nations that surrounded her. Seen in this light, Jesus' ministry *is* characterized by conflict with the *real* enemies of his people; namely, the demons who corrupted and dominated them. Jesus' ministry could be characterized as spiritual warfare with the devil and his demons.

In this connection it is significant that after he was anointed by the Spirit and publicly identified as God's Son by the voice from heaven (Matt. 4:1ff. and parallels), he was led to the wilderness to be tempted by Satan, the great enemy of mankind. Unlike Israel, which was also God's "son" according to Hosea 11:1 and which succumbed to temptation in their wilderness wanderings, and unlike Adam and Eve, who succumbed to the devil despite living in paradise, Jesus resisted the devil and proved to be loyal to God. He is a worthy leader and a model for his people. In his conflict with the devil, Jesus succeeded where others had failed. After his successful encounter with the devil, Jesus' first miracle was casting a demon out of a man in a synagogue (Mark 1:26–28, so also in Luke 4:31–37). The motif of spiritual warfare is found repeatedly in the gospels (e.g., Matt. 8:28–34; Mark 9:14–29) and is occasionally highlighted by the military terms and Old Testament imagery employed by New Testament writers.[6] In every instance of conflict, however, the engagement turned out to be rather one-sided: Jesus vanquishes the spirits with a word.

Also connected to the Old Testament idea that the coming of the Lord would bring judgment on the wicked in Israel is the issue of Jesus' conflict with the Jewish religious leaders. The rulers of the people, particularly their religious leaders, came in for heavy criticism from Jesus. Ideally, the priests and scribes would have led the people to a deeper knowledge of God (Lev.

10:8–11; Deut. 17:8–11; Mal. 2:4–7). In Jesus' day, however, these leaders proved to be obstacles between the people and their God. Jesus openly criticized them for their hypocrisy and failure to observe the most important elements of Old Testament law (Matt. 23:1–36; Luke 11:37–54). He said they needed to repent, lest God visit judgment on them. Indeed, in John's Gospel the connection between the unrighteous leaders of the people and Satan is made explicit. In John 8:44 Jesus charged, "You are of your father, the devil, and you want to do the desires of your father." Ultimately, these leaders stood in peril of losing a place in the kingdom (Luke 13:22–30). In his dealings with Israel's leaders, Jesus' words had a familiar ring to them, for he echoed many of the criticisms that Old Testament prophets made of the leaders of their day (e.g. Isa. 1:23; 28:14–22; Jer. 2:26–37).

As to the fate of these various enemies, it is not merely reserved for the future—it is also experienced in the present. Perhaps the most famous passage in the Bible is John 3:16 ("For God so loved the world that He gave His only begotten Son, that whoever believes in Him should not perish, but have eternal life"). Less famous is verse 18 which says, "He who believes in Him is not judged; he who does not believe has been judged already." According to this verse, standing under the judgment of God is just as much a present reality for the nonbeliever as is standing in the grace of God for the Christian.

Similarly, in the well-known opening chapter of Romans, the apostle Paul outlined the tragic consequences of mankind's depravity. He said, "The wrath of God is being revealed from heaven against all the ungodliness and wickedness of men" (Rom. 1:18 NIV). The present tense verb *apokaluptetai* ("is being revealed") indicates that the outpouring of God's wrath is a present reality for those who oppose him. Likewise, in 1 Corinthians 1:18 (NIV) Paul said, "The message of the cross is foolishness to *those who are perishing*" (*tois apollumenois*). To outward appearances, to the "rulers of this age" and the so-called wise, well-born, and powerful (1 Cor. 1:26–28; 2:6), the good news that God has revealed his power to rescue those alienated from God by sin through the death and resurrection of Jesus is considered silly and contrary to received wisdom. But Paul not only thought unbelievers were wrong, he said they "*are* perishing." The point is this: though unbelievers might be regarded as clever in this world, Paul concluded that they are *even now* passing from the scene. They are, in other words, in the midst of being judged by God. Their present expectation and experience of judgment is a foretaste of the wrath to come (1 Thess. 1:9–10). This means that the important end-times theme at judgment is not realized solely in the future—it is also a present reality.

If the New Testament picture that judgment has begun is clear, it is infinitely more obvious that God's salvation has also come. Jesus' ministry is filled with stories depicting the salvation of God—from the forgiveness extended to sinners (Luke 7:36–50) to the restoration of sick and broken bodies (Mark 2:1–12) to the calming of chaotic winds and seas (Luke 8:22–25). Jesus spoke of the present reality of God's salvation. In John 5:24 (NIV) he said, "I tell you the truth, whoever hears my word and believes him who sent me has eternal life and will not be condemned; he has crossed over from death to life." Note that Jesus said the person who believes God sent him "has"—that is, possesses as a present reality—"eternal life." The apostle Paul also referred to the Christian's present experience of salvation: "For you did not receive a spirit that makes you a slave again to fear, but *you received* the Spirit of sonship. And by him we cry, 'Abba, Father.' The Spirit himself testifies with our spirit that we *are* God's children" (Rom. 8:15–16 NIV italics added; see also Eph. 2:8–9; 1 Cor. 1:18).

Both the prophetically anticipated salvation and judgment of God began through Jesus and continue to this day, even though they are not yet experienced as fully as they will be some day. The kingdom, the era of God's salvation, has begun.

Resurrection. Among those miracles reported in the New Testament, none is more important than Jesus' resurrection. His resurrection is the event that, if true, establishes him as God's unique Son and his words as the words of God. If Jesus was not raised, then—as Paul says—the apostles were wrong, Christianity is false, and Christians are pitiable because they base their lives on a lie (1 Cor. 15:12–19). The New Testament scholar C. F. Evans observed, "To a greater extent than it is anything else, Christianity—at least the Christianity of the New Testament—is a religion of resurrection; and it is this to a greater extent than is any other religion."[7] The question for us at the moment, however, is not the historicity of Jesus' resurrection, but how it relates to the notion of the kingdom as present.[8]

As seen in chapter 2, one element of the Old Testament picture of the end involves resurrection from the dead. A number of passages hint at resurrection, but it is perhaps most clearly expressed in Daniel. He wrote, "Many of those who sleep in the dust of the ground will awake, these to everlasting life, but the others to disgrace and everlasting contempt" (Dan. 12:2; also Isa. 26:19, Ezek. 37:11–14).

Jesus' resurrection is further evidence that "the last days" have begun. His resurrection amounts to a down payment or guarantee that the general resurrection of the dead promised in Scripture will come to pass. This is the point made by the apostle Paul in 1 Corinthians 15:20–28, where he called Jesus "the firstfruits." The firstfruits were just that—the firstfruits of a harvest. They were typically gathered several weeks before the whole crop was ready to collect. The expert farmer could draw some conclusions about the quality and quantity of the harvest to come on the basis of its firstfruits. Paul noted that through Christ the resurrection came, and through him "all shall be made alive" (v. 22). Thus, Jesus' resurrection not only established the credibility of his claim to be God's unique son, it also demonstrated—within the framework of Old Testament expectations of a new age—that the era of salvation had begun.

Summary. Taken as a whole, the New Testament affirms the arrival of God's reign, his "kingdom," in the life and ministry of Jesus. Furthermore, its arrival was not rescinded with his death; rather, his death proved to be another element in the kingdom's inauguration, for it led directly to his resurrection and the coming of the Spirit on God's people.

This understanding of the kingdom as present establishes a theological justification for many of the practices of the early church, some of which continue to the present time. Early Christians continued the ministry of Jesus by casting out demons, praying for the sick, raising the dead, and hearing the prophetic Word of God. They preached the good news about Jesus and the kingdom of God (Acts 19:8; 20:25; 28:23, 31). Paul noted that God was calling believers into his kingdom (1 Thess. 2:12). This is not to say these miraculous experiences were commonplace, for they seem not to have been (i.e., the book of Acts speaks often of miracles, but it must be kept in mind that it covers events in various places over a period of about thirty years). But Christians were and are emboldened to ask for God's intervention by the words and example of Jesus.[9]

Having surveyed briefly the evidence for the inauguration of the kingdom in the ministry of Jesus and the life of the early church, it is clear that those modern writers who speak of the kingdom only as a future reality are sadly, perhaps even tragically, mistaken. The tragedy is in the failure to recognize that in Jesus the most profound moment of human history—the end of the old age and the beginning of the new—has taken place. Further, this historical shift took place according to the Scriptures—that is, it took place according to God's plan. It was part of God's design in and for history.

THE FUTURE KINGDOM

We have argued that both Jesus and the early church believed that the era of God's salvation began with the coming of Jesus and the events at Pentecost. "If the kingdom has come," someone might ask, "why does the world around us often seem so bad? If this is the kingdom, is it really much different than what preceded it? Is this as good as it gets?" It would be wrong to think that New Testament writers emphasize the presence of the kingdom against its future fulfillment. In fact, in most places where the phrase "kingdom of God" is found, it refers to something in the future.

Jesus, for example, spoke of a future time when people "from east and west, and from north and south and will recline at the table in the kingdom of God" (Luke 13:29). As he neared Jerusalem, he told a parable to suppress expectations that his arrival there signaled the immediate, full coming of the kingdom (Luke 19:11ff.). The parable connected the return of the king to the total establishment of his reign. If we think of this parable in relation to Jesus, it teaches that his return will mark the consummation of the kingdom. This is the point made by several New Testament writers (1 Thess. 4:13–5:9; 2 Thess. 1:6–9; 2:1–12; 1 Cor. 15:23–28; 1 Pet. 1:5–9; Rev. 19:11–20:10). In subsequent chapters we will look more closely at these future expectations. For now, it is enough to point out that an important element of New Testament theology is the understanding that God's kingdom will be fully revealed and experienced in the future.

THE MYSTERY OF THE KINGDOM

Old Testament authors tended to see history, or at least the history of this world, as divisible into two eras: the present or wicked time and the future or blessed time. The two were radically different and fundamentally incompatible. The prophets seemed to view the collision of these eras in very stark terms. The wicked era was to be suddenly overtaken by the new, promised one, and all the elements associated with the latter (e.g., the coming of the Spirit, the exaltation of Israel, the destruction of her enemies) were to fall into place at once.

We have seen, on the one hand, that there is ample evidence to suggest the kingdom began with the life and ministry of Jesus; it is equally clear, on the other hand, that the kingdom has not come in its fullness. It is one of the major tasks of theologians, pastors, and laypeople to discern how these apparently incompatible realities are to be put together. In doing so, we have the teachings of Jesus to guide us. Biblical scholars often use the phrase "already-not yet" to describe this tension between the present and not-yet-present aspects of the kingdom.[10] But Jesus had another word to describe this enigma: mystery.[11]

Jesus revealed that the coming of the kingdom involves a few new twists. These new twists touch on almost every area of prophetic expectation, but they have in common the prophetically *unexpected* overlapping of the ages. They were conveyed by Jesus in a series of parables in which he referred to the mystery or "mysteries" of the kingdom. In the modern world the word *mystery* is often associated with things that are strange, eerie, or beyond comprehension. But this is not how the Bible uses the term. The word *mystery* refers to the revelation or amplification of a truth previously unknown or only partially known.

For example, in the parable of the wheat and the tares, Jesus taught that rather than experiencing sudden and irreversible judgment, the wicked would be allowed to mingle with the righteous once the kingdom has begun. In fact, they may even take on the appearance of the righteous and have their true identities revealed only at the end (Matt. 13:24–30, 36–43). In other parables we learn that kingdom begins small and grows large, begins almost inconsequentially yet makes its influence felt everywhere (Matt. 13:31–32).

The mystery is not that the Old Testament promises *won't* be fulfilled, but that they won't be fulfilled as many people expected them to be. Instead of the new era suddenly and completely replacing the old one, the two are allowed to coexist for a time. Their coexistence does not imply any uncertainty about the eventual outcome of history, for once events have been set in motion there can be no turning back. The Resurrection of Jesus and the coming of the Spirit—to cite only two examples—mean that the presence and growth of the kingdom are guaranteed as irreversible; nevertheless, to those steeped in the Old Testament prophetic hope, the New Testament picture of the kingdom as "already and not yet" is somewhat surprising.

Conclusion

The Old Testament prophetic hopes for an era of salvation began to be realized in the life and ministry of Jesus. Indeed, we may rightly regard his coming as signaling the most profound moment of human history—the end of the old age and the beginning of the new. But even during his lifetime Jesus recognized and taught that the complete coming of the kingdom, its consummation, lay in the future.

New Testament scholars have illustrated the tension between the "already" and the "not yet" elements of salvation by pointing to events from World War II. On June 6, 1944, Allied forces began their assault against Germany. After that date there was no question about the ultimate outcome of the war. Between D-day and the German surrender in the autumn of 1945, the Allies engaged in many battles, won many victories, and suffered a few significant setbacks. Yet events guaranteeing the eventual defeat of Germany had been set in motion.

In a similar way, the coming of Jesus—his life, death, and resurrection— set in motion the eventual and inevitable defeat of all people, powers, and things opposed to God. Since the first century the cause of the kingdom has experienced great victories and lamentable losses. But the eventual outcome of history is not in doubt—God's ultimate victory has been secured by the death and resurrection of Jesus. The era of salvation has begun.

As Christians we are subject to selfishness and temptation; we also sing praises to God and relish the experience of his forgiveness. We are dismayed by our inconsistencies, but they stem from a profound theological truth: the "already and not yet" aspects of the kingdom of God introduce tension into almost every element of Christian belief and practice. These tensions have a direct bearing on how we view the Christian life and how we think of our eschatological hopes.

The Christian story could be regarded as triumphal when its past is considered, particularly the event that signaled its historical validation: the Resurrection of Jesus. It is equally triumphal in its conception of the future, the time when Jesus returns and the kingdom comes in its fullness. But Christianity is not triumphal in the sense of guaranteeing protection to Christians from the suffering that is the common lot of mankind. In this regard Christianity is realistic: it neither denies the fact of evil, suffering, and death in the world, nor does it deny the historical evidence for the Resurrection. The Resurrection is an event that affirms one man's (Jesus') deliverance from a very real experience of suffering and death.

Even though the kingdom has been inaugurated and is present in part, the old, unredeemed element of this world retains considerable influence. In the New Testament we find the specter of God's innocent Son being put to death by unrighteous people. In addition, he warned his disciples that they must be prepared to share his fate at the hands of a hostile world (e.g., Luke 12:11; fulfilled in Acts 4–8 and elsewhere). In John 15 Jesus warned, "If the world hates you, you know that it hated me first. If you were of the world, the world would love its own, but because you are not of the world, but I chose you out of the world, because of this the world hates you" (vv. 18–19; also 1 Thess. 3:3; 2 Thess. 1:4–5; 2 Tim. 3:10–12; 1 Pet. 3:17).

Suffering can be anticipated by those who follow Jesus. This is not to deny God's power to intervene in the present age—he often does. We need only think of examples from the book of Acts such as the miraculous release of Peter from prison and Paul's resistance to the bite of a venomous snake (Acts 12:1–17; 28:1–5). Many Christians in our modern world could testify to an experience of God's power in their lives. But alongside these examples we also find the story of Stephen's murder at the hands of those who had a part in Jesus' death (Acts 7). We also hear of Paul languishing in prison for two years because of a corrupt Roman magistrate (Acts 24:25–27).

One of the great tensions between the old and new eras concerns Israel. One of the most clearly understood and widely held expectations regarding the era of salvation involved the exaltation of Jerusalem and the nation Israel. That hope was one of those things that did not happen at Jesus' first coming. Though it was a basic ingredient of the Old Testament picture of the kingdom's arrival, nothing like national deliverance for Israel took place in Jesus' lifetime. Indeed, he seemed on occasion to go out of his way to suppress such expectations.

But does this mean that such deliverance is not to happen in the future? How does the New Testament depiction of the kingdom as "already and not yet" relate to God's plan for Israel? Does the coming of the kingdom and the ever-expanding spread of the gospel to the various peoples and nations of the world imply that the people once called "chosen," the Jews, no longer hold that favored position? That is the question to be addressed in chapters 4 and 6.

✧ Chapter Four ✧

The Restoration of Israel Part I

✧

What about Israel? The question has vexed the minds of statesmen and politicians in the modern era; it has perplexed theologians and students of the Bible for centuries. What does the Bible have to say about Israel's future? Should we regard modern Israel as the fulfillment of prophecies of Jewish restoration? What is the relationship between the theme of Israel's future and the notion of design in history? What, indeed, is Israel?

Many popular books are adamant that Israel stands at the center of God's plan for the future. The case is typically made in this way:

1. God's covenant with Abraham (and his descendants) was unconditional.
2. The Old Testament promises of a great and everlasting future for Israel have not been fulfilled in the past in the anticipated way.
3. *Therefore*, the promises must be fulfilled in the future.

By taking this approach, Christian writers can pile unfulfilled Old Testament prophecies (or those that seem not to have been fulfilled) on top of one another, creating the impression that a mountain of evidence exists to support the view that Israel has a bright, distinct, and prominent future in God's plan. The flaw in this approach is the assumption that a prophecy not fulfilled in the expected way hasn't really been fulfilled. Though undoubtedly well-intentioned, this idea is mistaken.

New Testament writers occasionally seem to understand prophecy as fulfilled in unexpected or nonliteral ways. In Romans 9:25 Paul quotes Hosea 2:23, "I will call those who were not My people, 'My people,' and her who was not beloved, 'beloved.'" In Hosea the words refer to a time in the future when God would renew his love for those in Israel who had been estranged from him; yet Paul applied the promise to Gentiles, "whom He also called, not from among Jews only, but also from among Gentiles. As He says also in Hosea" (Rom. 9:24–25). The prophet Amos forecast a time in which God would first judge Israel, then restore it by restoring a Davidic king to office (Amos 9:7–15).[1] In Acts 15:15–21 James announced that Amos's prediction came to pass not by the restoration of Israel as such but by God's gracious selection of Gentiles. We should be cautious in assuming that because some prophecies seem not to have been literally fulfilled, they have not been fulfilled at all.

With respect to Israel, I am not suggesting that those Old Testament prophecies not fulfilled literally have all been fulfilled some other way. As we shall see, certain prophecies indeed await fulfillment. What I am suggesting, however, is that there is a better place to begin thinking about Israel's future than the Old Testament. Instead of looking there, we will first explore whether the New Testament points to a future for Israel. If New Testament writers think there is a future for Israel, we are on solid ground in talking about it as well. However, prior to a consideration of Israel's future it will be helpful to recount briefly the history of modern Israel.

Modern Israel[2]

The twentieth century witnessed the establishment of the nation-state of Israel in Palestine. The return of Jews to the land is a fascinating story, a history which contains the promise of future disputes and, perhaps, future resolution.

ITS ESTABLISHMENT

There is no need to rehearse fully the events that resulted in the establishment of the modern nation-state of Israel in 1948. At the human level it is clear that world sentiment (or at least the sentiment of those who held the reins of power in the United Nations) had tilted in favor of the Jews once the horrors of the Nazi Holocaust became widely known. The bleak history of anti-Semitism in general, and revulsion at Hitler's atrocities in particular, evoked support for the notion that the Jews needed a homeland where they could live securely. The Zionist movement, which had begun at the turn of the twentieth century and had encouraged a steady influx of Jews to Palestine, put pressure on the great powers to support a Jewish homeland. Great Britain, which controlled the land, was reluctant to cede it to the Jews. The establishment of a Jewish homeland in Palestine was also resisted by Arab nations and others who thought such an annexation amounted to thievery.

In the end the United Nations recommended partition of the land into Jewish and Arab states. The dominant powers—the United States, Great Britain, and the Soviet Union—agreed to the partition which was approved on November 29, 1947. A few months later (May 14, 1948), David Ben-Gurion declared the state of Israel. At the time of partition about 650,000 Jews lived in Palestine. Over the next ten years, Arab states, none of whom offered diplomatic recognition to Israel, expelled nearly 700,000 Jews, most of whom settled in Palestine. Those Arabs who vacated or were expelled from Israel in the course of these early years (also numbering around 700,000) became known as Palestinians.

The day after its establishment in May 1948, Israel was attacked by Egypt, Syria, Lebanon, Iraq, and Trans-Jordan (known now as Jordan). In this war, as in the subsequent war of 1956, Israel emerged victorious and succeeded in enlarging its territory. In between the conflicts of 1948 and 1956, Jordan annexed about two thousand square miles of territory originally intended for Palestinians under a United Nations plan. This land later became known as the West Bank.

Prior to 1964, various factions representing differing political and military philosophies claimed to speak for the Palestinian people. These were brought together in 1964 under the umbrella organization known as the PLO (Palestinian Liberation Organization). It was established to represent Palestinians in the struggle to "liberate Palestine."

THE EVENTS OF 1967 AND 1973

By 1967, Jews had come to Israel from at least eighty-six different countries. Its Jewish population had more than doubled since 1948. In the spring of 1967, led by the Egyptian president Gamal Abdel Nasser, the Arab states cooperated to devise another assault on Israel. On June 5, as the armies of Egypt, Syria, and Jordan prepared to attack, Israel launched a preemptive strike on three fronts.[3] With astonishing speed they overwhelmed their enemies, destroying soldiers, tanks, and airplanes and taking land. In a mere six days the Israeli armies on the southern front had advanced troops far into Sinai and Gaza; in the north the Israelis had wrested control of the strategically located Golan Heights from the Syrians; and in the east they captured the West Bank territory from Jordan. Perhaps the most significant feature of the operation was the Israeli capture and occupation of the whole of Jerusalem (which they subsequently annexed). For the first time in nearly two thousand years Jerusalem was under Jewish sovereignty. The armies of the

Arab states lay shattered and their leaders disgraced by the scope and speed of Israeli victory. In six days (June 5–11) the territory of Israel grew from about eight thousand square miles (roughly the size of New Jersey) to thirty-three thousand square miles.[4]

Egypt and Syria achieved some measure of revenge in 1973 when they launched a surprise attack on the Jewish holy day of Yom Kippur. After the initial success based on surprise, the armies of Egypt and Syria were routed by the Israelis, who were assisted by prompt aid from the United States.

The Yom Kippur War, as it was labeled, demonstrated in an unprecedented way the importance of the Middle East, particularly Israel, for world peace. How so? The Arab-Egyptian attack was accomplished with the material support and encouragement of the USSR. In the early hours of the war, Israel faced the danger of being overrun. They appealed to their chief benefactor, the United States, for help. America responded, sending fighter planes and other equipment to assist Israel. As the war tilted clearly in favor of Israel, the USSR threatened to intervene directly in behalf of its allies, Egypt and Syria, to prevent territorial gains by the Israelis and the destruction of Arab tanks and warplanes. The United States warned that Soviet intervention would lead to direct United States involvement: the first head-to-head confrontation between the great powers in the post-World War II era. Israel was persuaded not to pursue its cause, and hostilities ceased.[5]

To this day, the world at large is intensely interested in the Middle East. There are three major reasons for this: (1) economically, the greatest volume of easily accessible oil is found there; (2) strategically, it sits at the crossroads of three continents, Europe, Asia, and Africa; (3) religiously, Israel is the birthplace of two of the world's most dominant religions, Judaism and Christianity, and is important for the world's third great religion, Islam.

THE PRESENT POLITICAL IMPASSE

To put it in a nutshell: Jews claim the land as theirs; Palestinians, with the support of most Arab nations, say it belongs to them and must be given back. Jews argue that the events of the past two thousand years, culminating in the Holocaust, make clear that a Jewish homeland is the best safeguard to their existence and security. Furthermore, Palestine is their traditional homeland and it is they who, since the late-nineteenth century, have worked to transform the land from desert to oasis.

In addition, although not many Jews are willing to invoke it, there are some who argue the land is theirs by divine right. Palestinians also claim a long tradition in the land and say that their land, houses, and farms were confiscated to make a safe place for Jews. They ask whether two wrongs, the Nazi Holocaust and the confiscation of their land, make a right. Palestinians have long sought the return of land and the destruction of the nation-state of Israel; in fact, these principles are enshrined in the founding charter of the PLO.

Each group can make a plausible case for its position before the tribunal of world opinion, but as things now stand, neither can make a compelling case. As a result, force prevails, and for now and the foreseeable future, Israeli military superiority is unlikely to be challenged successfully.

While it may be difficult to say that history is clearly on the side of Jews or Palestinians, it is true that history is unambiguously on the side of war. In what way? There have been four large, multinational conflicts and innumerable skirmishes over the past fifty years. And yet there are those within and outside Israel who hope for peace. But is this admirable hope well-founded? Only the most optimistic observer of the Middle East could suggest that the long-range position of Israel is anything but untenable. How so?

Israel's enemies are numerous, well funded, and ideologically opposed to their existence. For example, Jews in Israel number about 4 million. As of 1996 the population of the neighboring states of Syria, Jordan, and Egypt was 83.5 million (a ratio of about 21 to 1). If we go a little farther to include countries that border the neighbors of Israel (Iraq, Iran, Saudi Arabia, Libya, and Sudan), the ratio of Israel's enemies to Israeli is about 57 to 1.[6]

As to funding, while Israel has a relatively diverse economy, for sheer size of gross domestic product ($80.1 billion in 1996), it cannot compare with its neighbors and the surrounding oil-rich states ($893.3 billion in 1996). The $6 billion in foreign aid that Israel receives annually from the United States is small compared to these figures.

With respect to its relations with neighbors, Israel is surrounded by enemies and former enemies. Israel is ethnically distinct from its neighbors with whom they either maintain a fragile peace or are in a declared state of war.[7] To the southwest, a formal peace exists with Egypt, but within Egypt itself the rise of Islamic fundamentalism poses a danger to the stability of the government and, as a result, to the peace with Israel. Even under the peace treaty one sometimes hears derogatory statements about Israel by the Egyptian government.[8] In the north Syria has been ruled for years by President

Hafez al-Assad; it refuses to sue for peace with Israel until the Golan Heights are returned. In fact, Syria has apparently been developing weapons of mass destruction, something that causes Israelis to feel even more threatened.[9]

Israel enjoys a formal peace with its neighbor on the east, Jordan, but the peace was for years largely predicated on the influence of Jordan's King Hussein. With his death in 1999, Jordan's future position toward Israel is an open question. There are well-founded concerns about the rise of Islamic fundamentalism in Jordan. Should the fundamentalists come to power, Israel would find itself with an enemy on the eastern front. Other avowed enemies—Iraq, Iran, Saudi Arabia, Libya, and Sudan—are also situated relatively close to Israel.

David Dolan chronicles the religious foundations of the conflict between Israel and its Islamic neighbors. He argues that opposition to Israel has become part of the religious dogma of those Islamic and Islam-dominated states near Israel. If true, his conclusions suggest the conflict is even more unmanageable than some people might wish to think. It is conceded that the various countries near and surrounding Israel have their own national interests and agendas. They often have trouble getting along with one another. This lack of unity has greatly benefited Israel, and it is surely in Israel's self-interest to promote its neighbors' disunity where possible. Nevertheless, there is one area where these nations typically do agree: in their loathing of Israel. History has shown that for the purpose of opposing Israel, Arab unity *is* possible. It remains to be seen if and when this unity may again be achieved.

A MODERN RELIGIOUS REVIVAL?

Modern Israel is one of the most secular nations on earth. Zionism, the political philosophy on which the modern nation is based, is thoroughly secular in its outlook. It is one of the ironies of history that the "people of the book" are fundamentally irreligious today.

While religious Jews did not play a significant role in the reemergence of the nation in 1948, there has been a slow but steady increase in their number and influence in the past fifty years. They have played a crucial role in the last several Israeli governments. Although they are not numerous, their support can help one of the major political parties get a majority and achieve power. The fact that their numbers have increased does not mean they are well-liked—quite the opposite. To cite but one example, religious Jews refuse on principle to serve in the Israeli armed forces. This increases the burden on nonreligious Jews to serve. It also increases their resentment toward those who do not.

While only a fraction of Jewish Israelis is part of traditional Judaism, an increasing number is involved with nontraditional Jewish sects, with many others open-minded about New Age religion. This is especially true among the young, who have apparently become disaffected with the unbelief of their parents. Interestingly, the openness of the young to New Age religion has also translated into more openness to the previously forbidden fruit of Christianity.

It is impossible to determine how many messianic Jews there are in Israel, mostly because there is no will on the part of public officials to acknowledge conversions. Official figures from the bureau of statistics are next to useless because by the government's definition one cannot be at the same time a Jew and a Christian.[10] Although I am reluctant to put too much stock in it, I am aware through anecdotal evidence of the growing number of Christian Jews (= messianic Jews) and messianic congregations in Israel. It has been estimated that there were no more than two dozen messianic Christians in the land at the beginning of statehood in 1948 and around 250 when Jerusalem was retaken in 1967. Now there are in the neighborhood of six thousand believers in more than fifty congregations.[11] In fact, it is arguably the case that Jewish Christians are more numerous now than at any time since the first century.

The religious hierarchy of Israel has found the conversion of Jews to messianic Jews so unsettling that it has not only passed laws that forbid proselytizing, but also proposed laws which would forbid the possession of a New Testament.[12]

We have noted that many Bible teachers and commentators think Israel is the key to understanding God's plan for the future. We have also briefly surveyed the history of modern Israel, observing that its present political and religious condition is far from the biblical ideal. Does modern Israel play a role in God's plan for the last days? What does the New Testament say? Before we address these questions, we must explain what the biblical writers, especially New Testament writers, meant when they referred to Israel.

Who Is Israel?

In the modern world when we refer to "Israel," we automatically think of the modern nation-state located in the Middle East. It is now primarily a homeland for Jews. Nevertheless, within its borders and among its citizenry is a large number of non-Jewish people.

Historically, the word *Israel* has been used in various ways. In the Bible it was initially used as a second name for Jacob, the son of Isaac. It was given to him after his personal encounter with God and the blessing that resulted from it (Gen. 32:28; also 35:9–10).

Later, when the unified monarchy established by Kings David and Solomon was fractured (1 Kings 12), we find a second use of the word. The northern tribes of Israel were called "Israel" while the southern tribes were referred to as "Judah" or "Ephraim." In 721 B.C. the northern kingdom of Israel was conquered by the Assyrians and its existence as an independent nation ceased.

A third use of the term occurred after the exile of the southern kingdom to Babylon. Those who returned to the promised land were often referred to as "Israel" (Ezra 2:2, 70; 4:3; 6:16; Neh. 1:6; 2:10; 11:20; Zech. 12:1; Mal. 1:1). This is the way various New Testament writers, including Paul, often use the term: to refer to the physical descendants of Abraham, "the Jews," especially when they are thought of in the light of God's promises (e.g., Matt. 2:20; 10:6; Luke 1:68; John 1:31; Rom. 9:4).

The fourth use of the term is a narrowing of the third. While the third use is primarily an ethnic and political designation, the fourth use refers to those Jews who are part of the *elect remnant*. What does this mean?

In Romans 9 Paul defended the thesis that despite widespread Jewish rejection of the gospel, the Word of God had not failed (v. 6). He said that his "brethren" and "kinsmen according to the flesh" (v. 3) were "Israelites" (v. 4). This is the typical definition of Israel (the third use, above). However, in Romans 9:6 Paul contended that God's word has not failed because "they are not all Israel who are descended from Israel." What did Paul mean? Is Israel more than, or less than, the descendants of physical Israel? Paul said "Israel" refers not merely to the physical descendants of Abraham, but to those physical descendants who are in the promised line. He pointed to several Old Testament precedents for his narrowing of the meaning of the term. In Romans 9:7–9 he noted that it was Abraham's son Isaac who was *chosen* (i.e., not Ishmael, and therefore not just *any* descendant of Abraham). In Romans 9:10–13 he observed that although Isaac had two sons, only one (Jacob) was *chosen*. Finally, in Romans 9:27 he wrote, "THOUGH THE NUMBER OF THE SONS OF ISRAEL BE AS THE SAND OF THE SEA, IT IS THE REMNANT THAT WILL BE SAVED" (citing Isa. 10:22).[13]

In other words, Paul argued that his narrower use of the term *Israel* to refer to a remnant of believing Jews within the larger group of Israel was valid from a scriptural point of view. Nonetheless, even with this more narrow use of the term, all those referred to by the label "Israel" are ethnic Jews.[14]

This brings us to a possible fifth use of the term: can the word *Israel* refer to believing Gentiles? The term *Israel* appears almost seventy times in the New Testament. The vast majority of occurrences fall clearly under numbers one, three, and four above. In fact, I am not aware of any unambiguous application of the term to Gentile believers. Even those writers who, on other grounds, equate the church with Israel or true Israel recognize that the nearest Paul comes to this meaning is in Galatians 6:16 where he prays for "the Israel of God."[15] However, it is possible to take this as a reference either to Jewish Christians or to those in ethnic Israel who—though not now Christians—will eventually come to faith in Jesus.[16]

In the absence of a clear example to the contrary and the multiplied applications of it to ethnically Jewish people, we should be reluctant to say that Paul uses "Israel" to refer to Gentile believers or the church. Some would argue that although the term *Israel* is not explicitly applied to the church, the equation of the two is legitimate because the New Testament frequently applies words first directed at Israel to the church (e.g., 1 Pet. 1:15–16). Without offering a detailed defense of my position here, I would simply suggest that in this passage Peter does what Paul says we can expect: he applies Old Testament Scripture to Christians because Scripture was written "for our instruction" (1 Cor. 10:11; also Rom. 15:4). To the extent that we share a spiritual heritage with Israel, we can see ourselves as spiritually related. However, this is not the same thing as saying "the church is Israel."[17]

To sum up: the term "Israel" may refer to (1) the patriarch Jacob; (2) the northern kingdom; (3) the Jewish nation as a whole; or, (4) a believing remnant within the nation. The word always has in mind Jewish persons. Most occurrences of "Israel" in the New Testament refer to the Jewish nation as it existed in Jesus' day and at the time of the early church.

Jesus and the Pattern of Israel's Rebellion

In the Old Testament, at various times the prophets warned God's people to repent lest judgment come; the ultimate expression of this judgment under the old covenant was Jewish dispersion among the nations (see again Deut. 28:15–68). In the New Testament Jesus is depicted as, among many other things, a prophet *par excellence*. We noted earlier that Jesus came to preach the good news that God's new era of salvation was beginning. He preached almost exclusively to Jewish audiences. Although he and all the apostles were Jewish, most Jews did not follow him. Indeed, it was at the urging of the Jewish leadership that the Roman authorities put Jesus to death.

But Jesus had anticipated this rejection. Before his death, he had made predictions concerning the fate and future of Jerusalem and the Jewish people. He warned the nation to repent lest judgment come (e.g., Luke 13:1–9). He said the temple would be destroyed and Jerusalem besieged, that many of its people would be killed, and still others would be sent into exile among the nations (Luke 21:5–6, 20–24; see also the parallels in Matt. 24:15–28 and Mark 13:9–23). His words echo the warnings to Israel first sounded by the Old Testament prophets, who themselves often alluded to the curse section of Deuteronomy 28:15–68.

Jesus' predictions about Jerusalem began to come to pass about thirty-five years after his death, in the period of the Jewish War, A.D. 66–70. The reasons for the outbreak of the war are varied and complex—the abuse of power by Roman governors, the difficult economic situation in the region brought on by the famine of A.D. 48 and relentless Roman taxation, the actions of Jewish ultranationalists, whose murderous tactics provoked the Roman authorities, and so on.[18] Though there were many pockets of rebellion in the land, the trouble began at Jerusalem. The rebellion spread to the countryside and Rome sent its armies to establish order. After a long siege Roman armies broke through the walls of the city, destroyed the temple, and killed many inhabitants. The Romans then vanquished the remnants of Jewish opposition throughout Palestine.

Even though the temple was destroyed, the sacrifices ended, and the Sanhedrin dissolved, a circle of Jewish biblical scholars continued to meet outside Jerusalem to study the law and remember how the temple had operated. They apparently thought that restoration of the sacrifices would come soon. They sought to preserve knowledge of the sacrificial rituals for the time when it would again be needed at the temple. However, these hopes were not to be fulfilled. Around A.D. 130, the Roman emperor Hadrian proposed to build a city and pagan temple among the ruins of Jerusalem. This outraged the Jews in Palestine, and, in A.D. 132, a second revolt broke out. It was led by Simon bar Kokhba, who was regarded by many Jews as the Messiah. The Roman army stamped out the rebellion, and the war was over in

A.D. 135. Jerusalem became a Roman colony, and no Jew was allowed to enter it upon penalty of death.[19] Jews scattered to the four corners of the earth.

This dispersion of Jews, begun in A.D. 70 and intensified in A.D. 135, was to all appearances the ultimate fulfillment of the curses of Deuteronomy 28.[20] This chapter of the Bible indicated that God would punish his people by removing them from the land and exiling them among the nations when they did not "obey the Lord" (Deut. 28:15). The dispersion also fulfilled the words of Jesus, who nearly a hundred years earlier had predicted, "There will be great distress upon the land, and wrath to this people, and they will fall by the edge of the sword, and will be led captive into all the nations; and Jerusalem will be trampled under foot" (Luke 21:23–24). Worse yet, this dispersion signaled to some that God had put an end to his dealings with the nation.

It is useful to set the events of A.D. 70–135 in biblical-theological context. We noted in chapter 2 that Israel's history is marked by a cycle of events: blessings from God, disobedience to God, warnings from God to repent (given by prophets), judgment from God, leading to restoration and blessing . . . and so on. For example, before the exile to Babylon, God had sent prophets to warn his people to repent and turn to him in faith. Even though the warnings were not heeded in time to avert judgment, people did eventually repent. They returned to the land within 150 years of the start of the Exile. During this time the temple was restored, sacrifices were reinstated, and Jerusalem was rebuilt.

It is instructive to compare this state of affairs with what happened to the nation beginning in A.D. 70. If we take the view that Jesus was God's Son, prophet, and Messiah, we see a consistency in God's dealing with Israel. While they were oppressed by the Romans, God sent them Jesus, a savior and prophet like Moses. But they rejected this prophet and his message. Seen in this light, the words of Jesus provide a rationale for Jerusalem's destruction: it was God's judgment for their failure to recognize and follow him, their rightful king (Luke 19:41–44). On the other hand, if we accept a Jewish point of view that Jesus was neither prophet nor Messiah, these horrible events are not only catastrophic but nearly inexplicable, because they break the cycle of God's dealing with the nation. How so? If Jesus was not who he said he was, then before the events of A.D. 70 God had *not* sent a prophet to warn the people, had *not* offered additional promises of restoration, had *not* explained why he intended to bring a destruction that was unprecedented in scope and duration.

Banished from Jerusalem—without temple, sacrifice, priesthood, or king—the Jewish community focused on the Scriptures as a rallying point for its cultural identity. As they lived among the nations in Diaspora for the next 1,900 years, hope in the ancient promises faltered. This was especially the case after the Nazi Holocaust, where for many the question "where is God?" was answered with a resounding "nowhere." As Elie Wiesel wrote so poignantly,

> Never shall I forget that night, the first night in camp, which has turned my life into one long night, seven times cursed and seven times sealed. Never shall I forget the little faces of the children, whose bodies I saw turned into wreaths of smoke beneath a silent blue sky. Never shall I forget those flames which consumed my faith forever. Never shall I forget that nocturnal silence which deprived me, for all eternity, of the desire to live. Never shall I forget those moments which murdered my God and my soul and turned my dreams to dust. Never shall I forget these things, even if I am condemned to live as long as God Himself. Never.[21]

If Jews were bewildered by the apparent outcome of history (prior to 1948), many Christians seemed equally in the dark, at least as far as their relationship with Jews were concerned. There were many deplorable episodes of anti-Semitism on the part of Christians through the centuries, a fact that seems incongruous with their devotion to Jesus—a Jewish man and Israel's Messiah.

But some might argue that treating Jews harshly was warranted because of their role in causing Jesus' death; moreover, some say, God has also treated them harshly—so much so that as a people they have been written out of his plan for history. In the Old Testament, prophetic warning and divine judgment were means to an end. God chastised the people and exhorted them to renew their love for the Lord so that he might, in turn, restore them. But is this the goal that Jesus' words of warning and rebuke were meant to achieve? Has the cycle of blessing and disobedience that characterized Israel's history been broken completely with the coming of Jesus? When Israel rejected *this* prophet of God, did God reject them? Answers to these questions await us in chapter 6. In the meantime, there are other issues to consider.

PART II
FOREGROUND

That Which Lies Ahead

✦ Chapter Five ✦

UNCERTAIN SIGNS
IN UNCERTAIN TIMES

✦

As long ago as 4000 B.C. fortune-tellers used practices like reading tea leaves, astrology, numerology, and palmistry to divine the future. In the modern world such practices are widely regarded as relics of a superstitious world or as downright fraudulent.

But a longing for signs, omens, and special information is not confined to the past. Modern history affords us many examples of groups and individuals who have declared that they have "inside information" or special insight concerning the future last days. For example, in 1843 the American preacher William Miller taught his congregation that the world would end before March 21, 1844. This sensational message brought thousands into his church—and considerable embarrassment when events did not turn out as he had predicted.[1]

More recently a South Korean church leader's prediction that Christians were to be removed from the earth on October 28, 1992, led many to sell their belongings, others to resign jobs, and a few—when the prophecy failed to occur—to commit suicide.[2] Although this "inside information" allowed these leaders to gather many followers, it did not prove reliable—but that has not prevented others from taking their place with new claims of inside information and the almost inevitable assembly of followers who believe them. These teachers and leaders would remain unnoticed but for the natural desire of people to know how the future will unfold. As noted earlier, such concern is not new. Indeed, a few days before his death Jesus was asked what signs might precede his return and the end of the age (Matt. 24:3). It is clear that the last days was a topic of interest to the followers of Jesus in the first century, even before his death.

His followers continue to wonder about the last days and the signs of the times. Books, radio and television broadcasts, newsletters, and Internet websites publish warnings of Jesus' soon return at a record pace. Most of them point to various current events as irrefutable evidence that the end is near. Are there "signs of the times" that we can rely on to evaluate whether we are really living in the last days?

Signs of the End?

The Bible depicts the end times as characterized by various kinds of disasters. Thus, our obsession with them becomes, in the minds of some people, an implicit confirmation that the end is near. Popular books on the end times ask whether the persecution of the church, the apparent increase in the number of "natural" disasters, outbreaks of war, and the appearance of would-be messiahs are signals that the end is near. In what follows we will look at five categories of "signs" and ask if their occurrence in the modern world offers confirmation that "the end is nigh."

THE PERSECUTION OF THE CHURCH

Jesus predicted widespread and intense persecution of Christians at the end of days. According to Matthew 24:9, believers are to experience tribulation and death, and they will be "hated by all nations"—all in advance of "the end" (Matt. 24:14). The book of Revelation depicts many Christians martyred in the tribulation of the last days as seeking vindication from God, only to be told that others must share their fate before the end comes (Rev. 6:9–11). The late twentieth century has witnessed the bloodiest, most extensive persecution of Christians since the beginning of the church.[3] This fact is occasionally cited as proof that we are living in the last days.

The New Testament indicates that persecution is what believers may expect in the time before the return of Jesus. For example, in Luke 21 Jesus spoke extensively about the last days and said that before the terrible events of the end the enemies of the church "will persecute you, handing you over to the synagogues and prisons leading you before kings and rulers on account of my name" (v. 12). In fact, this is the very thing that happens to Christians in the book of Acts (4:1–23; 5:17ff.; 6:9ff.; 8:1ff.; 12:1ff.; 14:19ff.). Furthermore, the apostle Paul often referred to the tribulation faced by the church (Rom. 5:3; 8:35; 12:12; 2 Cor. 1:8; 7:4; Eph. 3:13; 1 Thess. 1:6; 3:3–4; 2 Thess. 1:4). He echoed the views of Jesus on the theme of persecution, declaring that "all who desire to live godly in Christ Jesus will be persecuted" (2 Tim. 3:12).

From the first century onward Christians have been persecuted for their faith. Though there were numerous localized persecutions during the first two centuries of the Christian era, it was the Roman Emperor Decius who instituted the first organized persecution throughout the empire in A.D. 250. It was short-lived, however, and had the effect of strengthening the church and even bolstering public opinion of believers who were seen as victims of a corrupt government. A century later Christianity gained official status under the rule of Emperor Constantine. In his considerable empire, official persecution of Christians faded away.

Persecution has occurred throughout history. It has never entirely ceased and will intensify in the last days. But it is important to keep in mind that although it is a necessary feature of the last days, it occurs at other times as well. Persecution cannot be interpreted as an infallible signal that the end times are near.

EARTHQUAKES, PLAGUES, FAMINES, AND HEAVENLY SIGNS

The world is fascinated by disasters. If a catastrophe or crisis occurs, you can bet it will be featured at the top-of-the-hour newscast or in newspaper headlines. And if authentic natural disasters fail to titillate, Hollywood will invent or recreate one to entertain us. It matters little whether the disaster is natural or man-made: we are fascinated by them all.

According to Jesus, before the end comes "there will be earthquakes in various places; there will also be famines" (Mark 13:8). In Luke 21:25 he warned, "There will be signs in sun and moon and stars, and upon the earth dismay among nations." In the book of Revelation after the "seven seals" begin to be broken (an event which may refer to the onset of worldwide tribulation in the last days), more than one-fourth of the earth's population dies as a result of disasters such as famine, plague, and earthquake (Rev. 6:8, 12; 8:7–10; 16:2–18). It is no wonder that many people want to know whether contemporary natural disasters are signs of the end. One newspaper featured this front-page headline: "Signs of the End?" The article went on to state, "The magnitude and frequency of natural disasters sure seem to be increasing. Scientists offer some reasonable explanations. But some high-profile religious leaders believe these disasters could be fulfilling biblical prophesies of approaching doomsday."[4] Over the next few pages we will survey evidence concerning several of these natural disasters to see if they warrant merely Christian concern or apocalyptic alarm.

According to the United States Geological Survey, the incidence of major earthquakes appears to be on the rise.[5] Scientists in California have forecast the likelihood of a major earthquake in one of the state's population centers in the next thirty years.[6] Does all this suggest that the biblical scenario of a world literally trembling at the return of the Lord is on the verge of being realized?

The "trend" just mentioned is based on observations over a short span of time. Indeed, the USGS notes that the number of earthquakes reported annually has steadily increased with the increase in the number of seismograph stations established to monitor quakes.[7] At present twelve thousand to fourteen thousand earthquakes are registered each year. The Scriptures do not indicate what a prophetically significant number of earthquakes might be. It is clear that we have no way to know whether, over the course of the last two thousand years, their frequency has increased.

Furthermore, even if we were to detect a statistically significant rise in frequency of earthquakes, there is no way to rule out the possibility that an equally statistically significant decrease might not occur one hundred or two hundred years from now. According to Matthew 24:8 earthquakes are only "the beginning of birth pangs." From this comment we may conclude that, just as birth pangs tend to increase in frequency and severity as the moment of birth approaches, so earthquakes and associated phenomena increase before the return of Jesus. But this increase is never quantified for us. Hence, even if there is an increase over a period of time, we do not know for certain that it is the increase signaling the last days.

But what about the threat of plagues? The explosion in the worldwide incidence of AIDS, along with its resistance to cure, has troubled medical researchers and politicians alike.[8] It is estimated that 22.5 million people are infected with HIV throughout the world.[9] Perhaps of even greater long-term consequence is the alarming proliferation of Hepatitis C (HCV). It is estimated that a staggering 170 million people are infected worldwide.[10] Furthermore, there is growing awareness in the scientific community of the adaptability of various bacteria and viruses. This adaptability may some day outstrip our ability to treat these aggressive microbes and diseases effectively.[11] As reported in *The Wall Street Journal*:

> Stuart B. Levy of Tufts University's medical school believes
> that current antibiotics will increasingly fail against common

bacteria, leaving some deadly diseases untreatable in the next few years. That raises nightmarish fears: Millions of people could die of once-routine and easily curable infections; common ear infections in children could rage into potentially brain-damaging meningitis; many forms of pneumonia would turn deadly.[12]

But alongside these ominous developments has come more positive news. Modern medicine and related technologies have led to a considerable increase in life expectancy and overall quality of life.[13] Multiplied billions of dollars are spent each year on medical research. The past twenty years alone have witnessed dramatic breakthroughs in the detection and treatment of various illnesses and injuries.[14] As to HIV and HCV, these diseases do pose grave health risks; yet each is, if not curable, largely preventable.[15] Furthermore, both HIV and HCV are relatively slow-acting viruses when compared with other more aggressive health menaces.

But even if the "superbugs" mentioned earlier were to emerge, would their appearance be a sure sign that we are living in the last days? It may be tempting to think so, but if we reflect on the history of plagues over the past two thousand years we see that the absence of plague is the exception rather than the rule. Hence, the recent experience of Western culture and the resultant expectation of a plague-free life turn out to be historical oddities. Plagues can appear and wipe out large numbers of people yet not be sure signs that the end has come. The so-called "Black Death" which ravaged Europe from 1347 to 1351 produced more fatalities than any previously known war or epidemic. Estimates are that nearly one-third of Europe's population died.[16] If a plague of similar proportion were to strike the United States in the early twenty-first century, nearly eighty million people would die! One can only imagine the panic that would accompany such an event and the number of doomsayers who would proclaim that "the end is nigh." As fatal and as frightening as various plagues and epidemics might appear, they are not clear indicators that the end times have arrived.

But Jesus also warned of famine. Is not the modern incidence of famine a cause for apocalyptic concern? According to published reports, tens of millions may die from famine in the near future.[17] Is this what Jesus warned about when he said that in the last days there would be famines (Mark 13:8; also Rev. 6:8)?

It is impossible to say. Famines have occurred since the time of Jesus. Indeed, in Acts 11:28 we read about the large-scale famine that occurred in the reign of the Roman Emperor Claudius in A.D. 46. Paul was acquainted with famine (Rom. 8:35).[18] More recently a drought-induced famine caused eight hundred thousand deaths in northwest India in 1837–38. In Ireland nearly one million people died in the potato famine of 1845–49. As many as five million people lost their lives in the USSR in 1921–22, while about one million people were starved in Cambodia in 1975–79.[19]

Yet over the past two hundred years the effects of famine have been mitigated by developments in transportation, communication, and agriculture. In the modern world, death from starvation is often caused by bad politics rather than by bad crops or bad weather. For example, the famine in Sudan in the late twentieth century was rooted in civil war, with troops from one side burning farms and equipment to terrorize and defeat their enemies.[20]

It is obvious that famines can occur in times other than the end times. We cannot infer that famines are in themselves clear signs that the last days have arrived.

Signs from heaven are a prominent feature of the last days. They figure into Jesus' description of the end in Luke 21:25–26 as well as in the book of Revelation (6:12–14; 8:10–12). This is not surprising. The notion that heavenly phenomena could serve as portents of a gloomy future was common both in the Old Testament and in Graeco-Roman literature. For example, in the Old Testament we learn that on the day of the Lord when Babylon will be judged, "all hands will go limp, every man's heart will melt. . . . The stars of heaven and their constellations will not show their light. The rising sun will be darkened and the moon will not give its light" (Isa. 13:7, 10 NIV). Similarly, the prophet Joel wrote:

> Blow the trumpet in Zion; sound the alarm on my holy hill. Let all who live in the land tremble, for the day of the LORD is coming. It is close at hand—a day of darkness and gloom, a day of clouds and blackness. Like dawn spreading across the mountains a large and mighty army comes, such as never was of old nor ever will be in ages to come. . . . Before them the earth shakes, the sky trembles, the sun and moon are darkened, and the stars no longer shine (Joel 2:1–2, 10 NIV).[21]

The first-century Roman historian Suetonius noted that the death of the Roman Emperor Claudius was preceded by omens: "The rise of a long-haired star, commonly called a comet; the striking of his father Drusus's tomb by lightning."[22] While a modern scientific person might not put much stock in such things, Scripture indicates heavenly signs *are* part of an end-times scenario. Are the recent reports from the Red Cross and reputable scientists about impending doom from climatic changes fulfillment of Jesus' words that in the end people will live in fear because of the "roaring of the sea" (Luke 21:25)?[23] Are modern fears about the destruction of the earth from a renegade asteroid an advance warning that the something like a burning mountain cast into the sea of Revelation 8:8 is a realistic possibility?[24]

Perhaps. Perhaps not. From time immemorial there have been heavenly phenomena that some people have interpreted as significant omens. But there is no way to know if the things we see now are preludes to or part of the heavenly signs mentioned in Scripture. We cannot regard them as certain signs that the last days have arrived.

There is no question that "natural" disasters are to occur often in the end times; the issue is, Do such disasters characterize only the end? We may note there is a certain affection between couples who are courting, and that courtship typically precedes a honeymoon; but it would be wrong to conclude that because a couple behaves affectionately, they will be married soon. Perhaps they are already married; perhaps the marriage is years away; perhaps the relationship will end next week. It is one thing to recognize a linkage of events; it is another to make that linkage absolute. In a similar way, there are serious questions about whether the apparent increase in disasters in the modern era is anything more than perception. There is the additional question, unanswerable in my opinion, of whether such an increase, even if real and demonstrable, should be understood as a sign of the end.

WARS AND RUMORS OF WARS
Some writers suggest the many wars and conflicts that have erupted in the past century are further evidence that the end is near.[25] After all, they note, in his lesson on the last days Jesus informed the disciples, "You will be hearing of wars and rumors of wars" (Matt. 24:6). Similarly, in the book of Revelation the second of the four horsemen of the apocalypse comes "to take peace from the earth . . . and a great sword was given to him" (Rev. 6:4). Additionally, they note that the twentieth century was the bloodiest in human history if the total number of war-related deaths is counted. Between forty million and fifty million people died in World War II alone. While the two World Wars engaged virtually all the major powers, innumerable smaller conflicts made war-related death and destruction almost ubiquitous.[26]

Moreover, we contemplate a future in which more and more nations will acquire sophisticated conventional weapons and, ominously, nonconventional ones. In 1945, the United States alone possessed a nuclear weapon. In 1949, it was joined in this lethal club by the Soviet Union. The British successfully tested an atomic weapon in 1952; the French in 1960. The world's two most populated nations developed nuclear weapons some time later: China in 1964, and India in 1974. During the 1980s it was learned that South Africa and Israel also had nuclear weapons capabilities. Pakistan exploded a nuclear device in 1998. At the turn of the millennium, nuclear weapons were under development in many other countries, including Iran, Iraq, and North Korea.

The Nuclear Non-Proliferation Treaty of July 1, 1968, was signed by the United States, the United Kingdom, and the Soviet Union. They, along with fifty-nine other nations, agreed not to assist other countries in obtaining or producing nuclear weapons.[27] The treaty has been bent and broken many times since its ratification. For example, evidence exists that China and Russia assisted in the development of these weapons by Iran and Pakistan.[28] This seems to have been done with the knowledge of other treaty signatories.[29] Other nonconventional weapons—chemical and biological—have been developed and stockpiled for years, despite international agreements barring these activities.[30] In the meantime, sales of sophisticated conventional weapons by major powers put lethal force in the hands of nations that would otherwise be unable to develop such weapons. Year by year the world becomes a more dangerous place.

The Roman Empire of Jesus' day enforced a peace—the *Pax Romana*—on its subjects. It was largely successful in maintaining peace for nearly two hundred years. Since then the world has rarely, if ever, enjoyed such tranquility. But as for the twentieth century, it is not clear on the basis of presently available data that it was the most belligerent on record *if* we take into account the percentage of total world population killed at war. In addition, there is simply no way to determine if the conflicts we see and hear about today are anything more than fallen humanity making its way from one historical moment to the next. We should not, indeed we *cannot*, conclude that what we see is unusual, much less a sign that the last days are here.

In fact, the Bible verse cited earlier *to connect* wars with end-time events can be interpreted to *discount* the immediate association of the ideas. After saying, "And you will be hearing of wars and rumors of wars," Jesus added, "See that you are not frightened, for those things must take place, *but that is not yet the end"* (Matt. 24:6, italics added). From this we can surmise that wars—even widespread and frequent ones—should not lead us to conclude that Jesus will return soon.

WIDESPREAD LAWLESSNESS

Jesus predicted that alongside persecution, natural disasters, and false prophets, lawlessness would increase in the last days (Matt. 24:12). Some people argue that an increase in lawlessness is a clear sign that the end is near.

There are two difficulties with this view. The first is common to many of the items we have explored in this chapter: it is the problem of quantifiability. How much of an increase in lawlessness would warrant the conclusion that the end is here? Would 4 percent be negligible and 28 percent prophetically significant? There is no way to know for sure.

A second difficulty has to do with what is meant by the term *lawlessness.* Does this mean crime? Is it immoral behavior?

Perhaps lawlessness is criminal behavior. Understood in this way, we can gauge whether lawlessness has increased by consulting crime statistics. But this leads to uncertain results, since crime seems to rise and fall over the course of many years. A severe increase over a period of years may lead some people to conclude that we are in the last days; that thesis may then be shattered by subsequent statistics which show crime has decreased. Further, what are we to conclude when crime increases in one culture and diminishes in others? In fact, the biblical notion of increasing lawlessness is probably not directly related to criminal behavior.

In the Old Testament there was a standard law code by which behavior could be judged (i.e., the books of Moses). To adhere to the laws was to be law-abiding; to break them was to be "lawless." Since deviation from that code was deviation from God's clearly expressed moral will, we can readily see that "lawlessness" equals "sin" (or "wickedness"). This connection influenced the way New Testament writers thought of lawlessness. In several modern translations the Greek word for lawlessness (*anomia*) is translated as "wickedness" (compare, for example, the NIV and NASB of Matt. 7:23; Rom. 4:7; 2 Cor. 6:14). So what does it mean that lawlessness will increase in the last days?

It probably means that sinful behavior, which in Jewish thinking would have been regarded as "lawless," will increase in the end. The world will be a place which has lost its moral compass. It does not mean that this bad behavior will be widely recognized as sinful—indeed, on account of its prevalence, it may not be condemned. The book of Revelation characterizes the last days as a time in which mankind is deeply involved in idolatry and immorality (Rev. 9:20–21; 18:3–5). These practices clearly fall under the Old Testament rubric of "lawlessness."

But who is to say that a given increase in wickedness would be the end-times increase envisioned by Scripture? Wise people from many cultures have lamented their own cultures' decline in morality and virtue. Indeed, these lapses have sometimes signaled the end of a particular culture. But the end of one culture, no matter how great it might have been, is not the same as the end of the world. It only seems like it to those in the midst of societal collapse. Perceptions about increased lawlessness may mislead us. But even if true, they would not by themselves permit us to conclude with certainty that "the end is near."

MESSIANIC PRETENDERS AND FALSE RELIGIONS

Non-Christian religions, sects, and cults have attracted many followers in the Western world in the twentieth century.[31] For a variety of reasons, it seems that the twentieth century has been a particularly fertile breeding ground for would-be Messiahs and prophets.[32] The emergence of these movements and leaders such as Rev. Sun Myung Moon, L. Ron Hubbard, and David Koresh has led some Christians to suppose that prophecies about false religious leaders are being fulfilled and that we are living in the last days.[33]

According to Scripture, the era between Jesus' comings would be marked by false religious leaders. Jesus taught that false prophets and messiahs would come soon after his departure (Mark 13:5–8). He said that some of them would have considerable powers of deception involving signs and miracles (Matt. 24:24). The apostle Paul warned the elders of the church at Ephesus, "I know that after I leave, savage wolves will come in among you and will not spare the flock. Even from your own number men will arise and distort the truth in order to draw away disciples after them" (Acts 20:29–30 NIV). In writing to Timothy, Paul warned that in the last days false religious leaders would appear and try to deceive believers (2 Tim. 3:1–8).

Nevertheless, there is no way to know if the current boom in messianic pretenders is another chapter in our march toward Armageddon or the final chapter before the end. Indeed, as early as the first century, the apostle John could write, "Even now many antichrists have arisen" (1 John 2:18). On a worldwide scope Christianity is attracting more adherents than non-Christian religions. This might surprise some Christians in the West who are accustomed to viewing the world through the decay of their own culture. But while believers in one culture may fear that it is losing its Christian heritage, what is true for them is not necessarily true for the world as a whole.[34] The church once flourished in North Africa but was supplanted centuries ago by Islam—yet the church's demise there did not signal the last days had come.

This belief about the world being overrun with false religions and messianic pretenders fails to consider the situation in the first century. Paul was a missionary to Jews, God-fearers, polytheists, and idolaters. To state the obvious, the world was not a Christian place! But its dominance by non-Christian religions did not mean the end had come. Thus, we should not conclude that the false religions, prophets, and messiahs in our world constitute clear signals that the last days have arrived.

Summary and Conclusion

The Scriptures lead us to expect the period between Jesus' first and second coming will be marked by persecution, disasters, wars, and lawlessness. To recognize this does not affirm a naturalistic view of the world—one that promotes the notion that everything continues now as it has from the beginning (2 Pet. 3:4). On the contrary, the phenomena mentioned in this chapter offer confirmation of the biblical worldview that the earth is a place deeply marred by the effects of the Fall.

There will be a rise in frequency and severity of disasters and troubles toward the end. This is part of the biblically anticipated end-times scenario. But as we have noted, even if we could demonstrate that natural disasters occur more frequently now than in the past, who is to say that they are sufficiently frequent for us to conclude that "the end is nigh"? I am not denying the link between disaster and the end times. What I am pointing out though is our inability to quantify that link and hence our ability to recognize it with certainty.

Does this mean that no clear signals will precede the end? It does not. In the following chapters we will investigate what these clear signals might be.

Chapter Six

THE RESTORATION
OF ISRAEL
PART II

✧

G od is involved with our world in the most essential way: he is its Creator. He is not the god of the Deists—a god who creates the world,
then walks away from it. He is not content simply to speak about himself—
he also reveals himself by intervening in human affairs. The God of Scripture is the God of history. His dealings with Israel make this point in an
especially powerful way: the Jews were not only given the Scriptures; they
also experienced both his hand of blessing and his rod of discipline. These
occurred not in the abstract, but in concrete historical phenomena.

To return to a question posed at the end of chapter 4: has God put an end
to his relationship with Israel? In what follows I argue that he has not. But
it is worth noting that although the theme of Israel's repentance and restoration is a major feature of modern speculation about the end times, it was
a relatively minor issue judging from the amount of space devoted to it in
the New Testament. Only two writers, Luke and Paul, seem to give it much
attention. We will deal with their writings consecutively.

A Future for Israel in Luke-Acts

We cannot be sure precisely when Luke-Acts was written.[1] It is clear,
however, that it was written in response to misunderstandings about Jesus
and the fledgling Christian movement. In the prologue to his Gospel, Luke
indicated that the issues important to Theophilus, i.e., "certainty of the
things you have been taught" (Luke 1:4 NIV), had not been satisfactorily
addressed by other writers, presumably *Gospel* writers.[2] Luke undertook to
clarify for Theophilus the issues which were troubling him. Since Luke has
more to say about a future for Israel than any other New Testament writer
(with the possible exception of Paul's discourse in Romans 9–11), we may

surmise that one of the issues Luke wished to clarify for Theophilus was the status of Israel.[3]

Why would Israel's status have been an issue for Luke? Because it touched on the question of God's faithfulness. Israel was the chosen nation. Yet in Luke's gospel we see the Jewish leaders' complicity in the death of Jesus. Furthermore, in Acts we observe continued Jewish hostility to Jesus' followers (both in Jerusalem and elsewhere). And, to top it all off, we have the record of Jesus predicting the destruction of Jerusalem and the death and scattering of its people. So, the question had probably emerged even as early as the first century, "Had God put an end to his dealings with the nation?" If the answer to the question was "yes," a problem would have remained for both Luke and his first audience: Did not God make unconditional promises to Israel in the past that now seem to have been changed? How could Christians have confidence that God might not change his mind about them, if he did so with Israel? No wonder Luke addressed the status of Israel!

The following passages indicate that, at least from Luke's point of view, God would make good his promises to Israel (although not precisely, perhaps, in the way anticipated by the prophets of old). In fact, Israel would continue to figure in God's plan of redemption to the extent that what the apostle Paul called the blessed hope of all Christians—the second coming of Jesus (2 Tim. 2:13f)—depended on the repentance of Israel.

ACTS 1:6

The resurrected Jesus taught the disciples for forty days about "the kingdom of God" (Acts 1:3); afterwards, he spoke of the coming baptism with the Holy Spirit (Acts 1:5). Then, in Acts 1:6 Jesus was asked by the disciples, "Are you restoring the kingdom to Israel at this time?" This question seemed to come out of nowhere; after all, we are told that Jesus had been talking not about Israel but about the "kingdom of God." What could they have been thinking?

Actually, it is not difficult to imagine what led the disciples to ask about the restoration of the kingdom to Israel. In certain Old Testament passages the coming of the Spirit (the topic just mentioned by Jesus) and the exaltation of Israel are linked. For example, Joel 2:28–3:2 speaks prophetically about a time when God will pour out his Spirit on Israel in an unprecedented way, with the result that mighty miracles will occur and the fortunes of Judah and Jerusalem will be restored. Similarly, in Ezekiel 39:25–29 God speaks of the time in which he will pour out his Spirit on Israel, a time at which he will also "restore the fortunes of Jacob, and have mercy on the whole house of Israel" (v. 25).

The disciples' question might also have stemmed from a misunderstanding with respect to Jesus' teaching. For example, in Luke 19:11–27 Jesus told the parable of the nobleman going to a far country to receive a kingdom. Perhaps the disciples thought that Jesus' death was equivalent to "going to a far country," and that now that he had been resurrected the time had finally come for him, the nobleman of the parable, to establish his rule. Especially in the light of the Old Testament Scriptures just surveyed, it is no wonder that the disciples were asking about the restoration of Israel. But what sort of "restoration" did they have in mind, and why did they think Israel needed it?

By Acts 1 the disciples have probably had time to recall Jesus' harsh pronouncements: Jerusalem would be destroyed and its inhabitants killed (Luke 19:41–44); days of vengeance would come on the land, and its people would be exiled (Luke 21:20–24). Certainly by the time Luke wrote Acts (in the mid- to late-sixties), Jesus' words were on the verge of fulfillment. The nation was under threat of judgment and exile; its removal from its place of favor had been confirmed by the words of Jesus.

The "restoration" mentioned in Acts 1:6 refers to Israel's return to the place of promise and blessing. The verb translated "restore" in verse 6 (apokathistêmi) occurs forty-six times in the Greek translation of the Old Testament.[4] Of its forty-six occurrences, many have this connotation, often with the further mention in context of a return to the promised land itself (Jer. 15:19; 16:15; 23:8; 24:6; 27:19 [50:19 in English]; Ezek. 17:23; Hos. 11:11; also 1 Macc. 15:3). For example, Israel's restoration to the land is clearly in view in Jeremiah 16:13–15 NIV:

> "So I will throw you out of this land into a land neither you nor your fathers have known, and there you will serve other gods day and night, for I will show you no favor. However, the days are coming," declares the LORD, "when men will no longer say, 'As surely as the LORD lives, who brought the Israelites up out of Egypt,' but they will say, 'As surely as the LORD lives, who brought the Israelites up out of the land of the north and out of all the countries where he had banished them.' For I will restore [apokatastêsô] them to the land I gave their forefathers."

The same picture is found in Jeremiah 23:8, where Israel's restoration to its land is mentioned in connection with the last days and the coming of a Davidic (messianic) king. In some instances a spiritual dimension to Israel's renewal is mentioned or hinted at (Jer. 24:6; Hos. 11:11); in others it is not. In the writings of the first-century Jewish historian Josephus the verb *apokataistêmi* sometimes refers to political restoration.[5] It is found eight times in the New Testament[6]; only in Acts 1:6 does it appear to refer to national restoration. This connotation for the term makes perfect sense in a context where Jesus' teaching about the kingdom, his own messianic identity, and his promise of the Spirit would quite naturally have brought a vision of national restoration and splendor to the minds of the disciples.[7]

Rather than giving a direct reply to their question in Acts 1:6, Jesus urged the disciples not to be preoccupied with the issue of Israel's restoration (which is solely within the purview of the Father's providence, Acts 1:7) but to carry out the worldwide evangelistic mission once the Spirit came (Acts 1:8). We should regard Jesus' avoidance of a direct answer as implicit confirmation of the premise of their question. As the Lucan scholar Robert Tannehill observes, "Jesus' answer to the question about restoring the reign to Israel denies that Jesus' followers can know the time and probably corrects their supposition that the restoration may come immediately, but it does not deny the legitimacy of their concern with the restoration of the national life of the Jewish people."[8] Jesus anticipated a future for Israel.

ACTS 3:19–21

In Acts 3 Peter and John, emboldened by the Holy Spirit and, perhaps, by the success of their preaching at Pentecost, returned to the temple. There, after the healing of the lame man, a crowd gathered, and Peter began to preach. Toward the end of his sermon, he pleaded with the Jews to repent:

> . . . that times of refreshing may come from the presence of the Lord; and that He may send Jesus, the Christ appointed for you, whom heaven must receive until the period of restoration of all things about which God spoke by the mouth of His holy prophets from ancient time (Acts 3:19–21).

According to this passage, if the Jews heed Peter's exhortation to repent, two things will follow: seasons of refreshing and the return of Jesus, the Christ. According to Peter, Jesus is in heaven at present by divine necessity, but he will be sent (again) once the Jews repent.[9] Hence the restoration of the things mentioned by the prophets of Israel and the return of Jesus are linked to the repentance of the Jews.[10]

Peter's comment evokes memories of Acts 1:6 in that the theme of Israel's restoration is revisited (this time by the Spirit-empowered Peter). The noun translated "restoration" in Acts 3:21 is related to the verb translated "restore" which Luke used in Acts 1:6. As we have seen, the language in the earlier passage envisions national blessing for Israel. But in Acts 3 *more* information is offered. Whereas in Acts 1:6–8 the time of the restoration of all things is not explicitly revealed, in Acts 3:19–21 we *are* told when it will come—after the Jews repent. While the promise of restoration in Acts 3 is conditional upon the nation's repentance (v. 19), it is nonetheless clearly made.

LUKE 13:35

In this passage the topic of Israel's restoration is raised, although in a more subtle way than in passages from Acts. Luke 13 stands roughly in the middle of Luke's gospel. The chapter opens with Jesus warning Israel to repent lest God's judgment come (13:1–9). It closes with Jesus saying to Jerusalem, "You will not see me again until you say, 'Blessed is he who comes in the name of the Lord' " (13:35 NIV). How does this brief statement suggest a future for Israel?

At first glance, the casual reader is tempted to think that the greeting "Blessed is he" is fulfilled at the triumphal entry in Luke 19:28–48. Certainly the words are repeated there. The problem with this interpretation is that while Jesus' words look forward to a greeting by Jerusalem (i.e., its populace), this is *not* what happens at the triumphal entry. Even though these words are used at Luke 19:38, in Luke it is clear that *Jerusalem* does *not* welcome Jesus as he comes to the city. It is not the people and leaders of Jerusalem who cry out in faith, "Blessed is the King who comes in the name of the Lord." Rather, it is the crowd *of disciples* (19:37) who remember his works of power and authoritative teaching and greet him.[11]

If Jesus' words in Luke 13:35 about Jerusalem welcoming him are not fulfilled at Luke 19:38, when are they fulfilled? They aren't—or perhaps more accurately, they have yet to be fulfilled. Instead, they hang enticingly as a hint of future restoration for Israel. Jesus' words in Luke 13:35 should be understood to refer to Jerusalem's change of heart—its repentance—some time after the temple was destroyed. Jesus looked forward to a time *after the destruction of its temple* when Jerusalem would repent and say, "Blessed is the one who comes." In other words, Jesus spoke of a time when Jerusalem would turn to him after the desolation of its temple. In so doing Jesus anticipated a Jewish presence in Jerusalem beyond the destruction he predicted in Luke 13:35.[12] According to Luke, well before his death Jesus hinted at his rejection by Jerusalem as well as the eventual repentance (and restoration) of Israel.

Other passages might be enlisted to provide a more comprehensive picture of Israel's future in Luke-Acts.[13] Taken together, several passages in Luke-Acts indicate God has not put an end to his dealing with the nation. God has plans for Israel even after the destruction of Jerusalem and the captivity of its people. Indeed, their repentance is an essential condition for the return of Jesus. But does Luke stand alone in his thinking about a future for Israel?

A Future for Israel in Paul

Paul is the second (Luke is first) most prolific New Testament writer. It is not surprising, therefore, that he has more to say about eschatology and the last days than anyone else. However, despite the fact that in almost every one of his books we find comments or teaching about the end times, in these same books there is little discussion of Israel.

The exception to this is found in Paul's letter to the Romans. The book of Romans may be divided into two parts. The first part, Romans 1–11, deals primarily with matters of doctrine and theology. The second section, Romans 12–16, concerns matters of practical living. One of the high points of the letter—perhaps the high point for many readers—is the strong affirmation of God's enduring love made in 8:35–39. It is worth repeating:

> Who shall separate us from the love of Christ? Shall tribulation, or distress, or persecution, or famine, or nakedness, or peril, or sword? Just as it is written, "FOR THY SAKE WE ARE BEING PUT TO DEATH ALL DAY LONG; WE WERE CONSIDERED AS SHEEP TO BE SLAUGHTERED." But in all these things we overwhelmingly conquer through Him who loved us. For I am convinced that neither death, nor life, nor angels, nor principalities, nor things present, nor things to come, nor powers, nor height, nor depth, nor any other created thing, shall be able to separate us from the love of God, which is in Christ Jesus our Lord.

But this word of comfort raises a question. According to the Scriptures, the Jews were the chosen people, the special objects of God's affection and promises. Yet in Romans 1–8 Paul talked about the common plight of Jews and Gentiles (e.g., Rom. 1:13–16; 2:9; 3:9, 29). Individuals in each group are sinful and must embrace by faith the Savior, Jesus Christ. Furthermore, by the time Paul wrote Romans, the Jews as a whole had become the enemies of the gospel, the persecutors of Christians, and the people whom Jesus predicted would face God's judgment. How then, in Romans 8:35–39, can Paul speak of God's faithful and enduring love? Does it still extend to the Jews? Paul has some explaining to do.

Paul immediately takes up these issues in Romans 9. He noted that Israel divides into two groups: the physical descendants of Israel, and the line of promise (the believing remnant). He observed that much of physical Israel was unbelieving. In the words of Isaiah, "ALL THE DAY LONG I HAVE STRETCHED OUT MY HANDS TO A DISOBEDIENT AND OBSTINATE PEOPLE" (Rom. 10:21, citing Isa. 65:2). What is the implication of this for ethnic Israel? Does Jewish rejection of the gospel mean that God has rejected his people (Rom. 11:1)?[14]

Paul gave a lengthy answer (Rom. 11:2–36). The part that interests us most is toward the end of the chapter. There he said:

> For I do not want you, brethren, to be uninformed of this mystery, lest that you will not be wise in your own estimation, that a partial hardening has happened to Israel until the fulness of the Gentiles has come in; and thus all Israel will be saved; just as it is written, "THE DELIVERER WILL COME FROM ZION, HE WILL REMOVE UNGODLINESS FROM JACOB. AND THIS IS MY COVENANT WITH THEM, WHEN I TAKE AWAY THEIR SINS." From the standpoint of the gospel they are enemies for your sake, but from the standpoint of God's choice they are beloved for the sake of the fathers; for the gifts and the calling of God are irrevocable (Rom. 11:25–29).

The verses teach: (1) Israel is indeed for now the enemy of the gospel (v. 28); (2) this fact does not mean the ancient promises have been revoked (v. 29); (3) Israel's present hardness of heart with respect to the gospel is temporary, not permanent (vv. 25–26); and (4) at some point in the future God will save "all Israel" (v. 26). Points (1) and (2) are clear enough; certain features of points (3) and (4) require elaboration.

What is it in the passage that suggests that Israel's hardening is temporary? After all, it has lasted from Paul's day until now (almost two thousand years!). The crucial term is the "until" in verse 25. We saw the same Greek word, *achri,* in our discussion of Luke 1:20 and 21:24. The word often provides a pivot for the action in sentences. The action described before "until" is typically reversed once the action mentioned after "until" takes place.[15] As applied to Romans 11:25, we see that the hardening of the nation—its resistance to the gospel—will cease once the "fulness of the Gentiles has come in" (v. 25). This is presumably a reference to the full number of Gentiles whom God has elected to save in this era.[16] When is this number complete? No one knows. But once it was complete, Paul expected the hardening of Israel to be removed and, more positively, for "all Israel will be saved" (v. 26).

But could things really be so simple? What does Paul mean by "all Israel," and what does the word *thus* in verse 26 refer to? The word *thus* is equivalent to "in this way." Paul said "thus" or "in this way" all Israel will be saved. But what "way" is he talking about? The "way" he referred to is the order of events he has just described—first comes Jewish hardening of heart, then comes Gentile conversion until the fullness is arrived at, followed by the salvation of all Israel.

In other words, the "way" or "manner" has to do with the conditions or timetable set forth in verse 25. What does it mean that "all Israel" will be saved? Does "all Israel" refer (1) to all Christians (both Jew and Gentile), (2) to Jewish Christians, (3) to every Jew alive after the full number of Gentiles has come in, or (4) is the word used to designate an unspecified, but large number (something like "most" or "lots")?

Possibility (1) is unlikely because Paul did not use the term *Israel* to refer to a collection of Jewish and Gentile believers (for this he typically used the word *church*). Possibility (2) is equally unlikely because it amounts to Paul's saying that all Jewish Christians will be saved—something so obvious that it's not worth saying. Either of the other options, (3) or (4), is possible. According to Professor C. E. B. Cranfield, the latter (option 4) is most likely because "all Israel" is often used to refer to a large number of Jews rather than to "every Jewish person."[17]

For example, in 2 Samuel 16:22 we learn that David's son Absalom pitched a tent on the roof of David's palace and there "went in to his father's concubines in the sight of all Israel." Did every Jew from the northern and southern tribes witness Absalom's actions? No—but *many* would have. Similarly, in 1 Kings 12:18 we read that Adoram, an agent of King Rehoboam, was stoned to death by "all Israel." It is obvious not every Jew participated in this stoning, though a large number did (also 1 Sam. 4:5; 18:17; 1 Kings 12:1; 2 Chron. 12:1).

To return to Romans 11, Paul readily conceded that Israel was at present an enemy of the gospel (11:28). But he remained hopeful about its future, because (1) his own conversion demonstrated that God hadn't totally forsaken the Jews (11:1); (2) God was able to reinstate them into the place of blessing if they repented and believed in Jesus (vv. 23–24); and (3) God would someday bring "all Israel" to faith (vv. 25–26).[18]

There can be little question that Paul found the prospect of the salvation of "all Israel" amazing. He expressed his wonder at the end of Romans 11, where he wrote:

> Oh, the depth of the riches both of the wisdom and knowledge of God! How unsearchable are His judgments and unfathomable His ways! For WHO HAS KNOWN THE MIND OF THE LORD, OR WHO BECAME HIS COUNSELOR? OR WHO HAS FIRST GIVEN TO HIM THAT IT MIGHT BE PAID BACK TO HIM AGAIN? For from Him and through Him and to Him are all things. To Him be the glory forever. Amen (Rom. 11:33–36).

This benediction is not only a fitting conclusion to the first major division in Romans; it is also his comment on the immediately preceding material of Romans 11:1–32.

Many contemporary Christians, aware of how secular the modern nation of Israel is, repudiate the idea that it could still be part of God's redemptive plan.[19] I suspect that Paul would have shared, at least in part, their skepticism. But at the end of the day he rested his case for Israel's salvation not on national righteousness, but on the election of God. And as he rhetorically asked elsewhere (Rom. 9:20–21), who can argue with that?[20]

A Future for Israel in Other Passages

Both Paul and Luke—whose writings make up about half of the New Testament—point to a future for Israel (though I readily concede that neither provides much detail about this future). What do other New Testament writers have to say about it? Very little. For example, the word *Israel* does not even appear in the letters of James, John, Jude, or Peter. The book of Hebrews makes no reference to a future for Israel as such, nor does the Gospel of John. Matthew and Mark have even less to say about it than does Luke.

With that in mind, it is worth asking whether Israel appears in the New Testament book that many people consider the blueprint for the end times, the book of Revelation (for cautions about interpreting and using this book, see Appendix C). Whatever Revelation has to say about a future for Israel, it says it with subtlety. The word *Israel* appears three times in the book (Rev. 2:14; 7:4; 21:12). Of these references, only Revelation 7:4 could possibly refer to God's dealings with Israel in the last days, and even this is far from clear.[21] But if there is little direct evidence that Revelation speaks of Israel, is there *any* reason to think Israel is being contemplated at all?

In fact, it is possible that the chronological framework of the book supports the idea that Israel is at least partially in view. On five occasions Revelation refers to a period of three and one-half years in which the action of the book takes place (Rev. 11:2–3; 12:6, 14; 13:5). This number may be the writer's subtle way of saying that at least some of the action described relates to Israel. How can the number function in this way?

Professor Harold Hoehner has argued that the prophecy of Daniel 9:24–27 on dealing with the last days, has been partially fulfilled, with seven years yet to be accounted for (for more details, see Appendix B). Many people look to a future seven-year period in which the remainder of Daniel's prophecy concerning Israel and the establishment of the kingdom will be fulfilled. Daniel 9:27 divides this "week" of years (i.e., seven years) into halves. In the first half, the coming "prince" makes a covenant with "the many." In the second half the prince causes sacrifices to stop. For now it is not important to describe in detail who this "prince" might be or what situation is envisioned by verse 27; the important point is that this last week of Daniel's is future and is divided into two three-and-one-half-year periods. And, moreover, this division corresponds to the three-and-one-half-year framework of the last days mentioned in Revelation.

Let me be clear: I am not saying Revelation refers *explicitly* to Daniel's seventieth week, nor am I trying to develop a precise chronology for events described in Revelation. What I am suggesting is that it is probably not coincidental that the three-and-one-half-year periods hinted at in Daniel's prophecy concerning "this people" (i.e., the Jews, and as yet unfulfilled) are mentioned in Revelation—a book largely dedicated to describing future events culminating in the return of Jesus (Rev. 19). Perhaps some of the action in Revelation also concerns Israel.

Why So Little Talk of Israel's Future?

If Israel is as important to the future as some modern authors suggest, why is its future role mentioned so rarely in the New Testament? There are several possible reasons for this.

First, to emphasize Israel's future might have undercut the efforts of the early Jewish Christians to evangelize Gentiles by reinforcing in their minds a central role for Israel. Perhaps the greatest challenge faced by the church in its early days was the issue of ethnocentrism—the reluctance of Jewish Christians to cross ethnic and racial boundaries with the gospel message. Jesus' apostles failed to heed his command to go out from Jerusalem (Acts 1:8; Matt. 28:18–20) until persecution came (Acts 8:1ff.). Time and again both in Acts and in Paul's letters we learn of the difficulties Jewish Christians had in accepting contact with Gentiles (e.g., Acts 10:9–48; Gal. 2:11–13). Many Jewish Christians retained a preference for their cultural and religious heritage, a heritage that typically looked down on social contact with Gentiles. Talk about a future for Israel might have given these Jewish believers the impression that the urgency of a mission to Gentiles was relieved.

Second, an emphasis on Israel's future could also have been misunderstood to affirm an abiding and central role of the Old Testament law in the life of believers, something Paul, in particular, would have wanted to avoid.[22] After all, he taught that both Jews and Gentiles needed to repent and that, having repented, they were united by virtue of their association with Jesus of Nazareth, not by conformity to Torah!(e.g., Eph. 2:11–22).

Third, it is possible that the link between Jewish repentance and Jesus' return would have caused some Christians to focus on the Jewish mission in hopes of hastening Jesus' return—to the exclusion of Jesus' mandate to go to all nations with the gospel message. Aware of these potential misunderstandings New Testament writers spoke sparingly of Israel's future.[23]

Modern Israel and God's Design for History

God has a future for Israel. According to Scripture, it involves the sovereignty of God and the choice of the Jews. Paul said this future will be fully realized when the full number of Gentiles comes to faith and God removes the partial hardening that Israel now experiences. According to Luke, when Israel repents Jesus will return. The repentance of Israel is a necessary precondition for the second coming.

Up to this point I have not described what this repentance might look like. Would it be a decision by nonreligious Jews to return to religious observance? Would it be a commitment by religious Jews to renew their dedication to God and Torah? Repentance refers to a change of mind and a change of allegiance. There is both a cognitive and volitional element in repentance. In the first century, nonbelievers, particulary those who had been idolaters, repented when they changed their minds about who Jesus was and made a commitment to follow him, to become his disciples. Future Jewish repentance would involve a recognition that Jesus of Nazareth was God's Messiah and a personal commitment to follow him. It would, in other words, be the sort of faith expressed by Peter, John, Paul, and other early Jewish Christians.

If God has a future for Israel—leaving aside for the moment the precise nature of that future—then they must survive. God's faithfulness to them is evidenced by their continued existence as a people. Despite the various attempts at a thorough genocide made throughout the centuries, the Jews have endured. So they must for the Scripture to be fulfilled and for God to bring his promises of restoration to completion. But his faithfulness is also evidenced by the unspeakable hardship they have endured. Jesus said the nation would suffer for rejecting him, and so it has. Their suffering speaks to the faithfulness and truthfulness of Jesus' words and God's promises. Obviously, this statement cannot begin to recall or empathize adequately with the hardships experienced over the years, but it does reaffirm the point that God reveals not only his blessing but also his anger in the arena of history with quite tangible results. Yet any outcome that did not in some sense fulfill the warnings of God through Jesus to the Jewish people would have mocked the words of Jesus and the prophets and called into question the truth of God's Word.

How does modern Israel relate to the ancient promises? The existence of the modern nation-state of Israel should not be disregarded in thinking about the last days. The fact that the Antichrist must come some day to a temple (this is examined in detail in chapter 7) hints that Paul foresaw Jewish national existence in conjunction with the Antichrist of the last days. It is possible that God could, apart from the existence of a Jewish nation, call to repentance the Jews dispersed throughout the nations so there would be the large-scale Jewish repentance mentioned in Romans 11. After all, from the first century onwards many Jews have recognized Jesus as God's Messiah. But the large-scale repentance envisioned in Romans 11 did not happen before 1948, and now the situation has changed. The conscientious modern person therefore must at least ask whether there might be a connection between national establishment (in 1948) and national repentance (in the future). How likely is it that the reestablishment of the nation is entirely *unrelated* to the predicted repentance?

Though it is but one feature of an end-times scenario, it seems reasonable to me that the existence of modern Israel is a precursor to the predicted end-times repentance because the large-scale repentance envisioned by Paul could most readily occur once the nation was reconstituted and relocated in the land—something that did not happen from the first century until the middle of the twentieth century. Furthermore, it is easy to speculate that the modern political impasse in Israel and the Middle East will persist or even worsen, and that an increased threat to Israel's security will ultimately lead many in the nation to pin their hopes for survival on the God of their fathers, since hope in anything else is destined to fail.

If the present existence of Israel could be related to God's design for the last days, what are the other features of that scenario and to what extent are they now present?

Chapter Seven

CERTAIN SIGNS IN
UNCERTAIN TIMES

✦

The apostle Peter said that in the last days people would mock Christians who looked forward to Jesus' return, asking, "Where is the promise of His coming? For ever since the fathers fell asleep, all continues just as it was from the beginning of creation" (2 Pet. 3:4). In chapter 5, I argued that many of the things people regard as "signs of the end" are not really that, or at least they are not infallibly that. Does their status as "uncertain signs" imply that the future will be just like the past and present, that there will not be a "great tribulation"? It does not. Although it was noted in chapter 5 that much of what we experience in the present era could be called "tribulation," things get worse in the end. Before we explore what the bona fide "signs of the end" might be, we must offer a brief note in defense of the idea that the Bible speaks of the end times as involving *particularly* difficult experiences for the earth and its inhabitants.

Is There a Great Tribulation?

Those who write about the end times often speak of the coming "great tribulation," a period of time in which the ancient prophecies about the last days are fulfilled. For many of these writers the phrase has become a technical term which refers to the seventieth week of Daniel (or a portion of that seven-year "week") during which time the events described in Daniel 9:26–27 and Revelation 6–18 unfold. However, that is not the way, or at least not the only way, the phrase "great tribulation" is used in the New Testament. For example, in Stephen's speech before the Sanhedrin in Acts 7:11 he referred to the conditions which led Jacob and his sons to Egypt as a "great tribulation." In Revelation 2:22 Jesus warned the first-century church at Thyatira not to be tolerant of the false teachers in their midst lest he send upon them "great tribulation" to purify the church. In Matthew 24:21 the phrase refers to the great hardship that accompanied Jerusalem's destruction in A.D. 70 (for an outline of Matthew 24, see Appendix D).

Although "great tribulation" is not a technical term, it is an apt description of the unusual hardship and difficulties which characterize the last days. According to Luke, Jesus envisioned a time of future tribulation. Although he did not use the phrase "great tribulation," he did speak of a future time after "the times of the Gentiles" is completed when

> there will be signs in sun and moon and stars, and upon the earth dismay among nations, in perplexity at the roaring of the sea and the waves, men fainting from fear and the expectation of the things which are coming upon the world; for the powers of the heavens will be shaken. And then they will see THE SON OF MAN COMING IN A CLOUD with power and great glory (Luke 21:25–27).

Likewise, the apostle Paul referred to the coming "day of the Lord" as a time of hardship and destruction, climaxing with the appearance of "the Lord" (1 Thess. 5:2–4; 2 Thess. 2:2–12). Finally, the book of Revelation is largely devoted to describing end-times events.[1] Revelation 6–18 should probably be understood as future oriented or, at least, as applicable to events occurring after the onset of "the great day of their wrath" (Rev. 6:17), culminating in the return of Jesus (Rev. 19:11ff., a clearly future happening).[2] The actions associated with the breaking of the seven seals (Rev. 6:1–8:1), the sounding of the seven trumpets (8:2–11:19), and the pouring out of the seven bowls (16:1–21) represent a gradual intensification of worldwide tribulation leading up to Jesus' return (in Rev. 19). In this respect, Revelation agrees with the picture of the end sketched by the Gospel writers and Paul.

To sum up: though Christians and others will face hardships, including martyrdom, in the period between Jesus' first and second coming, there is clearly an intensification of trouble in the form of persecution, natural disasters, and so forth just prior to Jesus' return. We are therefore justified in speaking of a future great tribulation.

Is it possible to be specific about the duration of the last days and of the great tribulation? Neither the Gospels nor Paul gives any indication of how long the last days might go on.[3] From a New Testament point of view, only in the book of Revelation is there a hint of how long the tribulation might last. Because it is not absolutely clear that these chronological references in Revelation are to be taken literally, it is with some caution that I suggest that

Revelation points to a period of three and one-half to seven years as the length of the tribulation. This is based on the idea explained in chapter 6 that certain events in the book of Revelation seem to occur within a chronological framework of between three and one-half and seven years (see pp. 99–100); although, as anyone familiar with commentaries on Revelation can attest, its chronological references have yielded a wide range of interpretations. Further, it seems that tribulation intensifies toward the end; during the last three and one-half years there is a great tribulation. However the question remains: Apart from the intensification of hardships (something impossible to quantify), how can we know when the days of tribulation are to begin? What signs mark the approach of the end?

Certain Signs

In chapter 6 we noted that the repentance of Israel *must* precede the return of Jesus. Scripture also hints that Israel will exist as a nation before he comes again. Their present national existence may be one element in the biblical scenario of the last days. But there are other features. The consummation of the last days is preceded by the appearance of the Antichrist, the emergence of "the apostasy," and the worldwide proclamation of the gospel. We will look at each of these in turn.

THE ANTICHRIST

It will probably be surprising to those who read popular books about the end times to learn that the biblical teaching about the Antichrist, if put into a single chapter, would be one of the shortest chapters in the New Testament. Only a few Bible passages refer to the Antichrist (Dan. 9:26–27; 2 Thess. 2:1–12; 1 John 4:3; Rev. 13:3–18; 19:19ff.). Furthermore, only one of these passages, 1 John 4:3, actually uses the term *Antichrist*. A detailed description of this sinister figure is not found in the Gospels; in fact, it is confined to a single chapter in 2 Thessalonians and, perhaps, Revelation.[4] This contrasts sharply with the attention given to other themes such as resurrection, ethics, even the return of Jesus. The word *Antichrist* provides little more than a hint of what else this coming figure might be: a surrogate or false Messiah.[5]

The most straightforward and detailed description is found in 2 Thessalonians 2:3–12, although the specific word *Antichrist* is not used. The first thing to notice in this passage is that the coming of the "man of lawlessness," in tandem with the emergence of apostasy, is a clear signal that the day of the Lord is near.[6] Once he comes there can be no doubt that the last days are upon us. Given the paucity of biblical data about the Antichrist, what can be said about him? How will we recognize him?

He is a political-religious figure. One noteworthy feature of the end-times scenario painted by many modern authors involves a worldwide empire presided over by the Antichrist. We are told that from this base of political power and religious influence he deceives the world and leads its opposition to God. It is further suggested that various twentieth-century phenomena—in particular, the founding of the United Nations, the establishment of the European Economic Community (now the European Union), and the creation and ongoing mission of NATO—are precursors to the one-world government that will eventually be led by the Antichrist.[7] Neither Jesus nor Paul made any explicit statement about the identity, the extent, or even the existence of the Antichrist's empire. Where do people who speculate about the Antichrist as a political leader get their material?

It is inferred from a handful of passages. According to 2 Thessalonians 2:4, the "man of sin" or "man of lawlessness" comes to God's temple and displays himself as God (or *a* god; see below for a detailed exploration of the passage). Although the comment in itself says nothing about the political nature of the Antichrist, Paul's words hint at this. He uses language that invokes images of other political figures who had already desecrated or would desecrate Jerusalem's temple. For example, the Syrian King Antiochus Epiphanes desecrated the temple in Jerusalem in 167 B.C. by demanding that a Jewish priest offer sacrifice to Zeus on its altar. This act was widely regarded as fulfillment of Daniel's mention of a coming one who would "desecrate" the temple (Dan. 11:31). Antiochus was a political-religious figure.[8] So too was the Roman emperor Gaius Caligula, who ordered his image erected in Jerusalem's temple in A.D. 40. Jesus seemed to build on Daniel's prophecy when he warned of an "abomination of desolation" that would come to the temple and desecrate it (Matt. 24:15).[9]

Given these backgrounds, in 2 Thessalonians 2:4 when Paul spoke of a man who would come and commit blasphemy in God's temple, we may infer that the man in view was a political figure. Furthermore, Paul's teaching and the background to it are consistent with the picture we get in Revelation 13:3–18, where "the beast" seems to wield tremendous political authority.[10] If Daniel 9:26–27 is future-oriented (for this, see Appendix B), it also speaks of a coming political leader (a "prince," v. 26) with the power to make treaties that involve temple worship at Jerusalem.

The extent of the Antichrist's authority is difficult to determine. Neither Paul (in his letters) nor Jesus (in the Gospels) spoke to the issue. Many contemporary writers think the Antichrist's power will be like that of the Roman Empire.[11] But neither the Roman nor the great empires which preceded it were, strictly speaking, one-world governments. Though dominating, alongside them all were nations with whom they competed, fought, negotiated, and cooperated. Even if we believe the Antichrist's empire is like the Roman Empire in its size and ruthless use of power, it does not follow that it will be a one-world government. Historically, the Roman Empire never was that and all the end-times talk of wars and conflicts runs counter to the notion of a single government which effectively controls the nations.[12]

This puts us in the awkward position of relying on the book of Revelation for information about the Antichrist's empire—a considerable difficulty (see Appendix C). Revelation 13, a passage which originally applied to the Roman Empire, speaks of the beast as having universal authority. The beast is given "authority over every tribe and people and tongue and nation" (Rev. 13:7). We are also told that "all who dwell on the earth will worship him" (Rev. 13:8) and that "all" will be forced to take his "mark" if they wish to "buy or to sell" (Rev. 13:17). If its imagery can be expanded and applied to the Antichrist, evidence from Revelation suggests the Antichrist wields considerable authority; nevertheless, this authority is limited in scope.

He promotes "lawlessness." It is conceivable that when Paul referred to a "man of lawlessness" in 2 Thessalonians 2:3, he had in mind someone who was literally a breaker of laws; that is, someone who breaks civil or criminal law. The problem with this view is that this is not the way the term *lawlessness* was typically used by Paul (as discussed in chapter 5, "lawlessness" for Paul is the equivalent of "wickedness" or "sin"). Furthermore, it is difficult to see how the "man of lawlessness" could proclaim himself divine (2:4) and successfully deceive the world (2:9–10) if he were widely viewed as a lawbreaker in the sense of a felon or criminal.[13]

There is a second way to interpret "man of lawlessness." The phrase could be understood to mean that the Antichrist is someone who *promotes* lawlessness.[14] This is consistent with Paul's later description of him as one who causes others to be deceived through satanically inspired miracles (2 Thess. 2:9–11). In Revelation 13 the Antichrist is similarly portrayed as one who has authority from Satan to murder God's people and compel others to engage in idolatry (Rev. 13:7–17). The Antichrist promotes lawlessness by making himself Lord in the place of and in opposition to Jesus and encouraging others to follow him.

Closely connected to the idea that the Antichrist promotes lawlessness is the notion that he is himself lawless.[15] His own perversity of character inspires his promotion of it in others. He is wicked. Those who are deceived by him will not regard him as such, but their lack of discernment notwithstanding, Paul's judgment is clear: The "man of lawlessness" is wicked.

He deifies himself. Politicians are not highly regarded in our culture—and often with good reason. The public tends not to associate them with cardinal virtues like honesty and integrity. But according to Paul, the Antichrist will do far more than claim to be good, virtuous, or honest. He will suggest that he is divine, that he is in some way the embodiment of God or a god (2 Thess. 2:4).[16] In conjunction with his self-glorification, the Antichrist will set "himself up in God's temple" and offer proof of his claim. His appearance there seems to intensify his blasphemy, since in the Old Testament it was God who resided at the temple in a special way (e.g., 1 Kings 8:13; Ps. 18:6; Hab. 2:20; indeed, the temple is often called "the house of God"). As F. F. Bruce wrote:

> The inner sanctuary of the Jerusalem temple . . . was the throne room of the invisible presence of the God of Israel: there, in the house which Solomon built for him, as earlier at Shiloh (1 Sam. 4:4), he was worshiped as "Yahweh of hosts, who is enthroned on the cherubim." . . . Although no ark surmounted by cherubim was to be found in the postexilic Holy of Holies, the God of Israel was still believed to have his dwelling there.[17]

The Antichrist's spurious claim to deity is bolstered by miraculous signs—signs produced by the power of Satan (2 Thess. 2:9; also 2 Cor. 11:14–15). The words Paul uses in 2 Thessalonians 2 to describe the mighty works of the Antichrist (*semeia, teras*) are the same words he used elsewhere to describe legitimate miracles performed in the power of the Holy Spirit.[18] By using terms that can apply to bona fide miracles from God, Paul hinted that the man of lawlessness counterfeits the legitimate miracles of God and thus deceives the world.[19] This large-scale deception is consonant with Paul's remark in 2 Corinthians 11:14–15 (NIV) that "Satan himself masquerades as an angel of light. It is not surprising, then, if his servants masquerade as servants of righteousness."

This is a breathtaking set of comments. What precisely did Paul have in mind in 2 Thessalonians 2? Does this passage suggest—are we to believe—that in the future some individual, some world figure, will have the audacity to make such claims for himself? We are hard-pressed to find integrity in leaders, much less divinity! Surely we are not to think that in our modern era someone would seriously make such an assertion. How would he be believed by a large number of people?

Perhaps this prophecy has already been fulfilled—if so, we can stop concerning ourselves with a coming Antichrist. Perhaps Paul's teaching about the Antichrist calls us to *remember* rather than *anticipate* his coming. Perhaps the man of lawlessness has already appeared in the temple! We must consider the historical background to Paul's remarks to see whether they have already been fulfilled.

As Paul would have known, the Jews had a long and unhappy experience of foreigners desecrating or seeking to desecrate their temple. For example, in 167 B.C. (nearly two hundred years before Paul wrote), Antiochus IV Epiphanes, the king of Syria, desecrated the temple by ordering sacrifices on its altar to Olympian Zeus.[20] Nearly one hundred years after that episode, the Roman general Pompey besieged Jerusalem, battered down one of its walls, and entered the city and the temple. This was regarded by the Jews as a desecration of their temple, though Pompey did not interrupt or replace the sacrifices as Antiochus Epiphanes had done.[21] Finally, roughly ten years before Paul wrote 2 Thessalonians, in about A.D. 40, the Roman Emperor Gaius (also known as Caligula) ordered that an image of himself be placed in the temple at Jerusalem.[22] This was due, in part, to his general policy of self-promotion (indeed, self-deification) and, in part, to his perception that the Jews were being particularly troublesome by refusing him divine honors and by insulting his representatives.[23] The veneration of the emperor was widespread in the eastern part of the Roman empire,[24] and the Jews' adamant refusal to participate in such veneration provoked Caligula to wrath.[25] However, before his plan could be implemented, he was assassinated (on January 24, A.D. 41). These are the most salient backgrounds to Paul's remarks—but they are only *backgrounds,* and it is clear that Paul spoke of *future* events in 2 Thessalonians. We must ask if any event subsequent to the early A.D. 50s, the date of 2 Thessalonians, could qualify as a fulfillment of Paul's words.[26] To return to an earlier question: Is it possible that Paul's prediction has been fulfilled, that "the lawless one" has already come and profaned the temple?

The magnificent temple of Jerusalem which stood in Paul's day was reduced to rubble by Roman armies in A.D. 70 near the end of the first revolt. At that time the Roman general Titus, soon to be emperor, entered the city and temple and made a spectacle of taking away its golden furniture and other valuable amenities. After this the temple was burned to the ground.[27] Was this the fulfillment of 2 Thessalonians 2:3–12?

There are serious flaws in viewing Titus' actions as fulfillment of Paul's words. First, Paul's "man of lawlessness" is clearly an eschatological figure in that he is eventually to be slain by the Lord at the "appearance of His coming" (2 Thess. 2:8). The "appearance of his coming" is a reference to Jesus' return, something which obviously has yet to occur.[28] It is apparent that no historical figure from the first century could be the man of sin Paul describes. Second, there is no evidence to suggest that Titus went to the temple in order to show himself as divine, as the lawless one in 2 Thessalonians 2:4 is said to do.[29] Whereas the man of sin goes to the temple to further his claims to deity, Titus went there to destroy it.[30] Finally, though the data are sketchy, there is nothing in the historical record to suggest that Titus was viewed as a miracle worker as "the man of lawlessness" is said to be. It is not possible, therefore, to make a convincing case that the lawless one has already come to the temple. Paul's words about the Antichrist remain unfulfilled.

But this leaves us with an interpretation whose chief drawback is its sheer implausibility: Are we to believe that there will again be a temple in Jerusalem to which the Antichrist will visit and exalt himself? Before we rush to this conclusion, we should explore more fully what Paul meant by the phrase "temple of God" (2 Thess. 2:4). Up to this point the discussion has assumed that Paul had in mind the desecration of the physical temple at Jerusalem. But is this assumption warranted?

The phrase "temple of God" (*naos tou theou*) appears six times in Paul's letters (1 Cor. 3:16–17 [3 times]; 2 Cor. 6:16 [2 times]; 2 Thess. 2:4).[31] In the Greek Old Testament this phrase and its equivalents ("temple of the Lord," "house of God," "house of the Lord") are found hundreds of times. It most often refers to the temple at Jerusalem. However, apart from 2 Thessalonians 2:4, in Paul's writings the phrase clearly and consistently refers not to a literal temple but to a metaphorical one.[32] For example, Paul used a simile to identify God's temple with God's people in 1 Corinthians 3:17: "God's temple is sacred, and you are that temple" (NIV). Just as the physical temple at Jerusalem was to be a place where God dwelled in a special way (e.g., 2 Chron. 6–7), so the Christian community is a place where God's Spirit dwells in a special way. Since Paul consistently used the phrase "temple of God" metaphorically, how could anyone think that he referred to a literal temple in 2 Thessalonians 2:4?

While conceding that "temple of God" is typically used by Paul in a metaphorical sense, there are good reasons to believe he referred to a literal temple in 2 Thessalonians 2:4.

In the first place, to understand "temple of God" as metaphorical in the present passage renders it senseless. If the phrase refers to the church or a temple in heaven, what would it mean for the man of lawlessness—who is evidently a human being rather than a spirit or power—to sit there and show himself as a god? He could scarcely take a seat in a heavenly temple. It is not clear what it would mean for him to take a seat at church and, even if he were to do so, it is far from clear how the action could be seen as furthering his self-deification. On the other hand, his assumption of a seat in a literal temple could easily be regarded as blasphemous, given the backgrounds discussed above. If "temple of God" cannot be used metaphorically here, we should understand that Paul had a literal temple in mind.

Secondly, the Old Testament background to the phrase suggests that we see Paul's use of it here as literal. "Temple of God" normally refers to the literal temple at Jerusalem, especially in prophetic texts which refer to a temple desecration (e.g., Dan. 9:26–27; 11:31; Jer. 5:1–17). In the present context where a desecration of the temple is in view, the Jewish background of desecrations by Antiochus IV Epiphanes and Pompey, and the one proposed by Gaius suggest that Paul had in mind a literal temple. Paul took over the normal Old Testament meaning of the phrase "temple of God" in 2 Thessalonians, one of his earliest letters.

But if this is true, how do we account for the transformation of the meaning of this phrase in letters Paul wrote later (i.e., 1 and 2 Corinthians, Ephesians)? The answer is that Paul changed his use of the term over time. Paul initially used "temple of God" to refer to the temple in Jerusalem, as the Old Testament and early Christian writers had done.[33] Later, he began to use the term figuratively and, once having done that, never again used it in a literal sense.

In conclusion, in 2 Thessalonians 2:4 Paul envisioned the man of lawlessness going to the temple in Jerusalem as part of his arrogant self-deification. But of course, there is no longer a temple, and this is problematic, to say the least, if we understand Paul to be referring to still-future events.

The reader of the New Testament passages that speak of the end times is impressed by the number of crises and disasters that characterize these days. They are unique in that they are unparalleled in scope by anything mankind has ever experienced. But perhaps no feature of the end seems more unlikely in the present political-religious climate than the suggestion that in the end a temple will be erected in Jerusalem. In fact, it is easier to imagine earthquakes, famines, and plagues on a global scale than it is to foresee a time when a Jewish temple could be built in Jerusalem. The reason for this is obvious: Virtually no one wants a temple built there.

Moslems, for instance, would surely oppose its construction. On the traditional site of the Jewish temple sits the Mosque of Omar (also known as the Dome of the Rock). Any attempt to supplant the Muslim mosque with a Jewish temple would surely lead to bloody conflict and, most likely, all-out war.[34] Further, it is hard to believe that enough Jews would be interested in the "old-time religion" to face the risks to peace that a rebuilding would involve. Most Jews in Israel are irreligious. This is not to deny that some are interested in rebuilding. Indeed, one small sect, the "Temple Mount and Land of Israel Faithful," has made it their ambition to build a third temple on the temple mount in Jerusalem. But they represent a fraction of modern Jews. Finally, the act would be abhorrent to Christians since we hold that Jesus was God's ultimate and irreplaceable sacrifice for sin (Heb. 9:23–10:13). Any rebuilt temple would presumably involve sacrifices, something to which Christians could not lend theological support because this could easily imply some deficiency in what Christ did as "the lamb of God."

Various solutions to this dilemma have been proposed. Certain Christian writers speculate that a rebuilt temple could appear only in the midst of world events so cataclysmic that the current political-religious landscape would be drastically altered. Many teachers suggest that the pretribulation rapture of the church (a topic explored in chapter 8) will produce massive chaos and confusion, resulting in the Antichrist's rise to power and the world's allegiance to him; he, in turn, will ensure the rebuilding of the temple and, ultimately, occupy it in order to exalt himself as Paul predicted (2 Thess. 2:4).[35] But to the extent that this theory presupposes a rapture of the church that occurs before the Antichrist appears, it is unlikely (see chapter 8). It is, of course, conceivable that the Antichrist's miraculous powers will enable him to persuade the natural and longtime opponents of temple construction to permit it; but as things now stand, nothing short of miraculous intervention would seem to be able to permit rebuilding.

Others suggest that a temple could be built in some place other than its traditional site.[36] Maybe so—yet those few Jews who long for a third temple insist that it should be built on its traditional site. Perhaps "tolerance," the chief virtue among the politically correct, will be elevated to the extent that Moslems can be encouraged to permit the Jews access to a place where they can freely practice their ancient religion. Perhaps.

To conclude: It seems ludicrous to think a Jewish temple will be rebuilt. Ultimately, however, it matters little how unlikely temple rebuilding might be; what matters is that a rebuilt temple seems best to correspond to the biblical end-times scenario. I am reminded of the logic of the fictional Sherlock Holmes, who pointed out that once all other solutions to a problem had proved impossible, the one remaining, however improbable it might be, had to be true. If a rebuilt temple seems highly unlikely, so too—in the minds of many—were the collapse of the Soviet Union, the tearing down of the Berlin Wall, and, perhaps more than these, the reestablishment of a Jewish nation in 1948. Some day the Antichrist will come to a temple.

THE APOSTASY

In 2 Thessalonians Paul sought to allay the fears of believers who were upset by the mistaken belief that "the day of the Lord" had already arrived (2 Thess. 2:1–2). He pointed out that "the day" could not have begun since its coming would be marked by two crucial events which had yet to occur: the coming of "the apostasy" and the appearance of "the man of lawlessness" (2 Thess. 2:3).[37]

Paul did not explain what he meant by "the apostasy." The word (apostasia) is used only twice in the New Testament—here and in Acts 21:21. In the latter verse it refers to allegations by Paul's opponents that as he preached and taught he encouraged Jews in his audiences to "forsake Moses." A careful reading of Paul does not support the charges, but for our purposes it is worth noting that Paul is alleged to have encouraged his hearers to forsake a well-known body of religious doctrine and practice.[38] This is consistent with the use of the term in the Greek Old Testament, a version of the Bible that Paul was familiar with (e.g., Josh. 22:22; 2 Chron. 29:19).[39] In 2 Thessalonians Paul envisioned a future time in which "the apostasy" would come.[40]

Although the term's rarity makes it difficult to pin down Paul's meaning in 2 Thessalonians 2:3, given what we do know, Paul likely had in view a defection—perhaps even a large-scale defection—from orthodox doctrine by those who were nominally part of the church. His teaching in 2 Thessalonians may be related to a comment he made years later in 1 Timothy 4:1 that "in later times some will fall away [*apostesontai*] from the faith, paying attention to deceitful spirits and doctrines of demons." Paul did not labor under the false impression that all people who attached themselves to churches were believers. His writings suggest that false Christians had and would continue to infiltrate the ranks of the faithful, with doctrinal defection becoming a benchmark of the end times.

The apostasy mentioned in 2 Thessalonians likely refers to a "falling away from" those doctrines that Paul held to be most crucial. Can we determine what these doctrines might be? Since Paul addressed so many doctrinal and ethical issues in his letters, it is not a simple task to discern which of them he regarded as most important. Yet we are given some indication of the relative importance of various themes by Paul himself. We can identify at least five of these.

The Resurrection of Jesus. Paul emphasized the centrality of Jesus' resurrection from the dead for Christian faith and life. Near the conclusion of his letter to the Corinthians, he wrote, "For what I received I passed on to you as of first importance: that Christ died for our sins according to the Scriptures, that he was buried, that he was raised on the third day according to the Scriptures" (1 Cor. 15:3–4 NIV). He went on to observe that "if Christ has not been raised, your faith is futile; you are still in your sins" (1 Cor. 15:17 NIV). Paul's emphasis on Jesus' resurrection is also found in 1 Thessalonians 1:9–10 where he summarized that church's response to his preaching: "You turned to God from idols to serve the living and true God, and to wait for his Son from heaven, whom he raised from the dead—Jesus, who rescues us from the coming wrath" (NIV). In Romans 10:9 Paul put the requirements for salvation quite succinctly, highlighting the central role of the resurrection in Christian faith: "If you confess with your mouth, 'Jesus is Lord,' and believe in your heart that God raised him from the dead, you will be saved" (NIV).

Based on the verses just surveyed, it is clear that for Paul the resurrection of Jesus is the central historical fact upon which the truthfulness of Christianity either stands or falls; one cannot regard it as anything but of the highest importance in Paul's theology (see also Gal. 1:1; Rom. 1:4; 8:34; 2 Cor. 4:14; Eph. 1:20; Col. 2:12; 2 Tim. 2:8).

The return of Jesus. Paul also spoke often of the Christian hope of Jesus' second coming. For example, in 1 Thessalonians 1:9–10 (one of Paul's earliest letters) he mentioned the Christian expectation that Jesus would return alongside his comment about Jesus' resurrection. In Titus 2:13 (one of his last letters) Paul referred to the grace and salvation God has brought to all through Jesus Christ, whose second coming is labeled "the blessed hope." Furthermore, as we shall see in chapter 8 Paul drew a connection between Jesus' return and the general resurrection of believers. The return of Jesus was accorded a central place in Paul's theology (see also 1 Cor. 1:7; 4:5; Phil. 3:20; 1 Thess. 3:13; 4:13–18; 5:23; 2 Thess. 1:7; 2:1, 8; 1 Tim. 6:14; 2 Tim. 4:8).

The divine Son of God. Related to the idea that God raised Jesus from the dead and will, in due course, bring him to earth a second time is a certain understanding of who Jesus is. For Paul and other New Testament writers Jesus is not simply a great prophet or Messiah, but the Son of God. He is deity incarnate. This is clearly expressed by Paul in Colossians 1:15–16: "He [Jesus] is the image of the invisible God, the firstborn of all creation. For by Him all things were created, both in the heavens and on earth, visible and invisible, whether thrones or dominions or rulers or authorities—all things have been created by Him and for Him." Coming from Paul the Jew, the remark that Jesus was the agent of creation must be taken as evidence that he regarded Jesus as divine (given the Old Testament doctrine of God as Creator; Gen. 1). Furthermore, the comment that he is "the firstborn of all creation" reinforces his identity as Lord over creation and Lord over the nations. When viewed in the light of Ps. 89:26–27 and God's comments there where David, God's anointed king, is similarly described. Jesus' deity is also suggested by the remarkable collection of verses in Philippians 2:5–7 (NIV), where Paul admonished the Christians at Philippi: "Your attitude should be the same as that of Christ Jesus: Who, being in very nature God, did not consider equality with God something to be grasped, but made himself nothing, taking the very nature of a servant, being made in human likeness."

Seen in the light of Old Testament passages regarding the uniqueness of God (e.g., Isa. 43:10–11; 44:6, 24; 45:5–7; Gen. 1:1)—and Paul's obvious familiarity with them—Paul is doing nothing less than affirming Jesus' deity. For Paul it mattered a great deal whom God raised from the dead.

Because he was the Son of God, Jesus was a suitable person to die for the sins of the world and extend God's offer of forgiveness to mankind. If Jesus had been something less than this, his death could scarcely have become the basis of salvation for the world.[41] We should understand the deity of Jesus as a fundamentally important doctrine for Paul.

Salvation by faith—for all kinds of people. Martin Luther and other Reformers followed apostolic teaching in making salvation by faith alone— *sola fide*—a centerpiece in their theology. They understood that mankind, left to its own devices, would never merit God's grace and salvation. For Paul, salvation by faith highlights the role of God's grace in salvation. This doctrine also proves to be a great equalizer of people in that by faith all kinds of people—Jews and non-Jews alike—experience God's salvation.

Near the beginning of the book of Romans, Paul cited the Old Testament prophet Habakkuk, "the righteous will live by faith" (Rom. 1:17 NIV). In this way Paul established for his readers the centrality of faith in the life of the believer—a point well understood in the Old Testament. Just before this statement, Paul linked the gospel's power to its ability to save both Jew and Gentile. In other words, the gospel isn't tribal religion—it encompasses all peoples. It transcends ethnic and racial boundaries. The same point was forcefully made earlier in his career when, concerned with certain false teachers who taught otherwise, Paul challenged the Galatians with these words: "A man is not justified by the works of the Law but through faith in Christ Jesus" (Gal. 2:16 (NIV); also Eph. 2:8; Phil. 3:8–9). The emphasis on salvation by faith sets Paul apart from various opponents of the gospel, who urged that believers must keep the Old Testament law to realize the benefits of the gospel. This emphasis on faith also sets Christianity apart from many world religions which consider that salvation is a matter of having one's good works outweigh one's shortcomings. It is faith which secures God's mercy and salvation. Accordingly, it is an indispensable feature of Paul's theology.

Ethical living for disciples. Finally, since Jesus is the Lord who sends his Spirit to transform the lives of his followers, there is a strong ethical dimension to Paul's teaching. In 1 Thessalonians 1:9–10, a passage to which we have already referred, Paul noted conversion involves people giving up idolatry and serving the true God. Elsewhere Paul said that God has saved us "and called us with a holy calling" (2 Tim. 1:9). God has set believers apart to do his bidding in the world rather than to live merely for ourselves. This is the sentiment behind his strong words in 1 Corinthians 6:9–11:

> Do you not know that the wicked will not inherit the king-
> dom of God? Do not be deceived: Neither the sexually immoral
> nor idolaters nor adulterers nor male prostitutes nor homosex-
> ual offenders nor thieves nor the greedy nor drunkards nor
> slanderers nor swindlers will inherit the kingdom of God. And
> that is what some of you were. But you were washed, you were
> sanctified, you were justified, in the name of the Lord Jesus
> Christ and by the Spirit of our God (NIV).

Paul could not envision a Christianity where converts were not transformed because all believers receive the Spirit (Rom. 8:1–11; Gal. 3:5–14)
and the Spirit is the agent of new life (Gal. 5:15–25; 6:8; 2 Thess. 2:13; Titus
3:5–6). His many exhortations to ethical conduct were based on the expectation that the *new* life given to believers results in *transformed* lives (Gal.
1:4; Col. 1:13; 2 Tim. 1:9; Titus 2:12).

Summary. These are cardinal tenets of the faith for Paul: the resurrection,
return, and deity of Jesus; salvation by faith for all kinds of people; and personal transformation through the power of the Holy Spirit. Each has been
enshrined in one or more of the historic creeds and statements of the
church.[42] To return to the issue of "the apostasy," we may surmise that Paul
envisioned a future time in which those who nominally identified themselves with Christianity would abandon its central doctrines. For Paul, such
doctrinal defection would signal the approach of the last days.

The early years of the Christian era were marked by doctrinal controver-
sies. These were largely settled by the various ecumenical councils that met
to discuss them. By the sixth century A.D., fundamental questions of doctrine had been widely agreed upon.[43] The past century, however, has witnessed defection from basic Christian doctrine on an unprecedented scale.
This is especially true in the so-called mainstream denominations which for
many years upheld orthodox doctrine. Has the apostasy Paul warned about
arrived?

Paul provided few details about the future apostasy. Thus, we cannot
confirm its appearance (indeed, its arrival is complemented by the appearance of the Antichrist). But this does not mean that we have nothing to say
about the apostasy. It is important, for example, to point out that never in
the history of the Christian church has orthodox doctrine been so widely
rejected by church members. This does not mean that those who have
departed the faith might not eventually return to it; perhaps God will yet
grant repentance to those who have rejected the truth. At the same time, it
may be that things will worsen, that more and more people who claim the

label "Christian" will reject those doctrines that believers of all ages have considered most important. If we moderns are not seeing the apostasy mentioned by Paul in 2 Thessalonians, we must be saddened by the prospect of an even worse departure from the truth in days to come.

What can we say in conclusion about the apostasy? (1) It is a certain sign of the end; (2) it is a doctrinal defection within the Christian church; (3) the *precise* nature of the defection is not spelled out for us, hence its identification with historical or contemporary circumstances cannot be established beyond doubt; and (4) Paul linked the apostasy to the emergence of the Antichrist.

WORLDWIDE PREACHING OF THE GOSPEL

Christianity is a missionary religion. The impetus for this came from Jesus himself. Before returning to heaven, he left his followers with a task: to make disciples of all nations. The mission was based on his own authority—an authority demonstrated by his ministry, death, and resurrection. In Matthew 28:18–20 Jesus said,

> All authority in heaven and on earth has been given to me.
> Therefore go and make disciples of all nations, baptizing them
> in the name of the Father and of the Son and of the Holy Spirit,
> and teaching them to obey everything I have commanded you.
> And surely I am with you always, to the very end of the age
> (NIV).

Furthermore, according to Acts 1:8, Jesus promised to send the Holy Spirit to enable his disciples to fulfill their mission ("But you will receive power when the Holy Spirit comes on you; and you will be my witnesses . . . to the ends of the earth") (NIV).

The importance of Jesus' remarks becomes clearer when we remember that before his death he indicated the worldwide preaching of the gospel *must* precede his return in the last days: "This gospel of the kingdom will be preached in the whole world as a testimony to all nations, and then the end will come" (Matt. 24:14 NIV; also Mark 13:10). The Greek word translated "nations" (*ethnê*) is normally used in the New Testament to refer to non-Jews and non-Christians; this may be a carry-over from the Greek Old Testament where the word refers to non-Jews.[44] The word *nation* usually refers to a group of people "bound by the same manners, customs or other distinctive features."[45] Jesus did not say that every person on earth must hear the gospel before his return, but that all people groups must be reached.[46] Has the gospel spread "to all the nations"? Is Jesus' mission about to be fulfilled?

Christians have taken the gospel to most of the world in the past two thousand years. From humblest beginnings—first Jesus, then his few disciples—Christianity has grown to become the world's most dominant and pervasive religion.[47] Even if the number of genuine Christians is far smaller than the number of those nominally affiliated with Christianity, it remains large. Moreover, in coming years the growth of Christianity is expected to outpace the growth of world population generally.[48] Meanwhile, the number of unevangelized people continues to shrink. In the year 1900 slightly over 50 percent of the world's population had not heard the gospel; by the year 2000 that number was slightly over 25 percent. Similarly, the number of unreached people groups is steadily decreasing, while an increasing number of people groups is receiving its own Bible translation. The groups are being reached by missionaries and Bible translators, and Christian broadcasting is also reaching an ever-larger number of people. Since 1970 the number of Christian radio and TV stations has more than tripled, from 1,230 to about 4,000. The increase in audiences has been equally prolific, from about 750 million in 1970 to over 2 billion in 1999. This has far outstripped the audience growth for secular stations.[49]

We are not in a position to say exactly when the mission to preach will have occurred, nor does the language of Matthew 24:14 demand the return of Jesus as soon as the last "nation" has been evangelized. Nevertheless, the church's mission is nearer fulfillment now than ever before. This is true not simply because Christianity's growth has matched population growth generally but because Christians have set out to evangelize the world. One could easily envision the accomplishment of the mission before the end of the twenty-first century. When that goal is met, one condition for Jesus' return will be realized. It is perhaps ironic what while Jesus warned that wars and rumors of war among "the nations" would accompany the years between his resurrection and return, it is when "the nations" hear of the Prince of Peace that he will return to establish it.[50]

Conclusion

We are now in a position to draw some conclusions from the various threads of data examined thus far. At the outset of this book, I cited the work of scientists and philosophers of science who use the criteria of specificity and complexity to argue for intelligent design. The Bible allows us a glimpse of specificity and complexity—hence design—in history. Time and again the Old Testament speaks of future events which come to pass. Its forecasts exhibit specificity and complexity, and they enable us to discount the possibility that they could have been predicted or foreseen from a purely human point of view. This is true for Daniel's prediction about the timing of the coming and cutting off of Messiah (as seen in Appendix B). It is true for Micah's prediction about the birthplace of Messiah (Mic. 5:2). It is true for the almost innumerable places where the prophets speak of impending national disaster (or deliverance) and their words come to pass. It is true for Jesus' prediction of his suffering, death, and resurrection.

But someone may object that the experience of Israel, Jesus, and the church is a slender thread from which to weave a theory about design in history. After all, the events described in the Bible are the smallest fraction of history—a history littered with apparently nonsensical and incomprehensible occurrences. And yet even this objection bolsters the biblical view of the world. According to Scripture, the role of God's people is to be a microcosm, model, and example of his intervention. We are to shed light on God's character in the midst of this spiritually darkened world. Along with the Scriptures, God's people testify to the fidelity of God and his engagement in history. And if God has intervened in the life of one nation and millions of individuals, does this not suggest his interest in and ability to engage the rest of the world?

So much for the past and present; what about the future? Given what we know about design in history past, it is reasonable to believe the future—the "end times"—is also designed. In chapter 1, I likened God's design for the future to the construction of a house and observed that a house would be ready for occupation once building materials like lumber, bricks, drywall, and paint had been put in place as called for in its blueprint. To complete a house it is necessary that materials be present in the same place and at the same time, but their mere presence does not mean the house is built. They have to be assembled in the prescribed way, according to a plan. An attempt has been made here to discover what God's "blueprint" is for the immediate future, a future culminating in the return of Jesus. Once this "blueprint" is known, it becomes possible to recognize more easily whether the raw materials characteristic of "the last days" are present or not, and if so, if they are present in the prescribed way.

As to the end times, we saw in chapter 5 that they involve many *uncertain* signs—things which do not in themselves *necessarily* signal the end is near.

Famines, plagues, earthquakes, false teachers, wars, and rumors of wars are no more signs of the end than loose lumber on a lot signals that a house is almost ready for occupation. While they are part of the biblical end-times scenario, they are not confined to it. To the contrary, they are characteristic of the entire period between Jesus' first and second coming. These hardships intensify in the end times, but we are not told what level of intensification accompanies or identifies "the end." Hence, we cannot say with any assurance on the basis of these uncertain signs that it has arrived. We must exercise caution in teaching that the so-called "signs" we may witness are extraordinary and point to an imminent end.[51]

But this is not to say there are no "signs of the times" worth taking note of. When we collect the various Scriptures and try to formulate a coherent picture of the end, we conclude that four things must happen before "the day of the Lord" arrives in its fullness: (1) the manifestation of the Antichrist; (2) the emergence of "the apostasy" (this apparently occurs in tandem with the Antichrist); (3) the worldwide proclamation of the gospel; and (4) the repentance of the Jews.[52] These events will be accompanied by natural disasters, plagues, and wars on a large scale. Humanity as a whole will be gripped by fear and an awareness of impending doom (Luke 21:25ff.; Rev. 6:15–17). The biblical picture of the last days is not pleasant.

Can we establish a timetable or order for the events described in this chapter? Probably not. All must precede the return of Jesus; beyond that, relatively little information is given.

The appearance of the Antichrist is the event which will most clearly signal the beginning of the last days. But how can we give assent to the notion that a satanically empowered human being will emerge and deceive the world? How can we moderns believe that a miracle worker will appear and under the guise of goodness lead the world astray spiritually? It seems unbelievable. Perhaps Jesus, Paul, and John speak metaphorically about the spiritual darkness that will characterize the last days. But this is unlikely. In the context where Paul predicted the coming man of sin, he also predicted the return of Jesus (2 Thess. 2:4–8). Are we to think he spoke metaphorically of Jesus' return? And if it is conceded that a literal return of Jesus is difficult to imagine, is it any easier to believe in his literal resurrection?

Paul had a supernaturalistic view of the world that expected God to intervene in history. The Antichrist is but one feature of this worldview. Events at the end are extraordinary. This is why they are hard to envision, especially if we buy into the notion that "all continues just as it was from the beginning of creation" (2 Pet. 3:4). Yet the uniqueness of events at the end is not a sufficient reason to discount the most likely meaning of the words of Jesus, Paul, and John. An Antichrist will come.

The reestablishment of a national Israel in 1948 may be a harbinger of the coming Antichrist. Although many people disagree with me, it is not unreasonable to believe the Jews' presence in the land of Israel now is a precursor to their repentance, particularly in light of Paul's teaching that the Antichrist must appear in "the temple."[53] As we observe events of the last two thousand years, it may be unwise to regard the establishment of a national Israel as wholly unrelated to the nearness of the Lord's return. Clearer than this, however, is the need for Jewish repentance to happen before Jesus returns.

The emergence of "the apostasy" will accompany the Antichrist. Apostasy is all around us; the church is even now plagued from within and without by false teachers, preachers, and leaders. Nevertheless, this "falling away" from true doctrine will become even more prevalent with the appearance of the Antichrist. We may regard present circumstances as dire—but even if that conclusion were justified, we could not say *the* apostasy has come; Paul did not qualify or quantify his statement sufficiently to allow its clear and indisputable identification.

The worldwide proclamation of the gospel is arguably the only one of the "certain signs" within the range of human control. It is likely that all the people groups of the world will have been reached with the good news about Jesus before the end of the twenty-first century. And yet Scripture does not require us to believe that the fulfillment of the mandate to preach results in the *immediate* onset of the day of the Lord. There could be delay between the two events.

No Antichrist has emerged to offer himself as the world's Savior and lord. It is undoubtedly true, as John wrote, that many antichrists have come (1 John 2:18; 4:3); but the one final incarnation of evil has yet to appear. When he does, the world will laud him as its deliverer, while believers will label him the deceiver. When he comes, the final act in this age will near its conclusion. When he comes, believers must gird themselves for unprecedented suffering. Or must they?

Chapter Eight

THE SECOND COMING

✧

W hat a movie they could make! If Hollywood would only apply its technological wizardry to the story of the last days! Imagine—the cunning figure of the Antichrist, natural disasters galore, global warfare on an almost unimaginable scale, and the courageous story of those who endure suffering for the sake of their noble leader, Jesus. And what a closing scene!

Movie or not, the horrific suffering to be experienced during the tribulation of the last days will culminate in the personal, bodily return of Jesus. For his followers, unprecedented suffering gives way to unprecedented deliverance. His return signals the end of the world as we know it. In its place comes a restored earth in which God dwells with his people forever. But before this transformation is complete, a series of interim events must occur.

Rapture or Second Coming?

The New Testament contains many references to the return or "second coming" of Jesus. He mentioned it before his death and after his resurrection; it is found in the earliest New Testament book and in the latest; it is taught in the Gospels, the Epistles, and the Revelation. A person cannot read the New Testament without recognizing that Jesus' return is a major theme.

Christians have traditionally held that Jesus will return bodily to earth at the end of the age to vanquish his enemies and reward his followers. In Luke 24 we learn of encounters between the risen Jesus and his disciples. After he miraculously appeared to them, their sorrow initially gave way to fear and the mistaken impression that they were seeing a spirit. Jesus countered this by inviting them to touch his body, saying, "Why are you troubled, and why do doubts rise in your minds? Look at my hands and my feet. It is I myself! Touch me and see; a ghost does not have flesh and bones, as you see I have" (24:38–39 NIV). To further demonstrate the reality of his presence, he asked for food and ate it in front of them. This picture of a bodily risen Savior is also found in John's Gospel, where the doubtful Thomas is invited by Jesus, "Put your finger here; see my hands. Reach out your hand and put it into my side. Stop doubting and believe" (John 20:27 NIV).

According to Acts 1, for forty days or so after his resurrection, Jesus taught the disciples until he ascended into heaven (Acts 1:1–9; the events described here follow the resurrection narrative in Luke 24). As they watched him go up into the clouds, the disciples were told by angels, "Men of Galilee, . . . why do you stand here looking into the sky? This same Jesus, who has been taken from you into heaven, will come back in the same way you have seen him go into heaven" (Acts 1:11 NIV). The phrase "in the same way" points to the personal, bodily return of Jesus. The bodily nature of his return is linked to the bodily nature of his resurrection. From these and related passages come the Christian doctrine that Jesus will return bodily some day from heaven to earth.

As to Jesus' returning visibly, this is also found in many biblical passages. Before his death Jesus taught that after tribulation "'the sun will be darkened, and the moon will not give its light; the stars will fall from the sky, and the heavenly bodies will be shaken.' At that time men will see the Son of Man coming in clouds with great power and glory" (Mark 13:24–26 NIV). Jesus was not describing a private appearance or secret revelation; his return would be open, obvious, and public. The book of Revelation says, "Look, he is coming with the clouds, and every eye will see him, even those who pierced him; and all the peoples of the earth will mourn because of him. So shall it be! Amen" (Rev. 1:7 NIV, citing the Old Testament prophet Zechariah).

From the first century onward Christians have taught that Jesus will someday return to earth, but in the past several decades another view of Jesus' coming has gradually developed alongside the traditionally held belief that he will return bodily and visibly. In *Left Behind*, a best-selling series of novels by Jerry Jenkins and Tim LaHaye, the world enters its darkest hour—the tribulation—after God removes Christians from the earth. They are taken in an event known as the "pretribulation rapture." After they are taken, the Antichrist reveals himself to a dismayed, deceived, and desperate world. The novels thus embrace a theological perspective known as "pretribulationalism." According to its proponents, Jesus' return involves two phases: a secret coming to remove his church from the hardships that will mark the last days, and an open "second coming" to execute judgment on the ungodly and establish his millennial kingdom. Used in this context, "the rapture" is a technical term for the secret coming of Jesus to deliver his church from impending tribulation.

Pretribulationalism is something of a historical oddity. It was virtually unknown in the first eighteen centuries of church history. Those who hold to it believe it was the theological orientation of Paul and other apostles, but it was not spoken of—or not clearly spoken of—by ancient church writers and historians.[1] The novelty of this view does not mean it is wrong, only that it warrants close examination. Its relative newness suggests there is a heavy burden of proof on those who believe it. What evidence is there for pretribulationalism?

I cannot hope to cover fully in this limited space all the arguments in favor of a pretribulation rapture. Others have written extensively on the subject; and I will attempt only to summarize, then critique their views.[2] According to John Walvoord, perhaps the premier exponent of pretribulationalism, the rapture was a crucial part of the message preached by Paul in the first century. Alongside the good news that Jesus was the crucified, buried, and risen Savior who alone offers salvation to the world, Paul taught the pretribulation rapture—or so it is thought.[3]

Pretribulationalists believe the rapture must occur before the tribulation. An argument for their position might run something like this:

✧ The great tribulation is a time when God pours out his wrath on the world and brings Israel to repentance (thus "wrath" is often a catchword for "great tribulation"); this time concludes with various signs and, eventually, the personal return of Jesus.

✧ Christians are destined not to experience God's wrath.

✧ Therefore, there must be some way by which believers are delivered from the time of tribulation (i.e., the time of wrath).

✧ This deliverance is effected through the pretribulation rapture.

This is a plausible argument—but will it stand up to closer scrutiny? Admittedly, the great tribulation is a time when God will make life on earth very unpleasant. It is also conceded that Christians are destined not to be the objects of God's wrath. But does it follow that believers will be absent from the earth during the tribulation? God protected Noah and his family from the Flood (Gen. 6:9ff.); he protected Lot's family from destruction in Sodom (Gen. 18:16ff.). In a similar way, it is argued, he will protect Christians from the tribulation by removing them from the earth. And yet the precedent of Noah's protection does not require that God keep us out of the tribulation. After all, God hasn't always protected his people by removing them from difficult circumstances. We note, for example, that God poured out his plagues on Egypt while Moses and the people of Israel were living there. The Jews were not taken out of Egypt before the plagues came; rather, they were preserved through them. And though they were preserved, Pharaoh continually made life harder for them, and they suffered (e.g., Exod. 5:1–9). Jesus didn't promise believers deliverance from the time of wrath. To the contrary, in his prayer for the church, Jesus asked specifically that it not be taken out of the world but be protected from the evil one (John 17:15). Jesus' statement advocating preservation from Satan rather than removal from the world is all the more striking when we remember that this age is a time when God's wrath is being poured out (Rom. 1:18). Moreover, the picture of Christians suffering for the sake of the gospel is commonly found in Revelation passages which may refer to the future great tribulation. In these passages Satan and those loyal to him persecute believers, often to the point of death (Rev. 6:9–11; 12:10–12; 13:7). Much of the book of Revelation points to future events. This indicates that large numbers of believers will suffer and die *during the tribulation*. If the pretribulational reply is, "Yes, but these are not Christian believers," then a question follows: "What kind of believers are they? Does God protect one class of believer from the time of his wrath but allow another class to experience it?" Believers have faced death in the past; they face it now; they will face it in the tribulation. Though it may be more widespread in the tribulation than at other times, can it be any more horrific? Consider the following account:

> There was one in particular the soldiers talked about that evening, a girl on La Cruz whom they had raped many times during the course of the afternoon, and through it all, while the other women of El Mozote had screamed and cried as if they had never had a man, this girl had sung hymns, strange evangelical songs, and she had kept right on singing, too, even after they had done what had to be done, and shot her in the chest. She had lain there on La Cruz with the blood flowing from her chest, and had kept on singing—a bit weaker than before, but still singing, and the soldiers, stupefied, had watched and pointed. Then they had grown tired of the game and shot her

again, and she sang still, and their wonder began to turn to fear—until finally they had unsheathed their machetes and hacked through her neck, and at last the singing had stopped.

Is this an excerpt from a novel about the end times describing the horrors the world will face after Christians are raptured and the tribulation begins? No, it is the report of the torture and death of a young Christian girl in 1993.[4]

Although believers may be preserved from God's wrath, this is not the same thing as saying they are protected from tribulation, even martyrdom, at the hands of God's enemies. There is no theological necessity for believers to be removed from the earth before the great tribulation, and there is biblical precedent for believers remaining in a given locale even while God's judgments are poured forth. God's wrath is being poured out now in some measure (Rom. 1:18), and believers are preserved from it even while others near them are not. It is true that the wrath mentioned by Paul is not being poured forth on *Christians* now, but then neither will it be during the great tribulation.

Alongside the theory that Christians must be taken out of the world before the tribulation, pretribulationalists also believe the rapture is imminent—that is, it could occur at any moment. Indeed, this seems to be the thrust of several biblical passages. For instance, in Matthew 24:36–44 Jesus taught that his coming will take the world by surprise much as the Flood did in Noah's day. Pretribulationalists ask, "How could this possibly refer to Jesus coming *after* the tribulation, since by then his return would not be a surprise?" Further, just as Noah's boarding the ark signaled the beginning of God's judgment on the ancient world, so—according to some pretribulationalists—the rapture at the beginning of the tribulation signals the beginning of God's final judgment on the world.

This belief in imminence influences the pretribulationist interpretation of several biblical passages. On the one hand, they recognize that the second coming will be preceded by various signs; hence it cannot come "at any moment." On the other hand, since passages like 1 Thessalonians 4:13–18, 1 Corinthians 15:50–57, and Matthew 24:36–25:13 seem to say the Lord could return at virtually any moment, it is thought these passages must refer to something other than the second coming.[5] Many pretribulationalists conclude that where a New Testament explicitly writer mentions tribulation and its attendant circumstances in connection with a coming of the Lord, the second coming is in view. Where a New Testament writer does not

mention tribulation in connection with the Lord's coming, the pretribulation rapture is in view. To cite a specific example, since Paul made no mention of tribulation in 1 Thessalonians 4:13–18 but did speak of the coming
of Jesus in the sky to meet his people, the passage must—it is thought—be
a reference to the pretribulation rapture. This inference assumes that Paul
and other New Testament writers would always mention prophetic events
in chronological order with thorough descriptions.

But this assumption is not warranted. In several instances Paul either did
not speak of the future in its chronological order or gave an abbreviated
version of it. For example, in 2 Thessalonians 1:6–10 he spoke of Christians
awaiting the return of the Lord "to deal out retribution." The mention of
"retribution" refers to Jesus' second coming (the time at which he deals out
retribution; see Rev. 19:11ff.). This is what we Christians are waiting for,
according to Paul. Yet he made this statement without mentioning the rapture *or* the tribulation—events which must precede Jesus' return, according
to pretribulationalists! Does this mean there is no tribulation or rapture
before the Lord returns? Was Paul inconsistent or absent-minded? No.
Paul's thought is consistent, just not always expressed in detail.

Imagine I were to come home one afternoon and be greeted at the door
by my curious daughter, "Daddy, where have you been?" I might answer, "I
took Ed to the airport." Somewhat later my wife might ask, "Why were you
gone so long?" I answer, "I had to buy gasoline, purchase a toll access card,
and get some groceries." The observer to these conversations could, but
need not, suppose that I had made two trips—one to the airport and another
for gasoline and groceries. In fact, I had made one. My original statement to
my daughter was not false, but it was incomplete.

In this respect 1 Corinthians 15:20–28 is similar to 2 Thessalonians
1:6–10 in that neither gives a complete description of future events. In
1 Corinthians 15:20–28 Paul mentioned Christ's coming in verse 23 (which
Walvoord understands as the rapture[6]) and "the end" in verse 24 (which
Walvoord sees as a reference to the millennial kingdom[7]) without mentioning events which on Walvoord's reckoning take place between the two (i.e.,
the tribulation, the second coming, and the judgment seat of Christ). Paul
clearly does not feel obliged always to describe fully prophetic events, and
we should not expect it of him. His letters are not theological treatises as
such; they are pastoral letters occasioned by particular circumstances. It
would be a mistake to expect a given passage to address fully all aspects of

Paul's doctrine of God or of the end times unless there is specific warrant for doing so.

If pretribulationalist teaching about Christians' physical removal from earth when God's wrath is poured out is open to question, and if the same thing can be said about the imminence of the rapture, what biblical passages lend greatest support to their belief? Although many texts are said to teach pretribulationalism, there are two which Walvoord regards as most crucial: 1 Thessalonians 4:13–18 and 1 Corinthians 15:50–57.[8] What do these passages teach about the rapture?

1 Thessalonians 4:13–18. First Thessalonians is one of Paul's earliest letters, composed shortly after his departure from the city of Thessalonica under duress in about A.D. 50.[9] Paul and his companions had been run out of the city at the instigation of Jewish authorities, who practically accused him of fomenting insurrection (Acts 17:1–10). Although his preaching ministry there was short-lived, it was successful, resulting in the conversion of some Jews and numerous God-fearing Greeks. After his departure Paul sent Timothy back to find out how the young church was doing (1 Thess. 3:1–10). Armed with Timothy's report, Paul wrote to the fledgling congregation to assure them of his well-being and to encourage them in their new-found faith. It seems that he also sought to address various questions or concerns they had. To cite a specific example, Paul wrote to clarify for them the fate of believers who die before the return of Jesus. This is the issue taken up in 1 Thessalonians 4:13–18. It says:

> Brothers, we do not want you to be ignorant about those who fall asleep, or to grieve like the rest of men, who have no hope. We believe that Jesus died and rose again and so we believe that God will bring with Jesus those who have fallen asleep in him. According to the Lord's own word, we tell you that we who are still alive, who are left till the coming of the Lord, will certainly not precede those who have fallen asleep. For the Lord himself will come down from heaven, with a loud command, with the voice of the archangel and with the trumpet call of God, and the dead in Christ will rise first. After that, we who are still alive and are left will be caught up together with them in the clouds to meet the Lord in the air. And so we will be with the Lord forever. Therefore encourage each other with these words (NIV).

Paul assured the Thessalonian believers that Christians who die before the Lord's coming ("those who fall asleep," v. 13[10]) will participate fully in the general resurrection from the dead. Indeed, Paul noted, they will return in spirit with the Lord at his coming and get resurrection bodies prior to those believers who haven't died. This apparently new teaching (new in that Paul introduced it with the comment, "But we do not want you to be uninformed," verse 13, implying that they had previously been uninformed) was meant to instruct and assure the church (vv. 13, 18).

This brief sketch of the background of 1 Thessalonians is agreed upon by commentators. But it is not immediately obvious why the passage is thought to support a pretribulation rapture rather than simply offer additional information about the second coming of Jesus (the traditional interpretation). To understand how the passage supports pretribulationalism, we must look further.

In arguing that the Thessalonians expected the rapture to come at any moment, Walvoord interprets the promise that they would be delivered from "wrath" at the coming of the Lord Jesus in 1 Thessalonians 1:10; 2:16; 3:13; 5:23 and, above all, 4:13–18 and 5:9 as reference to the great tribulation.[11] But this is probably *not* what Paul was talking about when he mentioned "wrath" in these passages.

As used by Paul the word *wrath* (*orgê*) most often refers either to the present pouring out of God's judgment (Rom. 1:18; 12:19; 13:4, 5; 1 Thess. 2:16) or to an unspecified future judgment, most likely the judgment carried out in the afterlife (Rom. 2:5, 8; 5:9; 1 Thess. 1:10). Even within 1 Thessalonians Paul used the term to describe a present reality. In 1 Thessalonians 2:14–16 (NIV) he wrote about those Jews who persecuted Jesus, Paul, and the church: "Wrath has come upon them at last." The tense of the Greek verb Paul used, "has come" (*ephthasen*), suggests the coming is something *already* accomplished.[12] In other words, the Jews of Paul's day had already begun to experience the wrath of God. If "wrath" can refer to something certain people in Paul's day were already experiencing, it cannot be a technical term that refers only to the great tribulation of the last days. Thus, the various promises of deliverance from wrath in 1 Thessalonians cannot be assumed to refer to promises of deliverance from the era of the great tribulation.

But if the preceding comments are valid, then 1 Thessalonians 4:13–18 says nothing about a pretribulation rapture as such. The verses do speak clearly about the resurrection of dead Christians and the transformation of living Christians at Jesus' return—but it cannot be assumed *this* return is anything other than the second coming and events associated with it.

Indeed, one feature of Paul's description favors interpreting the passage as pointing to a posttribulation rapture. What is it?

In writing to the Thessalonians Paul spoke of Jesus' return as a "parousia" (v. 15). While the term *parousia* might simply be translated as "arrival" or "presence," it often has richer connotations. The "parousia" began to be a notable feature of imperial practice during the first century.[13] The *parousia* was an event most ancient readers would have been well acquainted with. In the Hellenistic world a *parousia* often signaled the coming of a ruler or royal figure. That Paul had this in mind in 1 Thessalonians 4:13ff. is confirmed by the presence of a second word often used in descriptions of a *parousia*, "to meet" (*apantaô*, v. 17). What could the ancient observer have expected of the event?

At the approach of the dignitary, a band of municipal officials and other citizens, including the social, religious, and political élite, would proceed some distance from the city in order to meet the celebrity well in advance of the city walls. The whole population was to proceed in hierarchical order to greet the visitor. Once the dignitary had been met by a delegation from the city, speeches of welcome would be given by select members of the delegation. After this, the guest was escorted back into the city by those who had gone out to meet him. A *parousia* was frequently brought to an end by the visit of the guest to the local temple.[14]

Robert Gundry makes the point that the coming of Jesus in 1 Thessalonians 4:13–18 is likened to a *parousia* in that his arrival is signaled by a shout, he is accompanied by friends and allies (i.e., the believers who are said to be "asleep in the Lord"), and he is met in the sky by living Christians who welcome his appearance.[15] Gundry goes on to argue that just as a ruler in a *parousia* would continue into the city after his entourage was met outside, so this imagery of *parousia* leads us to expect that Jesus will continue his journey to earth after he is met by believers rather than stop and retreat to heaven, as the pretribulationalists would have us believe.[16] Additionally, this picture of Jesus' *parousia* in 1 Thessalonians 4:13–18 is similar to the description of Jesus' return in Revelation 19:11ff., where he is accompanied by the saints on his descent to the earth.

To conclude: 1 Thessalonians 4:13–18 speaks about the fate of deceased and living Christians at the time of Jesus' return. The former, who initially go to be in the presence of the Lord when they die (Phil. 1:20–24), will accompany the Lord at his return, and their spirits will be united with their bodies in resurrection at that time. Believers who are alive when Jesus returns will undergo a transformation—their mortal bodies will be made into immortal ones. The two groups of believers, once separated by death, will then be together with one another and with the Lord forever. The passage says nothing about a pretribulation rapture (or, for that matter, very little—if anything—about a posttribulation rapture); it deals not with the timing of the rapture vis-à-vis the tribulation but with the fact and timing of the rapture of deceased believers vis-à-vis the rapture of those alive when Jesus returns.

1 Corinthians 15:50–57. Scholars have long recognized 1 Corinthians 15 as the theological epicenter of Paul's first letter to the church at Corinth. In this chapter Paul reiterated for the Corinthians the fact and nature of Jesus' resurrection, then connected his resurrection to the fate of Christians on a wider scale. There were apparently some people in Corinth who had doubts about resurrection in general, a situation which led to doubts about Jesus' resurrection in particular. In addition to Corinth, this skepticism was found at other places where Paul preached, most notably in Athens where his philosophically minded audiences were dismayed by the proclamation that God had raised Jesus bodily from the grave (Acts 17:16–34; Athens and Corinth were located approximately forty-five miles apart). To the church at Corinth Paul wrote:

> Now, brothers, I want to remind you of the gospel I preached to you, which you received and on which you have taken your stand. By this gospel you are saved, if you hold firmly to the word I preached to you. Otherwise, you have believed in vain. For what I received I passed on to you as of first importance: that Christ died for our sins according to the Scriptures, that he was buried, that he was raised on the third day according to the Scriptures, and that he appeared to Peter, and then to the Twelve. After that, he appeared to more than five hundred of the brothers at the same time, most of whom are still living, though some have fallen asleep. Then he appeared to James, then to all the apostles, and last of all he appeared to me also, as to one abnormally born (1 Cor. 15:1–8 NIV).

Paul observed that Jesus' death and resurrection took place "according to the Scriptures"; that is, they were part of God's foreordained plan. He reminded the Corinthians that there were numerous, indeed hundreds of, witnesses to Jesus' resurrection. Paul further connected the fact of Jesus' resurrection to the veracity of the Christian faith:

> But if it is preached that Christ has been raised from the
> dead, how can some of you say that there is no resurrection of
> the dead? If there is no resurrection of the dead, then not even
> Christ has been raised. And if Christ has not been raised, our
> preaching is useless and so is your faith. More than that, we are
> then found to be false witnesses about God, for we have testi-
> fied about God that he raised Christ from the dead. But he did
> not raise him if in fact the dead are not raised. For if the dead
> are not raised, then Christ has not been raised either. And if
> Christ has not been raised, your faith is futile; you are still in
> your sins. Then those also who have fallen asleep in Christ are
> lost. If only for this life we have hope in Christ, we are to be
> pitied more than all men (1 Cor. 15:12–19 NIV).

For Paul as for all Christians the truthfulness of the Christian gospel is
directly related to the historicity of Jesus' resurrection. Apart from it, the
gospel is no gospel, and the faith is either an empty piece of deception or
hopelessly wishful thinking.

Toward the end of the chapter, Paul took up a different but related issue:
how mortal bodies can be made fit to "inherit the kingdom." His remarks in
1 Corinthians 15:50–57 resemble those made in 1 Thessalonians 4:13–18
and like the latter passage describe a future, practically instantaneous transformation of believers' bodies. Paul said:

> I declare to you, brothers, that flesh and blood cannot inher-
> it the kingdom of God, nor does the perishable inherit the im-
> perishable. Listen, I tell you a mystery: We will not all sleep,
> but we will all be changed—in a flash, in the twinkling of an
> eye, at the last trumpet. For the trumpet will sound, the dead
> will be raised imperishable, and we will be changed. For the
> perishable must clothe itself with the imperishable, and the
> mortal with immortality (1 Cor. 15:50–53 NIV).

In the early part of the chapter, Paul emphasized the bodily nature of
Jesus' resurrection; toward the end, he made it clear that Jesus' mortal body
was transformed by the power of God and made fit for eternity through resurrection. This is similar to what Paul said in Philippians 3:21, where he
remarked that Jesus "will transform our lowly bodies so that they will be like
his glorious body" (NIV). Paul said that we too must be outfitted with new
bodies in order to inherit the kingdom. God does this, according to 1 Corinthians 15:50ff., by transforming our mortal bodies in a moment of time.

Pretribulationalists think this passage offers strong support for their
case. They believe the "mystery" Paul spoke of in verse 51 refers to the

pretribulation rapture. Scholars recognize that the term *mystery* refers to something revealed in the New Testament which was unknown, or only partially known, in the Old Testament. Walvoord rightly notes that the Old Testament does teach the resurrection of believers (for more on this, refer back to chapter 2). He concludes that since the *fact* of resurrection cannot be the "mystery" in view of 1 Corinthians 15:51, Paul must have in mind the *timing* of the resurrection; that is, a pretribulation rapture.[17] But this is incorrect, for Paul explained here what he regarded as the mystery: the fact that some believers will not die and *then* be resurrected but will instead experience an instantaneous transformation while alive (vv. 51b–52; as in 1 Thess. 4:13–18). The Old Testament teaches that the dead will be raised; Paul here said some of the living will be raised at the same time. First Corinthians 15:50–57 does not teach a pretribulation rapture.

Furthermore, other passages understood by pretribulationalists as teaching imminence do not necessarily point to a pretribulational rapture. For example, 1 Thessalonians 5:2–3 need not teach a pretribulation rapture. The phrase "day of the Lord" (v. 2) might not refer exclusively to Jesus' coming but to a whole complex of events culminating in his return. After all, in the Old Testament the day of the Lord involved several features, one of which was the coming of the Lord (see chapter 2). Furthermore, when Paul spoke of th · day of the Lord in 2 Thessalonians 2:2–3, he said it must be *preceded* by the appearance of the apostasy and the man of sin. This is inconsistent with a pretribulation rapture, an event that takes place without such warning.

Likewise, in the passage where Jesus likened his return to the outbreak of judgment in Noah's day (Matt. 24:36–44), the word used for Jesus' coming in verse 37 (*parousia*) is used elsewhere in Matthew to refer to Jesus' second coming (24:3, 27). Matthew 24:36–44 need not imply anything more than a link between Jesus' coming and judgment on unbelievers. Noah and his family were warned by the prophetic word; the rest of the world was warned but chose not to believe. Stanley Toussaint writes, "The likeness [between Noah's time and the last days] is seen in the suddenness of the coming of the judgment and the unpreparedness of the world for it."[18] Where the story about Noah is told in Luke 17, the day of Jesus' coming referred to is the day he is *revealed* (*apokaluptetai*, v. 30), a term inconsistent with the notion of a secret return. Likewise, upon close examination, other passages that speak of imminence need not be understood as referring to a pretribulation rapture.[19]

I have argued that the biblical passages many pretribulationalists regard as strongly supporting their position do no such thing. Yet there are two other items to consider in favor of a pretribulation rapture. The first is evidence from the book of Revelation. For example, pretribulationalists observe that Jesus explicitly warned the churches to heed his word with the phrase, "He who has an ear, let him hear what the Spirit says to the churches" (Rev. 2:7, 11, 17, 29; 3:6, 13, 22). According to pretribulationalists, the rapture of Christians is not hinted at until Revelation 4:1; hence, the warnings just cited are in passages dealing with events before the rapture. Yet later in the book, where the familiar phrase, "If anyone has an ear, let him hear" is present, the expected tag line "to the churches" is strangely absent (Rev. 13:9). The phrase is absent (so the argument goes) because the church is absent—it has been raptured.

This is a worthwhile observation about phraseology in the book of Revelation—but it hardly constitutes proof for a pretribulation rapture. If the rapture could be established on other grounds, the observation from Revelation could supplement it—but it is not established on other grounds.

Likewise, some pretribulationalists argue that the rapture is alluded to in Revelation 3:10, where the church in the ancient city of Philadelphia is told by Jesus, "Since you have kept my command to endure patiently, I will also keep you from the hour of trial that is going to come upon the whole world to test those who live on the earth (NIV)." It is thought this passage helps the pretribulational cause because (1) the church at Philadelphia is typical of the church on earth before the great tribulation and (2) this church is promised to be "kept from the hour of trial," where this latter phrase refers to believers being removed from the earth before the tribulation.

It seems fair to ask if the promise of rapture is here made only to the church at Philadelphia and not to churches in Ephesus (Rev. 2:1–3) or Sardis (Rev. 3:1, 4) which, like the one in Philadelphia, are also commended. Would believers in those places not also be raptured? If the answer is that the promise of deliverance is made to the church at Philadelphia because it typifies the church that exists prior to the tribulation, we ask, "Where is the compelling evidence for that?" Further, what is it about the church at Philadelphia that typifies the pretribulation church? Is this church really more commendable or typical of the "last days church" than the church in Sardis or Smyrna? Why, if the raptured church must reflect the qualities found in the church at Philadelphia, does Paul in his letters speak of the rapture as applicable to all believers? Should he not have qualified himself?

These questions are not meant to demean the pretribulation position; they stem from my reluctance to use evidence from Revelation as proof of doctrines or ideas not clearly mentioned elsewhere (see Appendix C). It is not clear that Revelation 3:10 refers to a pretribulation rapture; in fact, to be fair it is anything but clear that John here refers to a rapture of any kind. Neither is it clear that the church at Philadelphia typifies the pretribulation church. But for the sake of argument, let us take Revelation 3:10 as speaking of the rapture. Does it help the pretribulation cause?

It is often argued that had John intended to say God would preserve believers *through* the tribulation (the posttribulation position) he would have used the Greek phrase *têreô dia* ("keep through") rather than the one he did use, *têreô ek* ("keep from"). But the situation is not that simple, for the phrase *têreô dia* may not have been known to the writer of Revelation. It is not found once either in the New Testament or in the Greek Old Testament. As to the phrase that is used, *têreô ek*, it appears just one other time in the New Testament (John 17:15). Yet in this passage Jesus explicitly asked God *not* to remove believers from the world (*ek tou kosmou*) but to keep them from the evil one (*têreô ek*) even while they are in the world.[20] Though the phrase is rarely used, it is possible that *têreô ek* was one Greek equivalent for "preserving through."

As to the nature of the preservation, Greg Beale notes that Jesus' remarks to the other churches in Revelation 2:3 "have focused only on spiritual perseverance, even at the cost of one's physical life (e.g., 2:8–11; 2:13). If 3:10 is referring to a promise of physical preservation before the final resurrection, then it is the only text in the whole book that does so."[21]

Finally, Beale observes that Revelation 3:10 may allude to the Greek version of Daniel 12:1, 10, suggesting that "the 'testing' in Revelation 3:10 has the double effect of purifying and strengthening believers and of divine punishment of others."[22] For believers to be purified and strengthened by the testing, they would have to be on earth to experience it. Given the objections just raised, I reiterate: one must be cautious about building doctrine on scarce evidence, particularly when that evidence comes from a book as often misunderstood and disputed as Revelation. I do not believe Revelation teaches a pretribulation rapture.

A final point in favor of a pretribulation rapture has to do with the nature of the millennial kingdom. Not all Christians think there will be a literal millennial kingdom, but many who do believe it to be a time when Jesus will reign on earth among mortals who are capable of procreation. If believers are given resurrection bodies when Jesus returns and nonbelievers are slain at his second coming, "who," it is asked, "will be left with a mortal body capable of procreating during the millennial kingdom?"

The key to resolving the apparent dilemma is this: Scripture does not teach that Jesus will slay all non-believers when he returns. In 2 Thessalonians 1:6–10 Paul said Jesus will deal out retribution to those who do not know God and to those who do not obey the gospel of our Lord Jesus when he returns. And yet this description modifies comments made earlier, where Paul described those who will be punished: "It is only just for God to repay with affliction those who afflict you." In other words, those who do not know God and get his wrath are those who have afflicted his church. This corresponds nicely to the scenario painted at the end of Revelation. In Revelation 19:18 we learn that at Jesus' return the birds are invited to feast on the "flesh of kings, generals, and mighty men, of horses and their riders, and the flesh of all people, free and slave, small and great (NIV)." In the following verses (19–21) we see that the birds' meal consists of the Antichrist, the kings aligned with him, and all their armies. In other words, not every unbeliever is slain by Jesus at his return, only those who actively supported the Antichrist and his persecution of God's people.[23] This corresponds to the idea that not every unbeliever in the last days is aligned with the Antichrist. If Jesus slays *all* unbelievers at his return, over whom does he rule "with a rod of iron"? (Ps. 2:9; Rev. 2:26–27; 19:15; the phrase implies the forcible imposition of his will).

As the reader will have observed, I do not believe the rapture occurs prior to the tribulation of the end times. The return of Jesus was a basic element of early Christian preaching and teaching and the church has upheld this doctrine for centuries without adding to it the teaching of a pretribulation rapture. Thus, I would suggest that from the outset odds favor the traditional—i.e., posttribulational—interpretation and require that competing ones be established with great care. I am not persuaded by pretribulational writers. I have listed certain criticisms of the pretribulation position above and will now explain in greater detail why I think the rapture will occur shortly before the second coming of Jesus.[24]

The close correspondence between passages that clearly point to the second coming and those that describe a rapture strongly suggests the two events take place at the same time. For example, one cannot fail to be impressed by the similarity in language that exists between Matthew 24:30–31, 1 Thessalonians 4:13–18, and 1 Corinthians 15:51–53 (see table next page).

Matt. 24:3, 30–31	1 Thess. 4:13–18	1 Cor. 15:52
3 the disciples were saying to him privately, "tell us, "when will these things happen and what will be the sign of your coming (*parousia*) and of the end of the age?" 30 The sign of the son of man will appear in the sky (*ouranos*); the son of man comes on the clouds of heaven	15 we who are alive and remain until the coming (*parousia*) of the Lord . . . 16 the Lord himself descends from heaven (*ouranos*) with those who have "fallen asleep"	
31 he sends out his angels to sound a great trumpet	16 with a shout, with the voice of the archangel, with the trumpet of God	52 in a moment, in the twinkling of an eye, the last trumpet is sounded
31 the angels gather together the elect	14–17 deceased and living believers are raised and transformed together	52 living and deceased believers, will be raised and transformed

Commentators agree the passage in Matthew deals with Jesus' second coming. Jesus taught here about his return (*parousia*) and the end of the age (see Matt. 24:3).[25] His coming in the sky (*ouranos*) and the gathering together of "the elect" (a general term for believers) are signaled by the presence of angels and the sounding of a "great trumpet." Though the context differs in 1 Thessalonians 4:13ff. (where the issue is not when Jesus will return but the fate of deceased believers at his return), the account shares several features with Matthew.

In each account the Lord returns from heaven (*ouranos*), in each an angel (or angels) accompanies him and signals the moment with a trumpet blast, in each believers are united with their Lord in the air, in each the coming of the Lord is described as a *parousia*. The passages are not *identical*, but we shouldn't expect them to be. After all, Paul prefaced his remarks in 1 Thessalonians with the comment, "We do not want you to be uninformed" (1 Thess. 4:13), thus suggesting that he was offering information not previously supplied.[26] And indeed his teaching about the instantaneous transformation of living Christians at Jesus' return *is* new.

As to the passage from 1 Corinthians 15, its context differs from Matthew 24 and 1 Thessalonians 4. As noted earlier, in 1 Corinthians the issue seems to be how mortal bodies can be made fit for eternity. In common with Matthew 24 and 1 Thessalonians 4, 1 Corinthians 15:50ff. says believers will meet the Lord when a trumpet is sounded and, like 1 Thessalonians 4:13ff., the passage indicates that this is the moment when deceased and living believers are raised and transformed.

Furthermore, these passages have much in common with other texts that deal with Jesus' second coming, thus bolstering the conclusion that they refer to the same event—i.e., the second coming. It is agreed that the phrase denoting the "coming of the Lord" in 2 Thessalonians 2:1 (*tês parousias tou kuriou*) and 1 Thessalonians 4:15 (*tên parousian tou kuriou*) refers to the rapture, yet a nearly identical phrase is used in 2 Thessalonians 2:8 and Matthew 24:3 to refer to the second coming. Similarly, Paul associates "the coming of our Lord Jesus Christ" with "our gathering together to him" (2 Thess. 2:1). The word Paul used in verse 1 to denote our "gathering together" with Jesus (*episunagôgê*) is practically the same one used by Matthew to speak of the angels "gathering the elect" (*episunagô*, 24:31). The latter passage clearly points to the second coming.

We have seen that phrases used in passages that clearly refer to the second coming also appear in passages dealing with the rapture.[27] Perhaps the pretribulationalists are correct to see these similar descriptions (Matt. 24:30f.; 1 Thess. 4:13ff.; 1 Cor. 15:50ff., etc.) as referring to two separate and distinctly different events, but it seems most unlikely to me.

A posttribulation rapture can also be inferred from other passages in Paul's letters to the Thessalonians. In 2 Thessalonians 1:6ff. Paul taught that believers will get relief from affliction "when the Lord Jesus shall be revealed from heaven with His mighty angels in flaming fire." It is not questioned that the Lord's coming "with his mighty angels in flaming fire" is a reference to his second coming;[28] what is sometimes not recognized is that Paul said it is *this* return—not some other event (i.e., a pretribulation rapture)—which brings relief to a persecuted church. If Christians are delivered from their enemies and from tribulation at the second coming, they must be experiencing tribulation on earth when Jesus returns—a scenario that fits perfectly with a posttribulation rapture. Similarly, Paul teaches that at his coming (*parousia*, 2 Thess. 2:8) Jesus will slay the Antichrist. The same word, *parousia*, is used in passages describing the rapture (1 Thess. 3:13; 4:15; 5:23).

Concerning imminence, Paul sought to quiet the apparently unsteady nerves of some believers in the church at Thessalonica with a reminder that the day of the Lord would not come until after the man of sin and the apostasy had been manifest (2 Thess. 2:1–5). He thus implied that "the coming of our Lord Jesus" and "our gathering together to him"—events which pretribulationalists think refer to the rapture—are not "imminent" in the sense of possibly happening at any moment but are instead preceded by other prophesied events. In 1 Thessalonians 5:1ff. Paul warned Christians that the day of the Lord—a phrase which refers to events culminating in the return of Jesus—would come suddenly, "like a thief in the night." And yet in the next few verses he warned *believers* that they should not be caught unawares (vv. 4–6).

How could Paul exhort believers to be spiritually alert for an event or time that—on the pretribulation view—they would not be present at? His comments make good sense, however, if they were directed at believers who might be on earth during the tribulation time which ends with the return of Jesus.

Finally, the many passages that speak of the visible return of Jesus call into question the notion of a secret, pretribulational return. Jesus taught that his coming would not be secret or private but open and obvious: "As the lightning comes from the east, and flashes even to the west, so shall the coming [*parousia*] of the Son of Man be" (Matt. 24:27). Further, "Then the sign of the Son of Man will appear in the sky, and then all the tribes of the earth will mourn, and they will see THE SON OF MAN COMING ON THE CLOUDS OF THE SKY with power and great glory" (Matt. 24:30). Angels inform the apostles who witness Jesus' ascension that "this Jesus, who has been taken up from you into heaven, will come in just the same way as you have watched Him go into heaven" (Acts 1:11). The apostle Paul described Jesus' return as obvious: "When the Lord Jesus shall be revealed from heaven with His mighty angels in flaming fire" (2 Thess. 1:7; also Rev. 1:7). Taken together, these passages cast serious doubt on the doctrine of a pretribulation rapture and instead bolster the posttribulation position.[29]

Summary. I do not relish the prospect of being a firsthand witness to the great tribulation should it occur in my lifetime; it gives me no pleasure to think my wife and daughter might experience the appalling conditions of those last days. But personal hopes aside, I do not think the church will be removed from the earth prior to the tribulation, nor do I believe our preservation through that time necessarily equates to *physical* preservation. But if this is so, how can believers look expectantly to the future—a future that may involve hardship, suffering, and death?

Perhaps the answer to this question is best hinted at with another: How have Christians throughout the ages maintained hope in the light of the hardships, sufferings, and martyrdom they experienced? How in the midst of life-threatening and hope-draining circumstances have believers endured? By their faith. The book of Hebrews defines faith as "the assurance of things hoped for, the conviction of things not seen" (Heb. 11:1). Christians believe they will ultimately be vindicated by God and rewarded for their loyalty to him. Their suffering may last for a moment, a season, or a lifetime, but their reward will last forever. It will be no different for Christians in the tribulation, although they—unlike their spiritual ancestors—can expect vindication quickly.

Because discussions about the timing of the rapture are often near to people's hearts, disagreement can be harsh. On occasion, people's motives for taking this or that position are called into question—a thoroughly unchristian enterprise (1 Cor. 4:5). If pretribulationalists are correct and Christians are delivered from the tribulation, I will rejoice—not in my error, but in the mercy of God, who spares us from such hardship. On the other hand, I fear that those who live in expectation of deliverance from the harsh tribulations of the last days have got it wrong and, to the extent that this expectation leaves them ill-prepared for the tribulation ahead, might not be ready to "be faithful unto death."

In any event, *excessive* preoccupation with the rapture can be seen as pointless, for either the rapture occurs prior to the tribulation and we rejoice in our deliverance from that dreadful time or it occurs afterwards and we endeavor to persevere spiritually. Hopefully, if we find ourselves in the tribulation, we will prove to be "faithful unto death" and will receive the approval of our Lord, "Well done, good and faithful servant!" (Matt. 25:21–23 NIV).

Some day Jesus will return in the skies in plain view of the earth and its inhabitants. He will come to a devastated planet—one wrecked by a final, extended, and nearly unconstrained outpouring of God's anger. One that has seen God's wrath and heard of his love through the preaching of the gospel. One that has killed his people and otherwise persecuted those loyal to him. For some people his appearance will be greeted with the sheer joy and enthusiasm normally reserved for the surprise visit of a beloved family member; for others his approach will evoke dread, loathing, and mortal fear.

Jesus will be accompanied by the spirits of deceased believers, who will be joined to resurrection bodies by the exertion of his mighty power; at nearly the same time the bodies of living believers will be instantaneously transformed—made indestructible and fit for eternity in a moment. This huge throng of resurrected saints will escort Jesus back to earth, where this Son of God will slay the Antichrist and his henchmen.

But although Jesus' return heralds the beginning of everlasting destruction for "the beast," it promises something quite different for the Messiah: reign in a transitional kingdom.

The Millennium

Attempts to unify Europe after World War II have been motivated, as least in part, by the belief that unbridled nationalism leads to war; hence, an effective deterrent to war involves the suppression of nationalism and, perhaps, the unification of nations. The noble aspiration for peace and unity is both praiseworthy and flawed. It is praiseworthy in that is seeks to avoid circumstances that have resulted in so much human misery, so much destruction, so much loss of life. It is flawed because it fails to appreciate the extent to which depravity is an individual and internal matter rather than something imposed by culture or ideology. As Jesus once remarked,

> That which proceeds out of the man, that is what defiles the man. For from within, out of the heart of men, proceed the evil thoughts, fornications, thefts, murders, adulteries, deeds of coveting and wickedness, as well as deceit, sensuality, envy, slander, pride, and foolishness. All these evil things proceed from within and defile the man (Mark 7:20–23).

Further, those who long for a utopian new world often fail to recognize the role played by evil spiritual forces in bringing misery to mankind. For these reasons, efforts to establish a utopian new world are destined to fail—but does that mean no such world will appear?

Time and again the Old Testament points to a future era in which God's Messiah will rule the nations in righteousness (e.g., Isa. 11:1–9; Jer. 23:5–6). But the ancient promises have not been fulfilled, or at least not fulfilled in the expected way, so it is worth asking: Are they still valid? Does Scripture teach there will yet be a time when God's Messiah, Jesus, will rule the world?

There is no consensus among evangelical Christians on this topic. Some believe there will be a literal millennial reign of Christ; others believe either that Jesus' current reign in heaven is fulfillment of the ancient promises or that his future reign will not take place on the present earth but in the new heavens and earth. The procedure here will be to take note of those passages which teach there will be a transitional kingdom, then to describe what it will be like, and, finally, to note its duration.

THE FACT OF A TRANSITIONAL KINGDOM

Although only one biblical text specifies the length of Jesus' reign after his return (Rev. 20:1–6), it does not stand alone in depicting a future wherein the Messiah is to exercise his royal power on the earth. In 1 Corinthians 15 the apostle Paul referred to a transitional kingdom. He wrote:

> But Christ has indeed been raised from the dead, the first-fruits of those who have fallen asleep. For since death came through a man, the resurrection of the dead comes also through a man. For as in Adam all die, so in Christ all will be made alive. But each in his own turn: Christ, the firstfruits; then, when he comes, those who belong to him. Then the end will come, when he hands over the kingdom to God the Father after he has destroyed all dominion, authority and power. For he must reign until he has put all his enemies under his feet. The last enemy to be destroyed is death. For he "has put every-thing under his feet." Now when it says that "everything" has been put under him, it is clear that this does not include God himself, who put everything under Christ. When he has done this, then the Son himself will be made subject to him who put everything under him, so that God may be all in all (1 Cor. 15:20–28 NIV).

Resurrection is the primary theme of these verses. In describing Jesus as "the firstfruits" in verse 20, Paul implied that other resurrections are to follow that of Jesus.[30] Beginning at verse 23 Paul noted the specific order of these resurrections:

1. "Christ the firstfruits,
2. then, (*epeita*) when he comes, those who belong to him,
3. then (*eita*) the end (*telos*) will come, when he hands over the kingdom to God the Father after he has destroyed all dominion, authority and power."

Everyone agrees that Jesus' resurrection (#1) and the resurrection of believers at his return (#2) are separate. The question is this: Does Paul suggest there is a clear temporal distinction between Jesus' return (#2) and "the end" (#3)? Does the "end" follow immediately the resurrection of believers at Jesus' coming, or are the events separated in time? If separated, Paul likely referred to a transitional kingdom in the intervening period.

There are good reasons to think the events are separated. First, the description of what will take place between Jesus' second coming and "the end" suggests there is a time interval between the two. In verse 24 Jesus hands over the kingdom to the Father, something that occurs after he (Jesus) "has destroyed all dominion, authority and power." The reason for the timing of the hand-over is explained in verse 25: "For he must reign until he has put all his enemies under his feet." In saying Jesus must reign, Paul's language hints at an unspecified interval of time between Jesus' return and the end—a time during which he reigns.

Second, a separation of events is also implied by temporal indicators Paul used. Within the context of 1 Corinthians 15, wherever we see the combination *epeita/eita*, events introduced by the terms are in temporal sequence. In verse 5 we learn that Jesus "appeared to Peter, then (*eita*) to the twelve, then (*epeita*) he appeared to more than 500 brothers at once." According to verse 7 Jesus "then (*epeita*) appeared to James, then (*eita*) to all the apostles." Later in the chapter Paul said, "The spiritual man [a reference to Jesus] did not come first, but the natural [a reference to Adam], and after that the spiritual" (v. 46). Thus, Paul's terminology indicates that Jesus' coming and "the end" are temporally distinct.

Other New Testament texts can be interpreted as implying or teaching there is a transitional kingdom. For example, in making a distinction between Jesus' coming and the end, with a "reign" taking place in the intervening period, Paul's teaching is similar to what we find in the book of Hebrews, where we learn that God did not subject to angels

> the world to come, about which we are speaking. But there is a place where someone has testified: 'What is man that you are mindful of him, the son of man that you care for him? You made him a little lower than the angels; you crowned him with glory and honor and put everything under his feet.' In putting everything under him, God left nothing that is not subject to him. Yet at present we do not see everything subject to him" (Heb. 2:5–8 NIV).

The writer of Hebrews drew upon an Old Testament passage in arguing for the superiority of Jesus; at the same time he indicated that Jesus does not *yet* reign in the prophetically anticipated way—the implication being that he

will some day reign in that fashion. Some might argue that Hebrews anticipates Jesus' reigning in a new heaven and earth—that, rather than a transitional kingdom, is when everything will be "subject to him." But the
resemblance between the language of Hebrews 2:8 and 1 Corinthians
15:24–28 is striking, and in the former the time when everything is subject
to Christ is distinct from "the end." Hebrews and 1 Corinthians both support the view that Christ will reign in a transitional kingdom.

Elsewhere, in Luke 22:14–30 Jesus taught his disciples that greatness in
the present era is defined by humility and service—but he also indicated
that such greatness will be rewarded in his future kingdom by the right to
rule alongside him (vv. 28–30). This, in turn, is similar to comments made
by Paul in 2 Timothy 2:11–13, where he cited what many scholars regard as
an early Christian creed or hymn.[31] Verse 12 reads: "If we endure, we shall
also reign with him." Believers will reign with Christ, probably during the
transitional kingdom mentioned in 1 Corinthians 15:20–28. This outline of
future events corresponds to what we find in Revelation 20:1–6:

> I saw an angel coming down out of heaven, having the key
> to the Abyss and holding in his hand a great chain. He seized
> the dragon, that ancient serpent, who is the devil, or Satan, and
> bound him for a thousand years. He threw him into the Abyss,
> and locked and sealed it over him, to keep him from deceiving
> the nations anymore until the thousand years were ended. Af-
> ter that, he must be set free for a short time. I saw thrones on
> which were seated those who had been given authority to
> judge. And I saw the souls of those who had been beheaded be-
> cause of their testimony for Jesus and because of the word of
> God. They had not worshiped the beast or his image and had
> not received his mark on their foreheads or their hands. They
> came to life and reigned with Christ a thousand years. (The
> rest of the dead did not come to life until the thousand years
> were ended.) This is the first resurrection. Blessed and holy are
> those who have part in the first resurrection. The second death
> has no power over them, but they will be priests of God and of
> Christ and will reign with him for a thousand years (NIV).

According to Revelation 20, the second coming of Jesus is followed by
one thousand years during which he will reign as King of kings and Lord of
lords. Further, believers have the enviable privilege of reigning with him.
The teaching of Revelation thus corresponds to other biblical passages we
have examined where Jesus reigns in a transitional kingdom.

The hope or expectation that God's Messiah would reign prior to the coming of an entirely new heaven and earth is not confined to the New Testament.[32] It was alive in some circles in Judaism in the first century A.D. For example, 4 Ezra 7:28–38 says that God's Messiah will reign four hundred years then die, after which a more general resurrection of the dead will occur, followed by the final judgment.[33] These nonbiblical Jewish writings do not present a consistent picture of the future and Messiah's role in it; but it is worth noting that many of them—taking their cue from Old Testament Scriptures—do envision a transitional kingdom ruled by Messiah. The various New Testament texts that teach about Jesus' (i.e., the Messiah's) future reign may thus simply offer further development of a theme already in existence prior to the coming of Jesus.

THE NATURE OF THE TRANSITIONAL KINGDOM

The transitional kingdom (or the millennial kingdom) will be characterized by the earthly presence of Jesus and the increasing extension of his rule into human affairs. The language of Jesus reigning and subduing enemies used in the New Testament echoes the language of Old Testament texts where God's Messiah rules the nations. Isaiah said:

> Then a shoot will spring from the stem of Jesse, and a branch from his roots will bear fruit, And the Spirit of the LORD will rest on Him, the spirit of wisdom and understanding, the spirit of counsel and strength, the spirit of knowledge and the fear of the LORD. And He will delight in the fear of the LORD, and He will not judge by what His eyes see, nor make a decision by what His ears hear; but with righteousness He will judge the poor, and decide with fairness for the afflicted of the earth; and He will strike the earth with the rod of His mouth, and with the breath of His lips He will slay the wicked. Also righteousness will be the belt about His loins, and faithfulness the belt about His waist. And the wolf will dwell with the lamb, and the leopard will lie down with the kid, and the calf and the young lion and the fatling together; and a little boy will lead them. Also the cow and the bear will graze; their young will lie down together; and the lion will eat straw like the ox. And the nursing child will play by the hole of the cobra, and the weaned child will put his hand on the viper's den. They will not hurt or destroy in all My holy mountain, for the earth will be full of the knowledge of the LORD as the waters cover the sea (Isa. 11:1–9).

We find the same image in Jeremiah 23:5–6:

> "Behold, the days are coming," declares the LORD, "When I shall raise up for David a righteous Branch; and He will reign as king and act wisely and do justice and righteousness in the land. In His days Judah will be saved, and Israel will dwell securely; and this is His name by which He will be called, 'The LORD our righteousness.' "

These passages are reminiscent of what the psalmist had earlier written about the rule of God's Messiah:

> Why do the nations conspire and the peoples plot in vain? The kings of the earth take their stand and the rulers gather together against the LORD and against his Anointed One. "Let us break their chains," they say, "and throw off their fetters." The One enthroned in heaven laughs; the Lord scoffs at them. Then he rebukes them in his anger and terrifies them in his wrath, saying, "I have installed my King on Zion, my holy hill." I will proclaim the decree of the LORD: He said to me, "You are my Son; today I have become your Father. Ask of me, and I will make the nations your inheritance, the ends of the earth your possession. You will rule them with an iron scepter; you will dash them to pieces like pottery" (Ps. 2:1–9 NIV).[34]

New Testament passages concerning the transitional kingdom do not begin to repeat, much less offer any elaboration on, the specific descriptions of the kingdom found in the Old Testament. There is no way to account for this fact with certainty. Nevertheless, since Paul's remarks about Jesus' future reign seem to echo those found in the Old Testament, it is no great leap to suggest that Paul and other New Testament writers intended their readers to understand that the transitional kingdom ruled by Jesus will be a time in which many previously unfulfilled Old Testament prophecies will come to fruition. Israel's Messiah, rejected by his own and by the world at large, will be vindicated at his return when he is given the right to rule by God the father, a rule he will exercise for some time in advance of "the end."[35]

Jesus will ensure protection for Israel and peace among the nations. God's promise to bless the nations through Abraham's offspring will continue to be realized through the reign of Jesus. He will presumably rule the world from Jerusalem in fulfillment of prophecies, but his rule will benefit and extend to all. Old Testament descriptions of the kingdom invoke images of a renewed and transformed earth. The earth in the millennial kingdom is a place where the deleterious effects of the Fall (Gen. 3) are minimized because the world "will be full of the knowledge of the Lord" (Isa. 11:9). To the extent that humanity is transformed by the knowledge of God, by the presence of the Lord, and by the power of his Spirit (cf. Jer. 31:31–34; Ezek. 37:14), it is capable of realizing God's original mandate to relate to him, to represent him, and to rule and subdue the earth (as noted in chapter 1).

Another factor that will produce a paradise-like environment during the transitional kingdom is the separation of Satan from humanity. According to Revelation 20:1–6, Satan will be bound during the millennium, unable to exert his ungodly influence on the nations.

It must be recognized that the Scriptures give us only an outline of life in the kingdom. Discerning this outline is made more difficult by the fact that in many instances the description of life in the millennium (the transitional kingdom) seems to overlap with descriptions of the new heavens and earth (the everlasting kingdom). For example, Isaiah 2:2–4 says:

> In the last days the mountain of the LORD's temple will be established as chief among the mountains; it will be raised above the hills, and all nations will stream to it. Many peoples will come and say, "Come, let us go up to the mountain of the LORD, to the house of the God of Jacob. He will teach us his ways, so that we may walk in his paths." The law will go out from Zion, the word of the LORD from Jerusalem. He will judge between the nations and will settle disputes for many peoples. They will beat their swords into plowshares and their spears into pruning hooks. Nation will not take up sword against nation, nor will they train for war anymore (NIV).

On one hand, the Isaiah passage sounds like the benevolent reign of Messiah during a transitional kingdom described elsewhere; on the other, elements of this passage are echoed in Revelation 21, where, after the new heavens and earth are described, we are told concerning the new Jerusalem, "The city does not need the sun or the moon to shine on it, for the glory of God gives it light, and the Lamb is its lamp. The nations will walk by its light, and the kings of the earth will bring their splendor into it" (Rev. 21:23–24 NIV).

In several other places the descriptions of the new heavens and earth and a transitional kingdom are practically indistinguishable.

THE DURATION OF THE TRANSITIONAL KINGDOM

Revelation 20:1–10 is the only biblical passage to mention specifically the length of Jesus' reign. Six times this passage specifies the transitional kingdom is to last one thousand years (vv. 2, 3, 4, 5, 6, 7). During this time Satan will be prevented from influencing the nations while Jesus rules the earth. His loyal followers will reign with him. However, Revelation 20:7–9 teaches that once the one thousand years have ended, Satan will be released to lead one last rebellion against Messiah and his people. The devil, in a familiar role, will initiate the insurgence by "deceiving the nations" (v. 8). We are given few details about the rebellion: it involves (1) nations from all over the earth (v. 8); (2) a great host of people (v. 8); (3) an assault against the city (presumably Jerusalem) where Messiah rules and near where his people reside (v. 9); and, (4) a final conflagration where "fire from heaven" is used to quell the rebellion (v. 9).

It is sometimes argued that the millennium mentioned here is not literal because the number John attaches to it in Revelation 20—one thousand years—is figurative. There are three responses to this observation.

First, even if the number "one thousand" is figurative, that would only lead us to conclude that the *length* of Jesus' future reign is unspecified. It would not, however, mean that the fact of his reign was in question because other passages—ones that do not specify its duration—teach that it will occur.

Second, the figure of a thousand years *is* used in passages that communicate figuratively, but the number *itself* is not *necessarily* figurative. Apart from Revelation 20 the figure of one thousand years is found in just three places in the Bible (Ps. 90:4; Eccles. 6:6; 2 Pet. 3:8). In Psalm 90:4 we learn that "a thousand years in your [God's] sight are like a day that has just gone by." The passage implies that God is not bound by time the way humans are; however the one thousand years mentioned must be literal, for if they are not, the metaphor cannot work. Similarly, 2 Peter 3:8 says that "with the Lord a day is like a thousand years, and a thousand years are like a day" (NIV). Here again the point is the timelessness or transcendence of God, a point that would be lost if the one thousand years mentioned are nonliteral. Thus, the mere fact that Revelation 20 uses the figure "one thousand years" cannot be taken to indicate that the entire passage speaks of a nonliteral one-thousand-year reign of Christ.

A third reason the kingdom should be regarded as literal (and future) concerns the events that are to characterize it. Those who think the millennium is figurative often argue that the one thousand years represent the present church age.[36] But according to Revelation 20:1ff. Satan will be bound and prevented from deceiving the nations during this era. This hardly squares with the New Testament picture of believers engaged in ongoing spiritual warfare with a deceitful and scheming Satan and his demons (2 Cor. 4:3–4; Eph. 6:10–12; 1 Pet. 5:8–9; 1 Tim. 4:1[?]). The idea that Satan is at present bound and unable to deceive the nations is also at odds with the notion of a coming Antichrist who will deceive the world (see chapter 7, also 2 Thess. 2:7–9). Furthermore, the absolute binding of Satan in Revelation 20:1–6 is followed by a period in which he is freed to deceive the nations. In this way the passage indicates there is a large difference between the period of his binding and the time of his loosing.

One other issue should be addressed—namely, the need for a transitional kingdom. After all, having been adored in heaven, would it not be a step backwards for Jesus to rule the earth, dealing with the sort of mundane issues that are often described in passages concerning a messianic reign? Would it not be anticlimactic for Messiah to rule mere mortals once the resurrection of his followers had already taken place? These are reasonable questions/objections, and more could be added to them. No one could protest were God to choose to move from the present world to a future world in a single step.

Yet from another perspective, there *is* a certain necessity for the kingdom. If God is true and if he has said there will be a transitional kingdom, then he is bound by his word and character to act accordingly. I have argued that Scripture indicates there will be such a kingdom, so the need for it is generated by God's obligation to act as he said he would. What precisely might be accomplished in it is difficult to say for sure. Some think it will be a time of special national exaltation for Israel, while others believe Israel will be only one beneficiary of Messiah's reign.

It is sometimes said this kingdom will produce a kind of utopia on earth—not the one ensured by the inherent goodness of man but the one established by the righteousness and power of Jesus Christ. At the end of it there will be one last human rebellion (Rev. 20:7–9). One result of the rise of Antichrist and his kingdom prior to the return of Jesus is the conclusion that government apart from God is imperfectable on account of mankind's inherent depravity and the influence of evil spiritual forces. Similarly, the rebellion at the end of the millennium will demonstrate that not even perfect government and the absence of wicked spiritual forces can produce righteousness in the hearts of fallen humanity.

Whatever else may be said of a literal millennium, it is indisputable that in the broad scheme of things it covers a fairly short period of time. After all, nearly two thousand years have separated Jesus' first and second advents (as of this writing). Because it is temporary, because it is transitional, we can hardly regard the millennium as the "ultimate" moment of human history. Yet it is an important aspect of the future because at that time the promises to Messiah will be completely fulfilled and the lamb of God will be vindicated in the eyes of the world as God's righteous king.[37]

Conclusion

Jesus will return to earth some day to defeat his enemies, to reward his friends, to establish his just and good rule upon the earth. Just as his death and resurrection were prophetically anticipated—and hence reflect God's design in history—so will his return. But as great and glorious as Jesus' reign may be, it is not "the end." One final and very long (indeed, unending) chapter remains in God's plan for the world.

✧ Chapter Nine ✧

Forever

✧

As a young boy I remember asking my father about heaven: If he died, would he go there? If I died, would I go there? Would we recognize each other? Was he sure about his answers? At an early age the prospect of a separation from loved ones caused by death was a source of concern for me, as it has been for millions of others throughout the ages. As I neared the completion of this book, questions from my five-year-old daughter and the death of my dear friend Joyce Schaerdel brought the issue of "forever" to my mind in a fresh way. Many of us know people who have lived to a ripe old age and others whose lives have been tragically cut short; yet our lives— even if they last a century—are only moments long when viewed against the broad expanse of history.

Like most world religions, Christianity teaches there will someday be a final reckoning where people's lives are evaluated. Christianity is occasionally criticized as offering an illusory "pie in the sky." Its promise of heaven is viewed by some as a sign of weakness, a failure to embrace this life to the fullest, or as a means of enforcing moral control (i.e., "you'd better conform to our beliefs and practices or God will be angry with you"). The criticism is warranted only if there is no "pie in the sky," only if there is no life beyond this one. But as we have seen, the Resurrection of Jesus testifies that at least one man *has* escaped death; and it is his testimony that beyond this world there is a heaven to be enjoyed and a hell to be avoided. Indeed, Jesus is our main source of information about the afterlife. What do he and others in the New Testament have to say about it? Who, according to Scripture, is our judge at the last day? How are we judged and with what result? How do our answers to these questions relate to the notion of design in history? We begin with the identity of the judge.

Who Judges?

The most recognizable symbol of the justice system of the United States is "Lady Justice"—a blindfolded goddess holding a pair of scales. She symbolizes our commitment to weigh evidence impartially and render an appropriate verdict. Many of us long deeply for justice, especially when so much of life seems unfair. We rejoice when the last scene of a popular movie or story unfolds and the hero, mistreated and perhaps misunderstood, vanquishes his enemies. It is satisfying to see justice done.

But it is helpful to remember that our society (particularly those members involved in jurisprudence) distinguishes what is *legal* from what is *just*. For many of us it is a maddening distinction because we have all heard of instances where a clearly guilty person has managed to escape justice based on some legal technicality. The technicalities are important because they represent an attempt to ensure the integrity of our process in arriving at justice, a process that is indispensable because none of us dares assume that what appears to be right and just really is. We pursue justice carefully because we are imperfect creatures, prone to errors in observation, reason, and judgment. But the administration of justice will be different in the end. It will be different because of the nature and abilities of the one who judges.

Those unfamiliar with the Bible often assume it teaches that God will be their judge some day. This is true as far as it goes, but Scripture is even more specific. The New Testament teaches that Jesus is God's authorized agent of judgment. According to the Bible, it is Jesus who will evaluate us. He came to earth two thousand years ago as "the lamb who takes away the sin of the world"; he will return as "the lion of the tribe of Judah" who judges the peoples with perfect justice. Jesus said, "The Father judges no one, but has entrusted all judgment to the Son, that all may honor the Son just as they honor the Father" (John 5:22–23 NIV).

According to Peter, Jesus commanded his followers "to preach to the people and to testify that he [Jesus] is the one whom God appointed as judge of the living and the dead" (Acts 10:42 NIV). Paul wrote, "In the presence of God and of Christ Jesus, who will judge the living and the dead" (2 Tim. 4:1 NIV; also Acts 17:31). In an ironic turn of events, the Son of God who was condemned by the world will return as its judge; the lamb becomes the lion; the victim, the avenger. What will his judgment be like?

Above all else, Jesus will render a fair judgment because he will not be limited by ignorance, prejudice, or favoritism.

He knows us completely. Our lives will be scrutinized in all their particulars—our motives, our words, and our actions. Paul noted that after the Lord comes he will "bring to light the things hidden in the darkness and disclose the motives of men's hearts" (1 Cor. 4:5). Jesus spoke of a future judgment when "every careless word that men shall speak, they shall render account for it" (Matt. 12:36). Paul also said we will be judged "for the things done while in the body, whether good or bad" (2 Cor. 5:10 NIV). In Revelation 20:13 the books were opened at the final judgment, and the people "were judged, every one of them according to their deeds" (also John 5:29; Rom. 2:5–8). Furthermore, in addition to our actions and motives, our faithfulness in using the talents and gifts we have received will be evaluated (Luke 19:11–27).

Although we may be capable of disguising our motives or hiding our actions from others, we will not be able to fool Jesus. According to Revelation 19:12, his eyes "are a flame of fire," that is, he possesses utter discernment and complete knowledge. Moreover, there will be no secrets on the day of judgment. The word Paul used to describe the judgment seat of Christ in 2 Corinthians 5:10 (*bêma*) elsewhere refers to the portable platform used by Roman magistrates to hear legal cases in public as they traveled among their constituents. Where it appears in the New Testament, *bêma* typically involves a public setting (Matt. 27:19; John 19:13; Acts 12:21; 18:12; 25:6). Hence, when Paul said we must appear before Christ's judgment seat, he probably envisioned judgment made in a rather open forum. Paul spoke that God would "bring to light the things hidden in the darkness" and "disclosing the motives of men's hearts" (1 Cor. 4:5).

The Greek words translated "bring to light" (*phôtizô*) and "disclose" (*phaneroô*) typically refer to making something obvious or open that was previously hidden (e.g., John 1:9; Eph. 1:18; 3:9; 2 Tim. 1:10; Heb. 6:4). These verses do not *necessarily* imply a detailed public disclosure of secrets—as if all our sins and private affairs would be available for public screening among the galleries of heaven—but they might. Jesus taught the principle that "nothing is hidden, except to be revealed; nor has anything been secret, but that it should come to light" (Mark 4:22).

Taken together, these passages imply at the least that God's evaluation of our lives will be done and made in public, even if all the data relevant to the judgment are not. Yet it is possible that our words, deeds, and motives *will* be on display in such a way as to commend or shame us among the throngs of heaven. In any event, Jesus is intimately familiar with our lives in all their particulars. He sees them entirely and clearly.

He will judge according to a fair standard. In the modern world the status and wealth of a defendant may give him or her special treatment before judicial authorities. Not so in the future, where neither the status, wealth, pedigree, nor any other factor will earn favorable treatment from the judge. According to Revelation 19:11, Jesus judges "in righteousness." He is not influenced by whim or prejudice; rather, he judges according to a righteous standard of conduct. What is the result of this judgment?

We moderns live in a fragmented world. Our society is fond of dividing people into groups based on sex, race, ethnicity, religion, political affiliation, socioeconomic status, education, and so forth. There are groups too numerous to count, yet in the end—after Christ returns—there will be only two: those who live forever with God, and those who do not.

Forever Without God

Individuals in our culture seem increasingly unwilling to accept responsibility for their actions. Almost everyone has a reason (an "excuse" in the old jargon) for his or her sin ("inappropriate behavior" in common parlance). Everything from bank fraud to child abuse to an exaggerated résumé is justified—sometimes in ingenious ways. In spite of this, there is a nagging suspicion that our tendency to blame has more to do with an age-old desire to avoid adverse consequences (remember Adam blaming Eve in the garden?) than with novel cultural stresses. We don't wish to hear that we are now and ultimately will be in the future held accountable; indeed, any talk of moral accountability and judgment smacks of intolerance—the most mortal of sins in modern culture. We are urged to avoid making judgments and, instead, to show tolerance. In many contexts this is sage advice, but it often carries with it the implication that no one can really know or do what is just. As we have seen, the Scriptures say otherwise when it comes to Jesus' final evaluation of us. That cautionary note shunning judgment will simply not apply as the final scene of history unfolds.

One occasionally hears that the Old Testament portrays God almost exclusively as wrathful and vindictive, while the New Testament is preoccupied with his grace and forgiveness. It may be surprising for some people to learn that according to the New Testament those who would not follow Jesus face a horrifying future—one that is unpleasant, unalterable, and unending. It is sometimes thought this apparently unyielding doctrine originated with narrow-minded Christians who forgot the message of grace and forgiveness preached by Jesus—and indeed, Jesus *did* emphasize those themes. But he did not confine his remarks to them alone; in fact, if there is a problem of "intolerance" on the issue of who is included and who is excluded from eternity with God, it appears to have originated with Jesus himself.[1]

It was Jesus who contrasted the broad gate through which "many" enter and which leads to destruction to the "narrow gate" through which "few" enter and which leads to life (Matt. 7:13–14). It was Jesus, in other words, who near the beginning of his ministry held out the possibility that some people would be "in" and some would be "out." He made explicit the connection between a faith response to him and eternal life. The night before his death he taught his disciples, "I am the way, and the truth, and the life; no one comes to the Father, but through Me" (John 14:6). According to Jesus, he alone is the provider of salvation; apart from him there is none. There is no alternate plan to get God's forgiveness and eternal life; there is no "reasonable compromise" to be reached. This highly restrictive view of eternal life was repeated by Peter in one of the earliest recorded sermons, "Salvation is found in no one else, for there is no other name [than Jesus] under heaven given to men by which we must be saved" (Acts 4:12 NIV).

Although Jesus set a narrow criterion for admission into the kingdom, he did *not* teach that those people traditionally thought to be "sinners" would be excluded from eternal life while religious ones would automatically be included. To the well-known harlot who wept tears of repentance at his feet, he said, "Your faith has saved you; go in peace" (Luke 7:50). Concerning the despised tax collector who admitted his sins, Jesus proclaimed, "Today salvation has come to this house, because he, too, is a son of Abraham" (Luke 19:9). In the story of the prodigal son, Jesus taught about God's persevering love for sinners (Luke 15:11–32). Jesus embraced all who came to him contritely, but he offered no solace to the proud, to those who viewed themselves as good and righteous, to those with no awareness of their own sinfulness and need for forgiveness. Such people criticized Jesus for associating with sinners, yet were sinners themselves, although in perhaps different and less obvious ways (Luke 11:37–12:10; 13:10–30; 16:14–31; 18:9–14).[2] Common to all these accounts is a response—either positive or negative—to Jesus.

The Christian doctrine that a faith commitment to Jesus Christ of Nazareth is essential to experience eternal life originated with Jesus himself. But

why was Jesus so narrow in his thinking? At one level, the question needn't
be addressed: if Jesus rose from the dead and thus spoke truly about how to
get eternal life, what difference does it make *why* he thought as he did? The
important thing for us to know is that he spoke truly! But if we probe a little
further, the idea that there might be invioable spiritual laws taught by Jesus
shouldn't surprise us. After all, modern people are accustomed to dealing
with narrow thinking and "absolutes." For example, if an airport runway is
situated north-south, planes can't safely land on it flying east-west. There's
simply no room for negotiation or compromise, and we wouldn't trust the
pilot who thought otherwise. Likewise computer code must be writtten precisely to work properly. Similarly, an inexact mixture of ingredients will
render the antibotic ineffective. If there are laws that govern the operation
of our physical universe, why should there not also be moral laws, and,
importantly, a moral lawgiver, who determines the moral rules of life? Jesus'
teaching—narrow minded as it might appear to some—reflects God's invioable moral rules. His convictions about heaven and hell were probably the
primary motivation behind his command that the church should preach the
gospel to the world (Matt. 28:18–20). Christians who repeat Jesus' views are
not intolerant or narrow-minded simply by virtue of their faithful recitation
and proclamation of his message. If fault is to be found in the message, it
should be laid at the feet of the person responsible: Jesus of Nazareth. Yet
the whole record of his life points to his care for the poor and brokenhearted
and his readiness to extend forgiveness to all who ask for it—but ask they
must.

But what about those who never ask? What happens to non-believers
when they die? Do they "go to hell"? Do they get a second chance at heaven?

As to second chances, they apparently all come in this life. The writer of
Hebrews asserted, "It is appointed for men to die once and after this comes
judgment" (9:27). The parable of Luke 16:19–31 suggests there is no coming back to this life from the dead. On this topic Scripture stands opposed
to the doctrine of reincarnation championed by many Near Eastern religions. They teach there are many opportunities beyond this life—indeed
many *lives* beyond this one—to attain true spirituality. The notion that there
may yet be a second chance after death cuts against clear scriptural teaching
and is reminiscent of the serpent's empty and false assurance to Eve that disobedience would not result in death, as God promised, but would instead
bring enlightenment (Gen. 3:4–5).

As to the fate of unbelievers, Scripture indicates it involves three phases. In the first, at death their spirits are consigned to what amounts to a holding chamber where they await resurrection and final judgment. Various words and images are used to describe it. For example, in the Old Testament *Sheol* (and its Greek equivalent *Hades*) is the abode of the dead. But while in some instances Sheol seems to be the place where all people go at death (e.g., Ps. 89:48), in many more it is seen as the dwelling of evildoers and the unrighteous (Num. 16:30; Deut. 32:22; Job 24:19; Ps. 9:17; 31:17; Prov. 5:5; Isa. 14:9; Ezek. 32:27). Indeed, Philip Johnston writes that Sheol "is used predominantly . . . of the fate awaiting the ungodly, a fate which the godly wish to avoid . . . , even if some like Job envisage it in their extremity of despair and abandonment by God. Peaceful death for the godly is never presented as descent to [Sheol]."[3]

In the New Testament Hades is typically seen in a negative light. (e.g., Matt. 11:23; Luke 16:23).[4] Hades is clearly distinguished from the "lake of fire and brimstone" (Rev. 20:10) and in the end will itself be destroyed by God (Rev. 20:14). Although he did not use the term Hades, Peter stated that ungodly persons are at present being held or confined as they await future judgment (2 Pet. 2:9). We may conclude by saying there is a place of temporary imprisonment for ungodly persons before their full and permanent experience of judgment.[5]

In the second phase of their afterlife, unbelievers are resurrected and judged. The prophet Daniel linked resurrection to judgment in Daniel 12:2, noting that in the end some would "awake" to everlasting life but others "to disgrace and everlasting contempt." Jesus also spoke of the resurrection of the unrighteous (John 5:29) as did Paul (Acts 24:15). Nonbelievers "come to life" (Rev. 20:5, a phrase that in context refers to resurrection [cf. Rev. 20:4–6]). Subsequent to their resurrection, unbelievers face evaluation by Jesus Christ. They will not fare well. What is the basis and outcome of their judgment?

As to the former, the thoughts, words, and deeds of unbelievers will be scrutinized. Up to now I have used the term *unbelievers* (or *nonbelievers*) to refer to those who ultimately will be punished by God. I use the term to make a distinction between those who believe in or depend on Jesus for forgiveness and new life and those who do not.[6] However, I do not mean to give the impression that unbelievers have merely failed to *believe* the right thing, as if their chief failure will have been cognitive in nature.

While the phrase "I believe" in the vernacular has often come to be an equivalent for "I think" or "I give intellectual assent to," this is not the way the term is used in the Bible. There undoubtedly is an intellectual or mental dimension to belief, but it is far more than that. Belief, or faith, involves a personal commitment, indeed allegiance, to a person (Jesus Christ). To return to the theme of unbelievers' judgment, the holistic nature of mankind—that is, our propensity to integrate thought, action, and commitment—makes it impossible that one could consistently do the right thing in God's eyes while having a religious commitment to something other than God.

But what is the standard of thought, word, and deed to which unbelievers are held? If, as Christians maintain, Jesus and the Bible represent our most complete revelation of who God is, surely not all people have had equal access to this revelation. This is indisputably true, but in the end unbelievers will not be judged by standards unknown to them, but by those revealed; namely, by the witness to God found in creation and by the witness to him found in conscience. The apostle Paul says the existence and power of God have been revealed to all mankind through creation itself:

> What may be known about God is plain to them, because God has made it plain to them. For since the creation of the world, God's invisible qualities—his eternal power and divine nature—have been clearly seen, being understood from what has been made, so that men are without excuse (Rom. 1:19–20 NIV; also Ps. 19:1–4; Acts 14:15–17; 17:22–29).

The evidence is so overwhelming, Paul says, that people must willfully undertake to deny it—they must "suppress" it (Rom. 1:18). In addition to the ubiquitous testimony of creation there is the further evidence of conscience. Paul referred to this in Romans 2:5ff., where he instructed Jews—those entrusted with the revelation of God's law through Moses—that they were not the only ones to whom God has revealed himself. He has also spoken to Gentiles, placing a sort of moral law, as it were, in their hearts (Rom. 2:5–16).[7]

Creation testifies to God's existence and mankind's moral obligation to honor him, yet we fail to do so. Each of us has violated the dictates of conscience or revelation or both. As Paul put it, "There is none righteous, not even one . . . all have sinned and fall short of the glory of God" (Rom. 3:10, 23). This is not a benign shortcoming, for as Paul later said, "The wages of sin is death" (Rom. 6:23). In their final reckoning at the throne of God, the evidence of their thoughts, words, and deeds will condemn unbelievers so that God will be seen as just in meting out punishment to them.

The third, final, and unending phase of their afterlife experience involves punishment. According to Revelation 20:15, after unbelievers are resurrected, evaluated, and pronounced guilty, they are cast into hell, the lake of fire. What is hell? Do people there burn forever in a lake of fire?

The Greek word translated "hell" (*geenna*) occurs twelve times in the New Testament.[8] Eleven of these are in the gospels (the exception being James 3:6); indeed, Jesus is our primary source of information on the topic. He said *geenna* was originally envisioned as a place of punishment for "the devil and his angels," yet added they would be joined there by a multitude of humanity (Matt. 25:41). It is a place of torment, which apparently involves both bodily and non-bodily aspects. There are two lines of evidence which point to a bodily dimension to it.

The first is the fact that people in hell possess a resurrection body. Although we do not have a great deal of information about what it will be like, according to Luke 24:36–43 and John 20:19–21:14, Jesus' resurrection body was capable of touching and being touched, of eating and working, of walking and disappearing at a moment's notice. There was, in other words, both continuity and discontinuity with his mortal body (also 1 Cor. 15:35–58).

In hell unbelievers' resurrection bodies will presumably be able to experience some sensations, so that—to move to our second line of evidence—the picture of hell as a fiery place implies intense anguish. The image of *geenna* as a place of fiery torment was mentioned often by Jesus, who warned that unbelievers would be thrown "into the furnace of fire" where there would be "weeping and gnashing of teeth" (Matt. 13:42, 50; also Matt. 5:29; 10:28; Mark 9:43, 48–49; Luke 12:5). That hell involves bodily torment is certainly the impression one gets from Luke 16:19–31 where the rich man surrounded by fire sought relief from his suffering.

But suffering in hell is also nonbodily in nature. In addition to the horrific picture of hell as a fiery place, Jesus also called it a place of "outer darkness" (Matt. 8:12; 22:13; 25:30; see also Luke 16:19–31). The weeping and gnashing of teeth also mentioned in these passages may be the product of bodily anguish, but the picture of "outer darkness" suggests extreme alienation, an existence without companionship, comfort, or hope. Paul referred to "everlasting destruction . . . shut out from the presence of the Lord" (2 Thess. 1:9 NIV), with the implication that all those things associated with the presence and goodness of God—things like love, fellowship, compassion, mercy, and hope—will be absent in hell.

Hell is permanent. Even among those who take Scripture seriously there is a school of thought that suggests the Bible equivocates when it talks about everlasting punishment.[9] They ask whether "everlasting" means "unending." Some argue that hell is everlasting in the same way that a fire which consumes a piece of paper is everlasting: once the paper is burned up, the fire is extinguished. Nothing else remains—yet this theory fails to do justice to the biblical data. According to Matthew 25:46, "these will go away into eternal punishment, but the righteous into eternal life." Here Jesus taught that "eternal punishment" lasts as long as "eternal life"—and no one suggests eternal life is limited in duration. Additionally, in Revelation 19:20 the beast and false prophet are thrown into the lake of fire; a thousand years later they are still there, facing even more punishment (Rev. 20:10). Finally, the indestructible nature of the resurrection body (1 Cor. 15:42) suggests the permanence of hell. Hell is a place of unending punishment. Its inhabitants are not burned up: they abide.

The very notion of hell is distasteful to the modern mind, and objections are often raised about its "fairness" with respect to duration and severity. Indeed, to some people it conjures up images of a spiteful God inflicting everlasting damage on practically defenseless creatures whose sins—however bad they may have been—seem not to warrant never-ending punishment. "How," it is asked, "can God punish for eternity those evils committed in the course of a lifetime of twenty, forty, or sixty years? The punishment seems all out of proportion to the offense." Must God punish forever those who offend him? Is he petty and vindictive? Is Jesus?

The complaint about the duration of punishment assumes two things: (1) that unbelievers cease to sin at death, hence punishment is entirely a matter of retribution for things done in this life; and (2) that the consequences of our sins and failures are temporary. Are these assumptions warranted?

We have precious little information about what unbelievers might do in hell, apart from suffer. Yet we may be justified in speculating they do not simply lament their fate but continue to sin against the God who imposed it. If heaven is a place where those who love God worship him with greater devotion and knowledge, perhaps it would not be unwarranted to speculate that hell will be a place where those who rebel against God will do so with more fervor and hatred. It may be that those in hell continue to sin, although perhaps not in all the ways available in the present life.

Furthermore, there is reason to believe that sins committed in this life have permanent consequences of their own. For example, when a child is murdered, do the consequences of the crime last only so long as the murderer is alive and punished, only so long as there is someone alive to grieve the child's absence, or do they last forever? They last forever. *Forever* the child will have been robbed of his or her life; *forever* the world will have been robbed of the contribution that this child could have made; *forever* the lives of parents, friends, and others will have been altered as a result of the crime. Because the consequences of the child's death continue in perpetuity, we cannot label it unfair for God to punish the criminal in perpetuity.

But of course most people are not murderers—so in what way could their sins merit eternal punishment? By the same principle: unending, if unforeseen, consequences flow from our actions in this life. There is an additional point to be made here. If the spirits and resurrection bodies of those in hell are extinguished or annihilated, in what sense could hell be regarded a place of justice and punishment for them? The consequences of their misdeeds go on forever, yet their punishment is over in a (presumably agonizing) moment. Hell would not constitute "punishment" apart from the conscious awareness of the guilty.[10]

So much for the duration of hell—what about its severity? There are two points to be made here: (1) its severity is related to the nature of the person we sin against, and (2) not everyone will experience the same hell.

As to the first point, if I sin against my neighbor there are limits to his outrage since he is a limited creature. His anger may be intense, and it may endure, but it is limited. Not so with God, for he is unlimited. If he is loving, he is infinitely loving; if he is just, he is infinitely just; if he is offended, he is infinitely offended. When we sin against God, we provoke his infinite and just outrage and rightly bear the consequences.

As to the assertion that not everyone in hell gets the same experience, Jesus pointed us in this direction when warning his audiences about the hypocritical religious leaders of his day: "They devour widows' houses and for a show make lengthy prayers. Such men will be punished most severely" (Luke 20:47 NIV; also Matt. 11:21–22). The comment that some are punished "more" implies that others are punished "less." People are judged for their deeds, and there may be as many varied consequences for these as there are deeds themselves. It stands to reason that the atheist who is a good citizen won't experience precisely the same fate as the mass-murderer.

There are surely many gradations of punishment hinted at by Jesus—all, however, within the broad context of hell mentioned above.

If we consolidate the various pictures of hell given in Scripture, it seems safe to say that hell is a place where unbelievers forever reap the consequences of their rebellious acts against God in both bodily and nonbodily ways. The fact that those in hell possess resurrection bodies together with certain descriptions of it as a fiery place suggests that bodily anguish is involved. A burning fire connotes bodily pain at the very least, yet because Jesus also spoke of hell as "outermost darkness"—something that seems irreconcilable with the notion of literal fire—it may be wise to suspend judgment concerning the literalness of the fire.

Let me hasten to add that this interpretation in no way denies or diminishes the reality of hell as the permanent and unpleasant abode of nonbelievers; it's merely an attempt to reconcile apparently disparate statements about it. Indeed, if there is not a literal fire, the image of it suggests a future experience almost too terrible to contemplate. There is likewise great nonbodily torment. Paul seems to encapsulate the totality of unbelievers' future anguish when he describes their fate as "everlasting destruction away from the presence of the Lord" (2 Thess. 1:9 NIV). Those who did not love God and neighbor in this life are left without either in the life to come, forever.[11]

Jesus wept at the prospect of Jerusalem's judgment even though it was justified (Luke 19:41–44). Paul lamented the Jews' alienation from God, though it too was justified (Rom. 9:1ff.). Scripture teaches that God will in the end do perfect justice. For many people his commitment to justice means he will commit them to hell. As Christians we review the biblical data with mixed reactions. We can rejoice that God is fair, that he will be vindicated, that his word will be proved true and his power absolute. At the same time we can feel sorrow for those who have chosen so poorly in this life, not because they are undeserving of their fate, but out of a wish that they had chosen otherwise. In so doing we reflect the heart of God, who doesn't desire "any to perish but for all to come to repentance" (2 Pet. 3:9).

Forever with God

If the fairly scarce information we have about life forever without God provokes fear, dread, and sorrow, information about life with him achieves just the opposite—intrigue, joy, and a sense of hopeful anticipation. Those who do not possess detailed information about heaven nevertheless often have a vague expectation of what it will be like: it's the place in the sky where we will go someday to sing praises to God and leave behind our earthly existence. But is this understanding of life forever with God the biblical one? What happens when Christians die? What is the biblical hope for the future?

Just as life after death occurs in phases for the nonbeliever, so too for the Christian. In the first, when believers die, they (absent their bodies) go immediately into the presence of the Lord. In 2 Corinthians 5:6–8 Paul wrote, "We are always confident and know that as long as we are at home in the body we are away from the Lord. We live by faith, not by sight. We are confident, I say, and would prefer to be away from the body and at home with the Lord" (NIV).

For Paul, absence "from the body" (i.e., death) would result in his presence with the Lord. Somewhat later, in the light of his uncertain future, Paul told the church at Philippi that if he continued to live he could continue to minister, while if he were to die he would "be with Christ" (Phil. 1:23). The book of Hebrews depicts heaven as a place where God and Jesus dwell along with "the spirits of righteous men made perfect" (Heb. 12:23 NIV). The idea that at death believers move into the presence of the Lord seems to be anticipated by Jesus himself, who told the repentant thief on the cross, "Truly I say to you, today you shall be with Me in Paradise" (Luke 23:43). When nonbelievers die, they await resurrection in a netherworld; when Christians die, they await resurrection in the presence of the Lord. There we will worship him, enjoy him, and prepare to return to earth with him. As good and satisfying as disembodied life in the Lord's presence will be, it represents only the first phase of our life-after-death experience.

The second phase involves our resurrection from the dead and evaluation by Jesus Christ. According to 1 Thessalonians 4:13–18, 1 Corinthians 15:50–58, Philippians 3:20–21, and several other passages, when Jesus returns he will clothe the spirits of previously deceased believers with resurrection bodies like his; he will also transform the bodies of living Christians, so that all his followers share in his resurrection. Jesus' resurrection confirmed him as God's unique Son, the firstborn from the dead, the leader of redeemed and restored humanity (Rom. 1:4; 5:12–21; 8:29; Acts 2:22–36). His resurrection body differed from his mortal one in several ways, not least in that it was indestructible and not limited as mortal bodies are (1 Cor. 15:42; Luke 24:36; John 20:19).

Nevertheless, his new body retained links to the old one. It was substantial (Jesus ate, drank, touched, was touched, and worked; Luke

24:36–43; John 20:20–28; 21:4–14) and bore resemblance to the first (Luke 24:39; John 20:20, 27). According to Scripture, when Jesus returns, *we* will be raised and transformed; *our* bodies will become like *his* (Phil. 3:21; 1 Cor. 15:42–57; 1 John 3:2). For us, what was by nature weak, sinful, and mortal will be exchanged for that which is strong, sinless, and immortal. We are not destined for an ephemeral eternity but one that is bodily, substantial. At Jesus' return our bodies will become like his, and our desire to know and serve God will be confirmed, purified, and intensified. The resurrection secures our future and makes the connection between body and soul complete and permanent.

Beyond that, our resurrection signals the onset of *cosmic* renewal! Paul hinted at this when he wrote:

> The creation waits in eager expectation for the sons of God to be revealed. For the creation was subjected to frustration, not by its own choice, but by the will of the one who subjected it, in hope that the creation itself will be liberated from its bondage to decay and brought into the glorious freedom of the children of God. We know that the whole creation has been groaning as in the pains of childbirth right up to the present time. Not only so, but we ourselves, who have the firstfruits of the Spirit, groan inwardly as we wait eagerly for our adoption as sons, the redemption of our bodies (Rom. 8:19–23 NIV).

Just as Adam's sin introduced havoc not only to mankind but also to the created order, so the return of the second Adam, Jesus, will bring restoration to mankind and the rest of creation.

What else lies in our future? As Christians we believe we will spend eternity with God. Jesus died for our sins, and because of his death in our stead, we no longer face the judgment of God. Our place in eternity is secure. But will we all enjoy the same eternity? Will the thief on the cross have the same heaven as the woman who faithfully served God for five decades? Will she have an eternity indistinguishable from the Christian who never seemed to grasp fully Jesus' call to be a disciple? Is it really correct to say we look to a future without the notion of judgment? If God is just, can he fail to evaluate the lives of his people?

The New Testament teaches that all Christians will be evaluated by their Lord at an event that Paul called "the judgment seat of Christ" (2 Cor. 5:10). This may be equivalent to the great throne judgment mentioned in Revelation 20:11–15.[12] It will be helpful to explain what is *not* at stake at this judgment, whenever it occurs. It is not an event where a Christian's fitness for heaven is evaluated. It is not the place where a Christian may "fail the test" and as a result end up forever separated from God. True Christians are those whom God has elected to eternal life and regenerated by his Spirit (John 15:16; Rom. 8:28–30; 9:14–18; Eph. 1:3–6; 2 Thess. 2:13; Titus 3:5; 1 Pet. 1:1–5). Their future salvation is assured by the faithfulness of God ·(John 5:24; 10:25–30; Eph. 1:13–14; 2 Tim. 2:11–13; Heb. 13:5–6). Accordingly, the issue discussed below concerns future rewards and losses for believers. What is the outcome of this evaluation?

All believers—not just a select few—will be subject to judgment. Paul said, "We must *all* appear before the judgment seat of Christ" (2 Cor. 5:10; also Rom. 14:10–12). Moreover, the judgment is inevitable—Paul said we "must" face it (2 Cor. 5:10). The future judgment is comprehensive, that is, it deals with every aspect of our lives—keeping in mind one important qualification; God promises to forgive sins when we come to him in faith (Heb. 8:12; Ps. 103:8–14; Col. 2:13–14). For this reason it seems likely to me that while our entire lives may be reviewed at the judgment seat, it is our life after conversion which forms the basis for any reward or loss.

According to Paul some believers will be rewarded while others will suffer loss as a result of appearing before the judgment seat:

> For no one can lay any foundation other than the one already laid, which is Jesus Christ. If any man builds on this foundation using gold, silver, costly stones, wood, hay or straw, his work will be shown for what it is, because the Day will bring it to light. It will be revealed with fire, and the fire will test the quality of each man's work. If what he has built survives, he will receive his reward. If it is burned up, he will suffer loss; he himself will be saved, but only as one escaping through the flames. (1 Cor. 3:11–15 NIV).[13]

What would it mean to be rewarded? What could be involved in suffering loss?

Reward for the believer involves at least two elements. The first is getting praise from the Lord. In parables Jesus recounted the praise given to loyal servants by their master upon his return: "Well done, good and faithful servant" (Matt. 25:21 NIV; also Luke 19:17). At first glance this seems a paltry reward for a life of service, a life which may have involved suffering and sacrifice for the cause of Christ. And yet we should not underestimate the value of commendation. We see its effect, for example, in children. C. S. Lewis observed, "Nothing is so obvious in a child—not in a conceited child, but in a good child—as its great and undisguised pleasure in being praised."[14] We are told to enter the kingdom of God as children; indeed, Jesus said that without this childlike faith it is impossible to please God (Matt. 18:1–4). If childlikeness is important to enter the kingdom, perhaps it characterizes other dimensions of kingdom life, including our enjoyment of commendation from the Lord. Praise from him will please and satisfy us into eternity.

A second element of future reward involves privilege and responsibility. In Matthew 10:37–40 two of Jesus' disciples request the honor of sitting near him in his kingdom. He answers that someday God will grant such honor to certain people. In the ancient world sitting close to the king not only involved honor (as in 1 Kings 1:19), it also suggested the privilege of intimacy with the king. If so, we might ask with reference to heaven how some people could have a deeper or more intimate experience of God than others in the future while all will have access to him. Perhaps—and here I speculate—perhaps the answer is that even now believers are being shaped and sized in their capacity to enjoy God in the future. Imagine two vases, one capable of holding a pint of water, the other able to hold ten gallons. Each one, when filled to the brim, is full. Were they able to speak, each might truly say "I'm full" and pronounce itself entirely satistfied. But clearly one would have a fuller (no pun intended) experience of water than the other. Perhaps believers in eternity will be like vases of different sizes, able to experience the presence of God to varying degrees based on their earthly lives, yet each also able to say "I'm full; I'm content; I'm statisfied." Intimacy with God will be one reward in eternity. Not everyone will have the same experience of it, and we should seek for the fullest one possible; yet at the end we will all be satisfied.

As to repsonsibility we note that in Revelation 2:25–26 Jesus urged the church at Thyatira, "Only hold on to what you have until I come. To him who overcomes and does my will to the end, I will give authority over the nations" (NIV). In Jesus' parable of the noblemen, after praising his servant for faithfulness in handling ten minas (roughly ten pounds of gold), the master rewarded him with governance of ten cities (a quantum leap in responsibility); Luke 19:11–27). While one must be cautious in pressing the details of a parable too far,[15] the fact that the faithful servant participated in reigning alongside his master is conspicuously similar to teaching found elsewhere in the New Testament that believers will share in Jesus' future reign (Luke 22:28–30; 2 Tim. 2:12).

To the faithful, especially those faithful in the absence of public recognition, there will be generous and public reward from the Lord (Matt. 6:1–6,

16–18). Details about our future reward are scarce, but what we do know suggests it will be generous, conspicuous, and long-lived. In the light of this teaching, believers can be properly motivated to dedicate their lives to God not only by our love for and gratitude to him but also by the hope of future reward. This—no less than a sense of gratitude—is noble motivation for service because it is rooted in the belief that God will do as he has promised.

But what about those Christians who fail to act appropriately in this life, those who have *not* been faithful? Their eternity is adversely affected. Jesus depicted such a one as being chastised by his master and losing privileges (Luke 19:20–26). Paul spoke of one who will "suffer loss" (1 Cor. 3:15) and used the same Greek word to describe his loss of status and privilege among his Jewish peers after his conversion to Christianity (Phil. 3:8). To cite the earlier example, perhaps "loss" involves a reduction in our capacity to experience God. As with rewards, information about "loss" is scarce. Nevertheless, it is apparently substantial and clearly to be avoided. We should, therefore, heed the words of John, "And now, little children, abide in Him, so that when He appears we may have confidence and not shrink away from Him in shame at His coming" (1 John 2:28).

What can Christians do to prepare for the judgment seat of Christ? Two things stand out. First, we should cultivate faithfulness. Jesus taught that servants are to be rewarded in proportion to their *faithfulness*, not merely their *fruitfulness*. Every Christian is supernaturally gifted by God to serve him and one another (1 Cor. 12:7; 1 Pet. 4:10). We should use these gifts and natural talents to engage in good works and, to the extent possible, do them in secret, since those done for God's eyes only will be especially rewarded (Matt. 6:1–6, 16–18). Second, we should cultivate mercy. Jesus said, "Blessed are the merciful, for they will be shown mercy" (Matt. 5:7 NIV). James wrote, "Judgment will be merciless to one who has shown no mercy; mercy triumphs over judgment" (2:13). When Christ reviews our lives, we will hope for mercy; we can ensure that we receive it *then* by showing mercy to others *now*.

Once believers have been resurrected and judged, phase three of their future will unfold. Where do we spend eternity? Will we be in heaven forever? Even nonbelievers think the Christian hope is "up there." To suggest otherwise would seem at first glance to invite a charge of heresy. Heaven is emblazoned in our consciousness as our eternal home. There is certainly scriptural support for this belief. During the last week of his life, Jesus taught that believers would eventually meet him in the sky (Matt. 24:31).

The night before his crucifixion he said he was going to "My father's house" to prepare rooms for his followers, who would eventually join him there (John 14:1–3). As he suffered on the cross, Jesus assured the believing thief, "Today you will be with me in paradise" (Luke 23:43). Paul was given a vision of the "third heaven"—a place he also labeled "Paradise" (2 Cor. 12:1–4)—and he later wrote, "our citizenship is in heaven, from which also we eagerly wait for a Savior, the Lord Jesus Christ" (Phil. 3:20).

Jesus is in heaven, and our future is with him (Acts 1:11; 3:21; 7:55; Phil. 3:20; Rev. 5:6–14); thus, it is thought we will live in heaven forever. This conclusion is reasonable and biblical, but upon closer examination we find that it is only *part* of the story. Heaven is *not* our ultimate destination. Instead, the Bible teaches that we are destined to live with God forever on a renewed earth. What is the evidence for this?

In several places Scripture teaches there will be a new heaven and earth. Peter, for example, looked forward to the establishment of a new heaven and earth "in which righteousness dwells" (2 Pet. 3:13). Similarly, toward the end of Revelation John had a vision of "a new heaven and a new earth" where God and his people would live (Rev. 21:1). Paul hinted at this development when he said, "The creation itself will be liberated from its bondage to decay and brought into the glorious freedom of the children of God" (Rom. 8:21 NIV). This expectation of New Testament writers was anticipated by the prophet Isaiah, who foresaw a day when God would create "new heavens and a new earth" (Isa. 65:17). If this is so, what is the relationship of the present earth to the coming new earth?

The relationship is characterized both by continuity and discontinuity. According to Peter:

> But they [skeptical nonbelievers] deliberately forget that long ago by God's word the heavens existed and the earth was formed out of water and by water. By these waters also the world of that time was deluged and destroyed. By the same word the present heavens and earth are reserved for fire, being kept for the day of judgment and destruction of ungodly men (2 Pet. 3:5–7 NIV).

Peter said the old world "was destroyed" (*apôleto*, v. 6) while the present one faces "destruction" (*apôleias*, v. 7). By this choice of words Peter hinted there will be some continuity between our present world and the new one. How so? Even though the world of Noah's day was destroyed—wrecked, as it were—by the flood, it was *not* annihilated. Noah and those with him did not repopulate a completely new earth. God did not destroy the old world entirely so that it had to be created afresh *ex nihilo*; it was purged, but not obliterated.[16] A similar destruction, Peter said, faces the present heaven and earth. In fact, by linking our resurrection to the renewal of creation (Rom. 8:19–23), Paul hinted that the fate of the latter is analogous to that of the former: our present physical bodies will be radically transformed, but they will still be *our* bodies.

What will life be like in the new heavens and earth? What will we do for eternity? The most outstanding feature of the new heavens and earth is the presence of God.[17] As a voice from heaven announced to John, "Now the dwelling of God is with men, and he will live with them. They will be his people, and God himself will be with them and be their God" (Rev. 21:3 NIV). John later observed that after the new Jerusalem descended to earth, "I did not see a temple in the city, because the Lord God Almighty and the Lamb are its temple. The city does not need the sun or the moon to shine on it, for the glory of God gives it light, and the Lamb is its lamp" (Rev. 21:22–23 NIV).[18]

God's throne is present, and his glory illuminates the earth (Rev. 22:1–5). Because God is there, every remnant and memory of sadness and mourning will be removed. As John wrote, "He will wipe every tear from their eyes. There will be no more death or mourning or crying or pain, for the old order of things has passed away" (Rev. 21:4 NIV). Because God is there, every unrepentant sinner will be banished: "Nothing impure will ever enter it, nor will anyone who does what is shameful or deceitful, but only those whose names are written in the Lamb's book of life" (Rev. 21:27 NIV; also 21:8). Because God is there, the city is secure—its gates will "never be closed" (Rev. 21:25).

But what about us? In the past some people have complained that heaven, or as I might put it, "life forever with God," must be an awfully boring experience. The fear, if that's the right word for it, seems to be that while life with God would undoubtedly be holy, free of turmoil, and generally pleasant, it might also lack creativity, beauty, excitement, and the pursuit of knowledge. In short, the prospect of singing praises *ad infinitum* is for some an invitation to sing *ad nauseum*. However, this apprehension is unwarranted on two counts.

First, it fails to appreciate the inherent joy that accompanies true worship. As a common grace God has enabled many of us to experience the pleasures of courtship and marriage, in particular, the sense of joy and excitement that is part of knowing and loving and being known and loved by someone special. Life forever with God is characterized by an increasing knowledge of and love for the Almighty—the ultimate 'someone special'— and yet, because we are limited while he is infinite, there will always be more for us to know and love (Rev. 22:4; 1 Cor. 13:12; Rev. 22:8; also Rev. 4:1–5:14). Indeed, those things that make life most worth living now—the knowledge of God, love, companionship, a sense of purpose and security— will be present in ever-increasing measure in the life to come. The presence of God is transforming, awe inspiring, and joyful—hardly the equivalent of "boring."

Apprehension about heaven is misguided on a second count; namely, in that it fails to consider certain extrabiblical data. It seems reasonable, for example, to suppose that a renewed earth will surpass the present one in beauty and intricacy. Why would this matter for us? To return to a theme discussed in Chapter 1, if we are newly equipped for immortality at the resurrection, perhaps our role as image-bearers—as those who relate to and represent God—will continue. Indeed, John's description of believers reigning in eternity (Rev. 22:5) may be related to man's original mandate to "rule and subdue," given the fact that Revelation 21–22 employs so many images from the creation account in Genesis (God creating a new heaven and earth, Rev. 21:1 = Gen. 1:1ff.; the tree of life, Rev. 22:2 = Gen. 2:9; the absence of the curse, Rev. 22:3 = Gen. 3:8–24).

We moderns may occasionally fall into the trap of unconsciously comparing this life and eternity to a sumptuous meal, with this life as the main course and eternity as dessert—but if we read the Scriptures aright, that comparison is precisely backwards. In reality, we should regard this life as the appetizer, and eternity as the main course, with (for those with a sweet tooth) dessert after dessert after dessert! This life is the shadow; the life to come is broad daylight. I suspect C. S. Lewis may be right when he suggests that heaven and hell begin in this life, that the future merely supplies confirmation and amplification of choices made now. As his teacher says in *The Great Divorce*:

> Both good and evil, when they are full grown, become retrospective. Not only this valley but all this earthly past will have been Heaven to those who are saved. Not only the twilight in that town, but all their life on earth too, will then be seen by the damned to have been Hell. That is what mortals misunderstand. They say of some temporal suffering, "No future bliss can make up for it," not knowing that Heaven, once

attained, will work backwards and turn even that agony into glory. . . . Both processes begin even before death. The good man's past begins to change so that his forgiven sins and remembered sorrows take on the quality of Heaven: the bad man's past already conforms to his badness and is filled only with dreariness. And that is why, at the end of all things, when the sun rises here and the twilight turns to blackness down there, the Blessed will say, "We have never lived anywhere except in Heaven," and the Lost, "We were always in Hell." And both will speak truly.[19]

This view certainly coheres with the New Testament teaching that eternal life is to be experienced both now and in the future. The same could be said for eternal death. In either event, consequences are experienced now and forever on the basis of choices made in this life.[20]

Forever and Design

Our story began with God, the powerful and personal Creator who made heaven and earth and devised a special, unique role for mankind: to enjoy fellowship with him and to represent him on earth. God's promises of blessings and warning against disobedience went unheeded, and the idyllic life in the garden was supplanted by a series of separations which resulted in mankind's alienation from God, others, himself, and the earth.

God promised to intervene and rescue mankind and the world from their plight. I have argued that apparently random contours of history are in reality shaped in large measure by God's efforts to make good this promise. History, especially the history encapsulated in the Bible, reflects complexity and specificity—hence, design. God chose Abraham, then Israel, then David and, supremely, his own Son Jesus Christ as agents of revelation and redemption. Christ died and rose, and in so doing inaugurated the final stage of God's involvement in history to redeem his people and punish his enemies.

These events unfolded according to God's plan, according to his design for history. Many of them were prophetically anticipated years before they took place and thus offer confirmation of God's involvement in and sovereignty over human affairs. Moreover, they show the imprint of God's gracious and redeeming hand. In the future the most persistent and pernicious foes of humanity will be vanquished: the devil and his followers will be punished; our bodies will be transformed; death will be destroyed; the curse will be removed. Life in a garden paradise once gave way to a world of thorns and thistles, but this latter will itself be replaced by a new heaven and earth in which there are no more tears, no more pain, no more death. Just as the past bears witness to his intentions and ability to act, so the future will unfold according to God's plan and bear witness to his grace, power, justice, and wisdom.

However, no matter how strong the evidence of design in history might be, no matter how well it may be presented (and this book is but a primer in assembling and presenting the evidence), it does not compel belief in the Creator. Evidence of design in history does not compel faith in the God who orchestrates it. It seems that God has worked so as to leave room both for faith and disbelief.

It is sometimes said that faith is irrational, that it requires a person to advocate one position as true while willfully ignoring and rejecting evidence to the contrary. But this is not the biblical notion of faith. Faith is rational; it is the kiss of commitment to a worldview that coheres, that accounts for apparently disparate facts in a reasonable way. Faith surely includes the hope that unfulfilled promises will come to pass, but such hope—though it be *hope*—is not unfounded, much less irrational. Yet faith is more than an ideological commitment. Above all else it represents personal allegiance to the God of Scripture and his risen Son. They are responsible for the design of history and for the two destinies which lie before those who read this book. Many readers will have already made their commitment to the Son of God and to the path of trial, tribulation, and eternal reward which is the lot of those who follow him; for others, what remains is to think carefully and to choose wisely which path to take.

Appendix A

The Language of Conflict in

Luke 8:26-39

L uke seems to highlight the conflict between Jesus and the demons by using military terms to describe it in Luke 8:26-39.

First, in the account of the demoniac's encounter with Jesus, the word translated "was met" in Luke 8:27 (*hupantaô*) frequently has military/conflict overtones. The verb *hupantaô* can mean "to meet" in a neutral sense, but it can also mean "to oppose." The latter sense is found in Luke 14:31 (the only other use of the term in Luke) where one king goes out "to meet" another in battle.

Second, when the man with the demon saw Jesus, "he cried out." In the Greek Old Testament, the verb translated "cried out" (*anakrazô*) is used thirteen times, almost always with overtones of battle or conflict. The Israelite army "shouted" (*anakragontôn*) at the walls of Jericho prior to their conquest of the city (Josh. 6:20), while Gideon and his companions sounded a battle cry (*anekraxsan*) before engaging the Midianite armies (Judg. 7:20). Jehoshaphat "cried out" in battle when faced with enemy soldiers and certain death (1 Kings 22:32). After he killed the apostate Jew and foreign officer at the beginning of the Maccabbean revolt, Mattathias "cried out" [*anekraxse*] in the city with a loud voice, saying, "Let everyone who is zealous for the law and supports the covenant come out with me" (1 Macc. 2:27). Thus, the exclamation of the demoniac sets the mood of the passage as one of hostility and conflict.

Third, the demons' label for themselves enhances the conflict imagery, since "legion" was a distinctly military term describing a large group of Roman soldiers.

Fourth, the term used to describe the pigs' rush into the lake (*hormaô*) often has military overtones. From classical times to the third century A.D.

it was commonly used to describe military movements. Xenophon, for example, tells of a bold Greek counterattack where the Greek soldiers took advantage of their superior training by "*charging* at them [their enemies] on the run" and engaging in man-to-man fighting. In the Septuagint, soldiers from Israel emerged from ambush and "rushed [*hôrmêsen*] against Gibeah" in battle (Judg. 20:37; also 1 Kings 15:19; Hab. 1:8; Jer. 4:28). The mood established by this choice of terms is emphatically hostile.

Fifth, the demoniac's question to Jesus, "What do I have to do with you?" contributes to the conflict motif (v. 28). The same phrase is used in the Septuagint in Judges 11:12, where Jephthah demanded to know of the Ammonite king, "What is between you and me, that you have come to me to fight against my land?" In another setting, David's commander Abishai wanted to kill Shimei for insulting David. In disgust David queried Abishai, "What have I to do with you . . . that you should this day be an adversary to me?" (2 Sam. 19:22). The same question had been put to Jesus earlier by the demons in Luke 4:34.

By using these terms Luke emphasized to his readers the conflict between Jesus and the demons.

APPENDIX B

DANIEL'S SEVENTY WEEKS

$$✧$$

According to Daniel 9:1–2, the prophet Daniel, who had been taken captive to Babylon years earlier (ca. the sixth century B.C.[1]), was reading from the prophet Jeremiah. There he learned the exile of Jews from Palestine was to last seventy years (Jer. 25:11–12). He realized these seventy years were almost complete, and in order to prepare for a return to the land, he prayed earnestly, confessing the sins of the nation and asking for God's mercy (9:4–19). His prayer was interrupted by the visit of the angel Gabriel, who said:

> Seventy "sevens" are decreed for your people and your holy city to finish transgression, to put an end to sin, to atone for wickedness, to bring in everlasting righteousness, to seal up vision and prophecy and to anoint the most holy. Know and understand this: From the issuing of the decree to restore and rebuild Jerusalem until the Anointed One, the ruler, comes, there will be seven "sevens," and sixty-two "sevens." It will be rebuilt with streets and a trench, but in times of trouble. After the sixty-two "sevens," the Anointed One will be cut off and will have nothing. The people of the ruler who will come will destroy the city and the sanctuary. The end will come like a flood: War will continue until the end, and desolations have been decreed. He will confirm a covenant with many for one "seven." In the middle of the "seven" he will put an end to sacrifice and offering. And on a wing of the temple he will set up an abomination that causes desolation, until the end that is decreed is poured out on him (9:24–27 NIV).

What are these "weeks," and why are they important for students of Bible prophecy? Gabriel revealed to Daniel God's plan for the nation—a plan that turned out to have been partially fulfilled with astonishing precision.

The prophecy can be divided into three parts. The first part, verse 24, sets the stage for what follows. It describes what the prophecy is about in broad terms and provides a chronological framework for its fulfillment. The second part, verses 25–26, hints that the seventy weeks will be interrupted after the initial sixty-nine weeks (the seven plus sixty-two). The third part, verse 27, refers to the last of Daniel's seventy weeks.

The seventy weeks in verse 24 refer to seventy weeks (literally "seventy sevens" in Hebrew) of years. Saying the "weeks" refers to "weeks of years" is based on the observation that Daniel had been thinking of Jeremiah's prophecies, which in turn relate to the weeks of years (the Sabbath years) that Israel had not observed (see Lev. 25:1–4; 26:31–35, 43; Jer. 25:11–12; 29:10).[2] If this is correct, then Daniel envisioned a period of 490 years (seventy times seven) to fulfill the prophecies made concerning the nation. Verse 24 describes, in effect, the complete—but not necessarily detailed—fulfillment of kingdom promises.[3]

Since verse 24 has in mind a period of 490 years, from what point are we to begin counting these years? Verse 25 tells us: when the decree is issued to rebuild and restore Jerusalem. Professor Harold Hoehner has demonstrated that this decree was given in connection with events mentioned in Nehemiah 2:1ff.[4] There Nehemiah, a Jewish official in the court of the Persian ruler Artaxerxes, got permission to return to Jerusalem to rebuild it (Neh. 2:5). He requested a letter from the king that would enable him to get provisions "for the gates of the fortress . . . for the wall of the city . . . for the house to which I will go" (Neh. 2:8). Artaxerxes gave permission and blessing in 445/444 B.C.

In other words, almost a hundred years passed between the time of Daniel's prophecy (sixth century B.C.) and the beginning of its fulfillment in Nehemiah's day (fifth century B.C.). In addition, verse 26 indicates that the 490 years will not run consecutively. They are interrupted after 483 years (seven plus sixty-two weeks = sixty-nine weeks; sixty-nine times seven years = 483 years) by the "cutting off" of the Anointed One (=Messiah, v. 26). If the prophetic clock began to run in 445/444 B.C. with the decree to rebuild Jerusalem and its walls, when did the sixty-nine weeks (the 483 years) end?

Before addressing that question, one important clarification must be made. It is likely that the 483 years Daniel would have had in mind were 360 days in length, not years that were 365 days long.[5] This means that we'll have to make some adjustments as we think about translating Daniel's years into years on our modern calendar. If Daniel's 360-daylong years are converted to 365-daylong years and added to 444 B.C., the end of the sixty-nine weeks takes place in A.D. 33.[6] What is so significant about that date? Professor Hoehner has argued persuasively that A.D. 33 is the most likely year for Jesus' death.[7] According to Christian tradition, he is the Messiah, the one who was eventually "cut off" (to use Daniel's terminology) from his people by his death.

If these calculations are correct, Daniel's prophecy about the first sixty-nine weeks was fulfilled with astonishing precision. He predicted the restoration of Jerusalem one hundred years before it occurred. He predicted several hundred years before Jesus' birth the year of his death.

So much for the first sixty-nine of Daniel's seventy weeks. What about the seventieth week of years? Have the events described in Daniel 9:27 taken place? Daniel mentioned an enigmatic figure (the "he" of v. 27a, most likely a reference to "the prince who is to come" in v. 26). This coming prince would make a covenant with "the many" (i.e., the Jews) and then break it halfway through the seventieth week (v. 27). This one who breaks the covenant is the "one who makes desolate" (v. 27). It is unlikely that the prophecies of Daniel's seventieth week have been fulfilled. In the first place, by the end of the seventy weeks the major aims to "finish transgression . . . and bring in everlasting righteousness" (v. 24) were to have been achieved, yet these things seem not to have been achieved in the life of Jesus, in the life of the early church, or at any time since. These promises have undoubtedly begun to be fulfilled (for more on this, see chapter 3), but Daniel had in view the consummation, not the inauguration, of the process.

It is unlikely that this final seven-year period mentioned by Daniel should be reinterpreted to refer to a figurative period of time, for it is not easy to see how the seventieth week could refer to a *figurative* time span when the first sixty-nine weeks were *not figurative*. It is reasonable to think that the same level of specificity found in the fulfillment of the first sixty-nine weeks will also be found with regard to the seventieth. Daniel's seventieth week has yet to occur.

APPENDIX C

INTERPRETING AND USING

THE BOOK OF REVELATION

The book of Revelation is difficult to interpret because it is filled with language and imagery foreign to the modern reader. In fact, many parts would have made for strange reading in the first century! Scholars have a special label for the literary genre of Revelation. They call it "apocalyptic" (it's the same label they assign to the book of Daniel in the Old Testament). The label applies to narrative literature that (1) displays an interest in the development of history, (2) is concerned with salvation and the end of the ages, (3) provides glimpses into heaven, and (4) is characterized by visions given to the writer of the narrative.

Interpreting Revelation

Even though Revelation is the one book of the Bible to promise explicitly a blessing upon those who read it (Rev. 1:3), those who read it usually end up feeling a little confused. Its structure is complex and difficult to determine—yet basic to any thorough interpretation of the book. There are nearly as many theories about its structure as there are commentaries—and there are plenty of commentaries! Greg Beale has set forth the various scholarly proposals concerning the book's structure, and a quick look at his work confirms the magnitude of the problem.[1] There are good reasons to be wary of developing a theory of the last days based solely on an interpretation of this enigmatic book, and yet it is possible to arrive at some general conclusions regarding its structure and contents. These will provide broad guidelines for understanding the book and using it to answer questions about the last days.

First, the book deals with the divinely ordained consummation of history, something which has already begun. The apostle John told us that the revelation given to him by Jesus concerns "things which must shortly take place" (*dei genesthai en tachei;* Rev. 1:1). The phrase *dei genesthai* has rich implications when understood in the light of its use in the Old and New Testaments. In the Greek version of the Old Testament it is found four times, all in Daniel 2 (vv. 28, 29, 45).[2] In each instance *dei genesthai* refers to events associated with God's plan for the consummation of history as revealed to Daniel in his dream and its subsequent interpretation. This phrase is not used anywhere else in the Old Testament. It is therefore noteworthy that the phrase appears most often in the New Testament in the so-called apocalyptic discourses—those passages where Jesus speaks about the end times (Matt. 24:6; Mark 13:7; Luke 21:9). By the time John wrote Revelation, the phrase had arguably become a catchword to designate divinely ordained events associated with the consummation of history. The revelation given to John focuses our attention on the last days.

Beale observes that while Daniel speaks of "what will take place in the latter days" (Dan. 2:28)—thus putting their fulfillment into the future—John's use of the word *shortly* in Revelation 1:1 signifies the nearness of fulfillment.[3] Indeed, the use of the term *shortly* (*en tachei*) in combination with the phrase "the time is near" (Rev. 1:3) indicates that prophesied events stand on the verge of fulfillment. Similar language is used in the Gospels to speak of God's kingdom as "at hand," meaning it has begun (for more on this, see chapter 3). This idea that the last days have begun is consistent with what the New Testament as a whole teaches—that God's prophesied era of salvation has begun.

Second, virtually the entire book of Revelation is future oriented from the writer's point of view, and much of it is future from the modern reader's point of view. After surveying the book as a whole, the scholar David Aune noted that John structured the book "because he intends the visions themselves to constitute *a single chronological narrative of the eschatological events that will soon begin to unfold* [his italics]."[4] Even the letters to churches, normally taken as evidence that John's message was for a contemporary audience, are future oriented from John's point of view. The churches were warned to deal with problems in the light of Jesus' warnings about how he might deal with them if they should fail to take his words seriously (Rev. 2:1–3:22).

Whether the Greek phrase translated "shortly" in Revelation 1:1 refers to *how* events unfold (i.e., once they begin, they unfold quickly) or, more likely, to *when* they unfold (in the near future), it is obvious they have yet to unfold—or to be more precise, they have yet to unfold completely. The second coming of Jesus (19:11ff.), together with the general resurrection of the dead (20:11–15) and the appearance of a new heaven and earth (21:1ff.) are clearly future events, not only from John's perspective but also from ours. Thus, even if it is conceded that much of Revelation refers to events already fulfilled (though this is debatable), it is obvious that some events—those described in Revelation 19:11–22:5—have not been.[5]

Third, much of the book is expressed figuratively; as a result, overly literal interpretations must be rejected not because they are "literal" but because they fail to take seriously the metaphorical nature of much of John's work. Twenty-five years ago I had just finished reading Hal Lindsey's *The Late, Great Planet Earth*, where the ten-headed beast of Revelation 13 was interpreted as a united Europe under the authority of the Antichrist. I was chatting with someone at school about it, and he remarked that the future scared him. I asked why, and he answered, "Because that beast is going to eat people—and I don't want to be eaten!" My acquaintance had taken the vision "literally." I had understood it metaphorically. Yet it may be that symbolic language is to be found not only in the visions in Revelation but also in many other places.

In the opening verse of the book John wrote, "The revelation of Jesus Christ, which God gave him to show his servants what must soon take place. He made it known by sending his angel to his servant John" (Rev. 1:1 NIV). The Greek word translated "made known" toward the end of the verse is *sēmainō*. As used by John the word has special connotations. For example, Jesus said, " ' But I, when I am lifted up from the earth, will draw all men to myself.' He said this to show [*sēmainō*] the kind of death he was going to die" (John 12:32–33 NIV). Jesus "showed" what kind of death he would experience by speaking figuratively of his crucifixion as a "lifting up." The same use of *sēmainō* is found elsewhere in John (18:32; 21:19). Not coincidentally, the verb is used in the Greek version of the Old Testament where Daniel thanks God for the vision and interpretation given to him: "I thank and praise you, O God of my fathers: You have given me wisdom and power, you have made known [*sēmainō*] to me what we asked of you, you have made known to us the dream of the king" (Dan. 2:23 NIV; also 2:30, 45). What was made known to Daniel? God's plan for the future, communicated symbolically in a dream. *Sēmainō* is used, in other words, not merely to talk about something as revealed but to talk about something as revealed in a particular way, i.e., through symbolism. If the opening statement in a biblical book is used to set its tone or list its purpose (as is the case in John 1:1–18; Luke 1:1–4), then the opening words in Revelation suggest that very much of what will be said is and should be taken as symbolic. Although some writers think Revelation should be interpreted literally in every place *except* where figurative language is plainly in view, Beale is probably right to conclude:

> we are told in the book's introduction that the majority of the material in it is revelatory symbolism. . . . Hence, the predominant manner by which to approach the material will be according to a nonliteral interpretative method. Of course, some parts are not symbolic, but the essence of the book is figurative. Where there is lack of clarity about whether something is symbolic, the scales of judgment should be tilted in the direction of a nonliteral analysis.[6]

I do not mean to suggest there are no objective historical events to which Revelation did or might yet refer. After all, it is important to appreciate that although Daniel's dream and vision used unusual and vivid imagery, there were historical referents to *them*. Daniel was not speaking in vague terms about the historical conflict between good and evil; he was referring to particular events that took place in history. The fact that Daniel learned of the future through unusual imagery did not mean what he learned was imaginary or unreal. In a similar way, the fact that Revelation speaks symbolically does not imply that events described there are "unreal."

In the light of what has been said, how will passages and teaching from Revelation be used in this book?

Using Revelation

Some popular authors who write about the end times give clear and specific identification to various figures and events mentioned in Revelation; for them, the book does *not* seem to present many interpretive difficulties. I am rather less confident in my ability to understand the book in all its particulars, and for this reason I will be cautious and selective in my use of it in talking about the end times. This caution stems not from any doubt about the veracity of Revelation, only from my inability to know with confidence what the writer meant in some of its passages. Furthermore, it must be noted that in wider Christian circles the futurist interpretation of Revelation often found in popular books about the end times is not universally accepted. In itself, of course, this does not mean these writers have it wrong, but it does supply a further reason for my caution.

My own view is that like Daniel, the book of Revelation will not be clearly understood until many of the events described, especially those in chapters 6–18, occur or are clearly past. The predictions about future world kingdoms and the Maccabean uprising described in Daniel 7, 8, and 11 (some of which took place in the 2nd century B.C.) would surely have been incomprehensible in their details to Daniel's first readers (i.e., in the 6th century B.C.); it is only with the benefit of hindsight that we see how accurately and specifically Daniel's words were fulfilled. In a similar way, I suspect we cannot clearly identify the persons and events mentioned in Revelation 6–18 unless we are present to experience them or can look back on their fulfillment. In this respect, Revelation really is for now something of a closed book—not in its larger themes and message, but in many of its details.

My approach throughout this book will be to look to Revelation to see the extent to which it may corroborate or amplify the picture of the end times found elsewhere in Scripture. At some points, of course, particularly where passages in Revelation give the only description of a particular event or phenomenon, I will of necessity have to use Revelation as *prima facie* evidence. But in those rare instances, I will take special care to justify my interpretation of the book.

Appendix D

The Structure of

Matthew 24:1–31

Jesus' most extensive teaching on the last days is found in Matthew 24, Mark 13, and Luke 21. Among these, Matthew's account poses the most challenges to the interpreter. More specifically, as the New Testament scholar D. A. Carson observed, "The most difficult interpretative questions [of Matthew 24] concern the structure of the discourse."[1] Numerous scholars have looked into the issue; their views are conveniently summarized by Carson.[2] I will not attempt here to set forth a detailed defense of my understanding of the chapter's structure; instead, I will contrast two major interpretive options, then state my view along with the chief evidence in its favor and major objections to it.

Significantly, this large block of teaching by Jesus took place outside the temple on the Mount of Olives (Matt. 24:1ff.)—a place, according to Zechariah 14:1–15, where God will come in the last days to fight against the nations on behalf of his beloved Jerusalem.

Among the many questions we might ask of Matthew 24:1–31, two of the most important are: (1) How many questions do the disciples ask in verse 3? and (2) Do verses 15ff. deal with the destruction of Jerusalem in A.D. 70, as is clearly the case in the corresponding section in Luke 21, or do they refer to a future (i.e., post A.D. 70) destruction of the city?

In Matthew 24 we read:

> Jesus left the temple and was walking away when his disciples came up to him to call his attention to its buildings. "Do you see all these things?" he asked. "I tell you the truth, not one stone here will be left on another; every one will be thrown down." As Jesus was sitting on the Mount of Olives, the disciples came to him privately. "Tell us," they said, "when will this

happen, and what will be the sign of your coming and of the end of the age?" (Matt. 24:1–3 NIV).

It seems that in the disciples' minds the three events mentioned—the destruction of the temple, the coming of Jesus, and the end of the age—were linked.[3] Why should this be so? At the end of Matthew 23 Jesus concluded his "woes" on the Pharisees and Jerusalem by predicting both the destruction of its temple and his eventual return (vv. 37–39). Here, then, in the near context of Matthew 24 we find the notions of temple destruction and Jesus' return first associated. There is no precedent for the linkage of all three events in Matthew, but it may be more readily comprehensible to us if we read the disciples' questions at Matthew 24:3 in the light of Jesus' comments at Luke 19:11–44. In the Luke passage, as Jesus approached Jerusalem (i.e., several days *before* the events narrated in Matthew 24), he mentioned to the disciples that there would be an unspecified time gap between his rejection and his victorious return (an event which would signal the full coming of the kingdom, i.e., the end of the age; Luke 19:11–27). Following this he prophesied the destruction of the temple (Luke 19:41–44). Thus, when Jesus mentioned the destruction of the temple subsequent to his entry (in Matthew 24:2), we can readily see how the disciples' minds might jump to the theme of Jesus' return and the consummation of the ages.

Moving on, in Matthew 24:4–14 Jesus spoke of world conditions before the coming of the end. Among the hardships believers may expect to face, he mentioned false religious leaders (v. 5), wars and rumors of war (vv. 6–7a), famines and earthquakes (v. 7). To the list of coming troubles, Jesus added widespread persecution (vv. 9–10), apostasy (v. 10), and lawlessness (v. 12). Though serious, these events do not signal the end; on the contrary, they are merely the beginning of the end (see vv. 6b; 8). The end comes, according to Jesus, only after the gospel has been preached to "all the nations" (v. 14). This brings us to the most perplexing element of the passage, verses 15–28. To what do these verses refer? There are two major interpretive options.

Matthew 24:15–28 Refers to a Great Tribulation Some Time after A.D. 70

As Professor Carson notes, Matthew 24 has been divided in many ways. Common to most theories is the recognition that verses 15–28 refer either to the events of A.D. 70 or to later ones.[4] Some interpreters think Jesus referred to the desecration of Jerusalem's temple that takes place in the last days. To take verses 15–28 as referring to events after A.D. 70—to a destruction of a temple in Jerusalem subsequent to the one which occurred in A.D. 70—is attractive for several reasons.

First, it enables us to harmonize Paul's expectation of a coming Antichrist who goes to the temple with Jesus' teaching (compare 2 Thess. 2:1–10 with Matt. 24:15ff.). According to Paul, the coming of the man of sin to God's temple will signal the arrival of the day of the Lord, a day that concludes with Jesus' return. In Matthew 24:15–28 the appearance of the "abomination of desolation" signals the onset of the great tribulation, a time that culminates in the return of Jesus (Matt. 24:29–31).

Second, it allows us to read the word "immediately" in Matthew 24:29 in a natural way—the second coming (vv. 29–31) comes "immediately" after the great tribulation (vv. 15–28).

Third, it lets the reader understand the unprecedented scope of the great tribulation in Matthew 24:21–22 as corresponding to the unprecedented end-times tribulation described in Revelation 6–19.

Fourth, on this interpretation the coming of the Antichrist to the temple is a signal for believers to flee Jerusalem, whereas if the passage refers to the events of A.D. 70, the coming of Titus to the temple occurred so late in the Jewish war that it could not have served to warn anyone to flee the conflict (which had run from A.D. 66–70). Finally, if Matthew 24:15ff. refers to the future, we can take the shortening of the days to protect "the elect" (in v. 22) as reference to God's intervening to spare the church before Jesus' return.[5] The church is often referred to as "the elect" (*hoi eklektoi*) in the New Testament (Rom. 8:33; Col. 3:12; 2 Tim. 2:10; 1 Pet. 1:1).

Despite the many strengths of this interpretation, it faces two practically insuperable difficulties.

First, the parallel passage to Matthew 24:15ff. is Luke 21:20–24; this latter passage clearly refers to events of A.D. 70. If we take Matthew as entirely future oriented (i.e., after A.D. 70), then we are forced to think that Luke and Matthew have Jesus teaching about two *different* things, despite the fact that the setting for his teaching is the same in each Gospel and his words are nearly the same. This is problematic.[6]

Second, in Matthew (like Luke) the disciples' questions include one about the destruction of the temple Jesus has just taught in and left (Matt. 21:23–24:1); if Matthew 24:15 deals with events after A.D. 70, then (1) Jesus never did answer their question about Herod's temple but instead (2) told them about a temple yet to be built. In principle there can be no objection to Jesus' predicting a future temple—after all, he was predicting the future destruction of an existing one. Furthermore, he wouldn't have been the first prophet to envision a rebuilt temple (e.g., Isa. 44:28 with Ezra 1:1–3). The problem lies not in Jesus' ability to see the future but in how such a prediction set in this context would be misunderstood. There is little in context to suggest that Jesus referred to anything other than the temple he had just walked out of. Would it not have been unusual for him to speak without hint or warning of a temple other than the one plainly in view of him and his audience?

Matthew 24:15–28 Refers to the Destruction of Jerusalem in A.D. 70

Another way to divide Matthew 24 is to regard verses 4–28 as dealing with the time period between Jesus' first and second advent—an era he labeled "tribulation" (*thlipsis*, vv. 9, 21). Within the general era of tribulation described in verses 4–28 is a subsection dealing with the destruction of Jerusalem in A.D. 70 (vv. 15–28), which Jesus labeled a "great tribulation" (*thlipsis megalē*). What arguments favor this division of the chapter, and what are its liabilities?

Verses 4–14 provide a general description of the time before Jesus' return—a time he characterized as "tribulation." False messiahs, wars and rumors of wars, famines, and earthquakes are signs—but they mark the beginning rather than the end of trouble (vv. 5–8). Persecution, betrayal, and death will also be common (v. 10ff.). Hence, "tribulation" is not too strong a word to apply to the entire period of church history which precedes Jesus' return. To characterize this whole era as tribulation fits well with Paul's experience (Rom. 5:3; 8:35; 12:12; 2 Cor. 1:8; 7:4; Eph. 3:13; 1 Thess. 1:6; 3:3–4; 2 Thess. 1:4) and that of believers generally (e.g., Acts 4:1–23; 5:17ff.; 6:9ff.; 8:1ff.; 12:1ff.; 14:19ff.; etc.).

Verse 14 anticipates the worldwide mission to proclaim the gospel with the fulfillment of the mission opening the door for the consummation of the ages ("then the end shall come"). The duration of the tribulation described in verses 4–14 is not specified. In the midst of this general time of hardship, a period of more intense difficulty arises. This period coincides with the coming of the "abomination of desolation" to Jerusalem and its temple (v. 15; in this verse we get an answer to the disciples' question about when the temple would be destroyed, v. 3). The localized nature of the suffering is reflected by verses 16–20, which specifically mentioned Judea and the

Sabbath. Jesus labeled it "a great tribulation" (v. 21; it is not best translated "*the* great tribulation," since the Greek article [= "the"] is not present) because of the unprecedented suffering people in the city would experience. According to Jesus, this great tribulation would produce false messiahs, who would attempt to lure people into the wilderness—something which took place during the Jewish war with the Romans during A.D. 66–70.[7] Thus, when Jesus said he would return "immediately after the tribulation of those days" (v. 29), he answered the second part of the disciples' question concerning *when* he would return: he would come *after* an (unspecified) era of "tribulation."

If this understanding of Matthew 24:4–31 is correct, it corresponds to the way Luke's major section on the end times is structured. According to Luke, before the destruction of Jerusalem there are troubles (Luke 21:8–19), troubles which include the destruction of the city (Luke 21:25–26) and continue until Jesus returns (Luke 21:27–28). But to take a contrary position for the moment, if our interpretation of Matthew 24:4–31 is right, what are we to make of Jesus' comments that "the son of man" (a self-designation) would come "immediately after the tribulation of those days" (Matt. 24:29)? If "the tribulation of those days" refers to the Roman destruction of Jerusalem, it is obvious that something is wrong: the Son of Man did not come immediately! How can we resolve this apparent difficulty?

The best solution is to take "the tribulation of those days" mentioned in Matthew 24:29 as referring to the entire time between Jesus' first and second comings. Verse 9 says believers will be delivered to "tribulation" well in advance of the end. Indeed, there is ample New Testament precedent to label the whole era as "tribulation." The chief difficulty with this view is that the specific tribulation mentioned in the immediate context has to do with Jerusalem's destruction. But this *needn't* be the case. As argued above, the term could refer more generally to church history.[8] To take Matthew 24:4–28 as referring to the entire tribulation period between Jesus' first and second coming, with verses 15–28 pointing to a time of particularly intense tribulation, is clearly not without difficulties, but on the whole it seems better than other options.[9]

GLOSSARY

✧

Amillennialism—a view of the end times which believes the "millennial kingdom" mentioned in Revelation 20:1–6 is already fulfilled by the advent of Christ, his present reign in heaven, and the present ministry of the church. It denies there will be a transitional kingdom (i.e., "millennial kingdom") during which Christ reigns on earth.

Dispensationalism—a theological system which emphasizes the distinctive natures and roles of Israel and the church. In this respect it differs sharply from other theological systems which emphasize either the merging of the two or the taking over of Israel's role by the church. Dispensationalism emphasizes that Jesus will return before the millennial reign of Christ and that this reign will last one thousand years. Most of its adherents think the rapture of the church will take place before the great tribulation of the last days.

Intertestamental—dealing with the period of time between the completion of the Old Testament and the onset of the New Testament era (traditionally, fourth century B.C. to first century A.D.).

Posttribulationalism—a theory concerning the last days which holds that Christians will be removed from the earth (raptured) after the great tribulation and just before the bodily return of Christ.

Premillennialism—a belief that Jesus will return to earth before his establishment of a transitional (i.e., "millennial") kingdom.

Pretribulationalism—a theory concerning the last days which holds that Christians will be removed from the earth (raptured) in advance of the great tribulation and the appearance of the Antichrist.

Rapture—the biblical doctrine that living and deceased believers will meet Jesus in the air before his bodily return to the earth; at this "meeting" the bodies of deceased believers will be resurrected while those of living believers will be transformed.

Endnotes

✧

Introduction

1. It reads in part, "who [Jesus] suffered and rose again on the third day, and ascended to the Father and shall come again in glory to judge the living and the dead."

2. For a good discussion of the historicity of the resurrection, see William Lane Craig's "Did Jesus Rise from the Dead?" in *Jesus Under Fire* (eds. Michael J. Wilkins and J. P. Moreland; Grand Rapids: Zondervan, 1995), 141–76; and by the same author "The Historicity of the Empty Tomb of Jesus," *New Testament Studies* 31 (1985): 39–67. For the possibilities of miracles more generally, see *In Defense of Miracles: a Comprehensive Case for God's Action in History* (eds. R. Douglas Geivett and Gary R. Habermas; Downers Grove: InterVarsity, 1997).

3. Dispensationalism (see glossary) was the theological orientation of Lewis Sperry Chafer, founder of Dallas Theological Seminary. The seminary has exercised a tremendous influence on popular thinking about eschatology, especially in the United States.

4. For two helpful, recent surveys of popular thinking about "the end," see C. Marvin Pate and Calvin B. Haines Jr., *Doomsday Delusions: What's Wrong with Predictions About the End of the World* (Downers Grove: InterVarsity, 1995) and Richard Kyle, *The Last Days are Here Again: A History of the End Times* (Grand Rapids: Baker, 1998).

5. See, for example, the systematic theology of Charles Hodge (*Systematic Theology*, 3 vols., Grand Rapids: Eerdmans, 1940, 3:713–880). See also the excellent book by Anthony Hoekema, *The Bible and the Future* (Grand Rapids: Eerdmans, 1979).

6. In contrast to its popularity among the laity and general reader, the thought that the Bible contains clearly understood predictions about the end times is widely rejected by biblical scholars. The rejection may well be traced to two sources: (1) the antisupernaturalistic worldview of many biblical scholars (i.e., there is no God or at least not a God involved with the world, how therefore can the Bible contain words from him that address current world conditions?); and (2) the widely held suspicion, even among those who are theologically conservative, that those who have promoted a Lindsey–like framework for biblical eschatology have frequently misused or misinterpreted Scripture in making their case.

Chapter 1

1. *Darwin's Black Box: The Biochemical Challenge to Evolution* (New York: Free Press, 1996). See also Michael Denton, *Evolution: A Theory in Crisis* (Bethesda: Adler & Adler,

1985); *The Creation Hypothesis: Scientific Evidence for an Intelligent Designer* (ed. J. P. More-land; Downers Grove: InterVarsity, 1994); and *Mere Creation: Science, Faith & Intelligent Design* (ed. William A. Dembski; Downers Grove: InterVarsity, 1998). For an especially read-able treatment of the problem with naturalism, see Phillip E. Johnson, *Reason in the Balance: The Case against Naturalism in Science, Law, and Education* (Downers Grove: InterVarsity, 1995).

2. *Darwin's Black Box*, 39.

3. "Science and Design," *First Things* 86 (October 1998): 23.

4. Ibid.

5. E.g., Gordon D. Fee and Douglas Stuart, *How to Read the Bible for All Its Worth: A Guide to Understanding the Bible* (2nd ed.; Grand Rapids: Zondervan, 1993); E. D. Hirsch Jr., *Valid-ity in Interpretation* (Yale: University Press, 1967); Grant Osborne, *The Hermeneutical Spiral: A Comprehensive Introduction to Biblical Interpretation* (Downers Grove: InterVarsity, 1992).

6. Not everyone uses the same terminology. The labels I use are my own.

7. If the objection is raised that the "son" in Isaiah 8 is not named Immanuel, the same point could be made about Jesus—he is named Jesus!

8. This kind of fulfillment raises a thorny issue: What did the author have in mind when writing the prophecy? Did Isaiah think there would be more than one fulfillment of his prophecy, and could he have imagined that its second fulfillment would involve a literal vir-gin bearing a child? Isaiah is not here to ask, but the biblical theory of inspiration involves two authors—the human and the divine (see 2 Pet. 1:20–21 and 2 Tim. 3:16–17). If we can-not know all that a human author might have in mind when he/she writes, how much less can we fathom all that God might have had in mind when he inspired the biblical writers to convey his words?

9. A different kind of patterned fulfillment is found in Matthew 2:13–15. There we learn that Joseph and Mary took Jesus to Egypt to protect him from King Herod the Great, who had ordered the murder of young boys in hopes of eradicating anyone who might threaten his rule (Matt. 2:16–18). While in Egypt, Jesus' parents learned of Herod's death and decided to return to Palestine. According to Matthew, they were in Egypt "until the death of Herod, that what was spoken by the Lord through the prophet might be fulfilled, saying, 'Out of Egypt did I call My Son' " (Matt. 2:15). At first glance it looks as though Matthew is citing an Old Testament prediction about God's Messiah. But a closer look reveals that the Old Testa-ment quotation is taken from the prophet Hosea, who refers clearly not to a particular indi-vidual but to the nation of Israel (Hos. 11:1, alluding to Exod. 4:21–22). Furthermore, there is no evidence to suggest that Hosea or his audience would have considered his remarks to be predictive. On the contrary, they looked backward to the Exodus accomplished in Moses' day, some five hundred years before Hosea lived. How then, can Matthew introduce Hosea's words by saying "that what was spoken by the Lord through the prophet might be fulfilled"? Apparently, Matthew's idea of "fulfillment" need not involve prediction as such. In this instance, at least, it refers to the repetition of a pattern of action or behavior. For Matthew the correspondences between certain features of the history of Israel and the life of Jesus point to the fact that just as God was active in the life of Israel, so he was involved in the life of Jesus of Nazareth.

10. Though they knew the prophetic Scriptures, and undoubtedly in some sense believed them, the scribes were apparently not motivated to act on what they understood.

11. Professor Bruce Waltke pointed out to me that the story also shows that although the star in the east brought the magi to Jerusalem, they could not have located Jesus without the Scriptures. For Matthew, therefore, first place is given to the role of the Scriptures in pointing to Jesus in a special and specific way.

12. Recent works on the formation of a biblical worldview emphasize this point. See, for example, Brian J. Walsh and J. Richard Middleton, *The Transforming Vision: Shaping a Christian World View* (Downers Grove: InterVarsity, 1984).

13. Among recent works, see Norman L. Geisler, *Philosophy of Religion* (Grand Rapids: Zondervan, 1974) and J. P. Moreland, *Scaling the Secular City: A Defense of Christianity* (Grand Rapids: Baker, 1987).

14. For example, if a person believes truth and virtue are relative, not absolute, he or she is hard-pressed to make a rational case against the exploitation of children. This does not mean that the person would favor something so awful, only that when push comes to shove he will have to acknowledge that child exploitation is something he doesn't personally favor and hopes that others take the same view. He cannot say, "It is wrong; it is immoral," because in so doing he appeals to some absolute standard of morality.

15. For penetrating critiques of various modern philosophies, including Postmodernism and New Age religions, see J. P. Moreland, *Scaling the Secular City*, and Donald A. Carson, *The Gagging of God: Christianity Confronts Pluralism* (Grand Rapids: Zondervan, 1996).

16. Liberal-critical scholars typically deny the Mosaic authorship of Genesis-Deuteronomy; conservative-critical scholars generally affirm it. For good discussions, see Raymond B. Dillard and Tremper Longman III, *An Introduction to the Old Testament* (Grand Rapids: Zondervan, 1994); Andrew E. Hill and John H. Walton, *A Survey of the Old Testament* (Grand Rapids: Zondervan, 1991); and Victor P. Hamilton, *The Book of Genesis, Chapters 1–17* (New International Commentary on the Old Testament; Grand Rapids: Eerdmans, 1990).

17. For these, see Foster R. McCurley, *Ancient Myths and Biblical Faith: Scriptural Transformations* (Philadelphia: Fortress, 1983), 18–25.

18. See Kenneth A. Mathews, *Genesis 1:1–11:26* (New American Commentary 1A; Nashville: Broadman and Holman, 1996), 160. Over the years readers have been puzzled about who the "us" in the account might refer to, since up to this point God has been doing the creating. The best explanation seems to be that already in the first chapter of the Bible we find a hint that there is more than one person in the Godhead. God is one, yet somehow God is at the same time "us." The Old Testament does not present a doctrine of the Trinity such as we find in the New Testament, where God the father, God the Son, and God the Holy Spirit are referred to as equally divine persons. Yet even in the Old Testament we find now and again suggestions that God exists in more than one person. For example, the Spirit of God is frequently mentioned (Gen. 1:2; Num. 24:2; 1 Sam. 11:6; 19:20; Job 33:4) as is the enigmatic "angel of the Lord" (Gen. 16:10; Exod. 3:2; Num. 22:32; Ps. 34:7; Zech. 3:1); Daniel's "One like a Son of Man" might also be seen to have divine status (Dan. 7:13–14). For more on this doctrine, see Wayne Grudem, *Systematic Theology: An Introduction to Biblical Doctrine* (Grand Rapids: Zondervan, 1994), 226–57.

19. D. J. A. Clines, "The Image of God in Man," *Tyndale Bulletin* 19 (1968): 70–90.

20. Ibid., 87.

21. Ibid., 86.

22. Note the repetition of the phrase "and he died" at Genesis 5:5, 8, 11, 14, 17, 20, 27, 31. This points to the veracity of God's original warning (2:17).

23. Professor Ken Mathews notes that the only other use of the phrase translated "its desire is for you" in Hebrew Scripture occurs in Genesis 4:7, where the Lord says to Cain, "And if you do not do well, sin is crouching at the door; and its desire is for you, but you must master it." Sin is personified as something which seeks to dominate Cain; he must refuse temptation and instead master it. If this same meaning for "its desire is for you" obtains in 3:16, it means the woman will seek to master or dominate the man. On this interpretation of the phrase "your desire will be for him" (וְאֶל־אִישֵׁךְ תְּשׁוּקָתֵךְ), see Mathews, *Genesis 1:1–11:26*, 48–52.

24. Throughout the ages some Christians have emphasized the other worldly character of the Christian faith, and to a certain extent this is understandable. After all, Jesus died and went to heaven; he said he would prepare a place for us there; and Paul said that when believers die they go to be with the Lord (Acts 1:11; John 14:2; Phil. 1:21–23). But this is only part of the story.

Chapter 2

1. For more on this, see John Stott, *The Cross of Christ* (Liecester: InterVarsity Press, 1986), 63–84, 111–32; also of interest, C. F. D. Moule, *The Origin of Christology* (Cambridge: Cambridge University Press, 1977), 107–26.

2. Almost everyone, and especially conservative Christians, ought to say "not necessarily." The "not" part of the response stems from principles of interpretation which state, in part, that the aim of interpretation is first of all to discover how the original readers of a given piece of literature would have understood it. Accordingly, a text must be interpreted against the background of its original culture and its original aim or intent. In this respect, it is obvious that we moderns cannot assume that when we read an ancient text it automatically means to us what it would have meant to its original audience. On the other hand (and here I come to the "necessarily" part of "not necessarily"), since we believe that the God who inspired the Old Testament also inspired the New, we must not dismiss the interpretations of the Old given by the writers of the New. Without ignoring what the New Testament says, in looking at the Old Testament we ought to strive first of all to understand it on its own terms.

3. Gordon J. Wenham notes, "Doubtless it is also deliberate that the promises to Abram fall into seven clauses in vv. 2–3, just as do the promises to Isaac and Jacob in 26:3–4; 27:28–29" *Genesis 1–15*, Word Biblical Commentary 1 (Waco: Word, 1987), 270).

4. On the meaning of "blessing," see Allen P. Ross, *Creation and Blessing: A Guide to the Study and Exposition of Genesis* (Grand Rapids: Baker, 1988).

5. On this see M. Weinfeld, "The Covenant of Grant in the Old Testament and the Ancient Near East," *Journal of the American Oriental Society* 90 (1970): 184–203, and by the same author, "בְּרִית," in *Theological Dictionary of the Old Testament: Volume 1* (eds. G. Johannes Botterweck and Helmer Ringgren; rev. ed.; Grand Rapids: Eerdmans, 1977), 270–72. The whole article, pp. 253–79, is worth reading.

6. This is one of the salient points made by Ronald W. Pierce in "Covenant Conditionality and a Future for Israel," *Journal of the Evangelical Theological Society* 37/1 (1994): 27–38.

7. Ezekiel 20 offers a good summary of Israel's history in the words of one prophet (see also the prayers found in Dan. 9:4–19 and Ezra 9:6–15).

8. Walther Eichrodt, *Theology of the Old Testament* (2 vols., Old Testament Library; Philadelphia: Westminster, 1961), 1:499.

9. Georges Pidoux, *Le dieux qui vient* (Neuchatel, 1947), 7, cited in George Beasley–Murray, *Jesus and the Kingdom of God* (Grand Rapids: Eerdmans, 1986), 3.

10. George Beasley–Murray, *Jesus and the Kingdom of God*, 24.

11. The "host of heaven" here being a reference to other gods (see John N. Oswalt, *The Book of Isaiah: Chapters 1–39* [New International Commentary on the Old Testament; Grand Rapids: Eerdmans, 1986], 454–55).

12. Richard N. Longenecker, *The Christology of Early Jewish Christianity* (Grand Rapids: Baker, 1981), 63.

13. Donald Gowan, *Eschatology in the Old Testament* (Philadelphia: Fortress, 1986), 97.

14. The dates are taken from Harold Hoehner's "Between the Testaments," in *Expositor's Bible Commentary* (Grand Rapids: Zondervan, 1979), 1:179–94.

15. For more information and content of the Old Testament canon, see the detailed analysis by Roger Beckwith, *The Old Testament Canon of the New Testament Church and Its Background in Early Judaism* (Grand Rapids: Eerdmans, 1985) and the rather more accesible work by F. F. Bruce, *The Canon of Scripture* (Downers Grove: Intervarsity, 1988).

16. D. S. Russell, *The Method and Message of Jewish Apocalyptic* (Old Testament Library; Philadelphia: Westminster, 1964), 263. It must be noted that Russell counts Daniel among the apocalyptic writers.

17. Ibid., 267.

18. Ibid., 319.

19. In a recent article Kenneth Atkinson argues that the violent messiah depicted in the psalm "was fashioned predominantly as a righteous counterpart to Herod the Great and subsequent Herodian rulers, whom he was expected to overthrow before inaugurating an eternal reign of peace" ("On the Herodian Origin of Militant Davidic Messianism at Qumran: New Light from *Psalm of Solomon* 17," *Journal of Biblical Literature* 118/3 [1999]: 435).

20. Some commentators think the predictions were not genuine in that they were actually made *after* events occurred; very often, however, this position is taken because of an *a priori* assumption that miraculous prediction of the future is impossible rather than on clear evidence that event preceded prediction.

Chapter 3

1. The Old Testament never uses the phrase "kingdom of God," either in Hebrew (the original language of the Old Testament) or in the Septuagint (an early Greek translation of the Hebrew Scriptures). For the sake of convenience I use the label "Septuagint" to refer to the Greek Old Testament as edited by Alfred Rahlfs. For more on the complex history of the text of the Greek Old Testament, see Ernst Würthwein, *The Text of the Old Testament* (Grand Rapids: Eerdmans, 1979), 49–73.

2. This is so because the Septuagint was the version of the Old Testament favored by most New Testament writers (see Everett Ferguson, *Backgrounds of Early Christianity* [2nd ed., Grand Rapids: Eerdmans, 1993], 407–10).

3. For more information on the word, see *Theological Dictionary of the New Testament* (ed. G. Kittel; trans. by Geoffrey W. Bromiley; Grand Rapids: Eerdmans, 1965), 3:623–25.

4. See *A Greek Grammar of the New Testament and Other Early Christian Literature* (F. Blass, A. Debrunner, Robert W. Funk; Chicago: University of Chicago Press, 1961),

§§175–76; Daniel B. Wallace, *Greek Grammar Beyond the Basics. An Exegetical Syntax of the New Testament* (Grand Rapids: Zondervan, 1996), 573ff.

5. See Frank Thielman, "Law and Liberty in the Ethics of Paul," *Ex Auditu* 11 (1995): 63–75.

6. For example, Luke has meticulously labored to strengthen the conflict motif through his choice of terms in Luke 8:26–39. On this, see Appendix A.

7. *Resurrection and the New Testament* (Studies in Biblical Theology, second series 12; London: SCM, 1970), 1.

8. See the material cited in note 2 in chapter 1 for further bibliography on the historicity of Jesus' resurrection.

9. For a contemporary exploration of the theme, see Jack Deere, *Surprised by the Power of the Spirit: Discovering How God Speaks and Heals Today* (Grand Rapids: Zondervan, 1993).

10. Those familiar with scholarly discussions of the kingdom will easily recognize my indebtedness here to the work of George Eldon Ladd (especially *The Presence of the Future* [Grand Rapids: Eerdmans, 1974]).

11. For a brief but excellent treatment of the issue, see the article entitled "Mystery," by Frank Thielman in *Evangelical Dictionary of Biblical Theology* (ed. Walter A. Elwell; Grand Rapids: Baker, 1996), 546–47.

Chapter 4

1. For a good exposition of the passage, see Douglas Stuart, *Hosea–Jonah* (Word Biblical Commentary 31; Waco: Word, 1987), 396–400; on the relative importance of differences between the Hebrew and Greek versions of Amos's text here, see F.F. Bruce, *The Book of Acts* (New International Commentary on the New Testament; Grand Rapids: Eerdmans, 1983[2]), 310.

2. The following summary is drawn from the *Encylopedia Britannica* CD, 1997 Edition and from David Dolan's excellent book, *Israel at the Crossroads: Fifty Years and Counting* (Grand Rapids: Revell, 1998).

3. How information for the attack was gathered and used is noted in Gordon Thomas's fascinating book, *Gideon's Spies: The Secret History of the Mossad* (New York: St. Martin's Press, 1999), esp. 44–48.

4. Most of this was located in Sinai and later returned to the Egyptians under the 1979–80 Camp David Accords.

5. For an in-depth but readable analysis of the recent history of the Middle East, see Dolan, *Israel at the Crossroads*.

6. *Wall Street Journal Almanac 1998* (New York: Ballantine Books, 1998), 501–608.

7. Former Israeli Prime Minister Benjamin Netanyahu noted that "with one or two exceptions, mostly relating to Israel, all wars in history generally break out from a condition of peace and even contractual peace. So the way to prevent future wars is not merely by signing peace treaties" (address to the Fifth International Conference of Jewish Ministers and Members of Parliament; January 8, 1998).

8. "Egypt and Syria warn Israel of war risk," *The Times of London* (Internet edition), March 20, 1997.

9. "Syrian nerve gas raises war fears," *The Times of London* (Internet edition), April 30, 1997.

10. For example, the Israeli Bureau of Statistics estimates there were 172,800 Christians in Israel as of 1998—but these are sharply distinguished from the Jewish population (from the Web Page of the Israeli Bureau of Statistics: www.cbs.gov.il/shnaton/st02–01.gif).

11. From the web page of the Messianic Jewish Alliance of America, "Freedom Report No. 53, October 8, 1998."

12. "Proposed Israeli Acts 'will outlaw New Testament,'" *The Times of London* (Internet edition), May 15, 1997.

13. He further argues, in Romans 9:24–26 that God even calls (chooses) Gentiles for salvation.

14. For more on this, consult the recent monograph by G. Harvey, *The True Israel: Uses of the Names Jew, Hebrew and Israel in Ancient Jewish and Early Christian Literature* (Arbeiten zur Geschichte des antiken Judentums und des Urchristentums 35; Leiden: Brill, 1996) and the important earlier work by Peter Richardson, *Israel in the Apostolic Church* (Society for New Testament Studies Monograph Series 10; Cambridge: Cambridge University Press, 1969).

15. Paul wrote Galatians in response to the false teachers, the "Judaizers," who were influencing the church in Galatia. Paul argued that to return to life under Jewish law as advocated by the Judaizers would be fundamentally at odds with the gospel (Gal. 1:6–7; 3:1–5; 5:1–6). Galatians 6:16 comes at the conclusion of this polemical book. In Galatians 6:11–16 Paul reiterated that neither circumcision (being a Jew) nor uncircumcision (not being a Jew) was most important. What mattered most was being a "new creation" (v. 15). Then he added, in a benedictory remark, "And as many as walk by this standard, peace be upon them and mercy also (be) upon the Israel of God" (καὶ ὅσοι τῷ κανόνι τούτῳ στοιχήσουσιν, εἰρήνη ἐπ' αὐτοὺς καὶ ἔλεος καὶ ἐπὶ τὸν Ἰσραὴλ τοῦ θεοῦ.). As Ernest De Witt Burton wrote years ago in his classic critical commentary on Galatians, "There is no instance of his [Paul] using Ἰσραήλ except of the Jewish nation or a part thereof. These facts favour the interpretation of the expression as applying not to the Christian community, but to Jews; yet, in view of τοῦ θεοῦ, not to the whole Jewish nation, but to the pious Israel, the remnant according to the election of grace." (International Critical Commentary; *A Critical and Exegetical Commentary on the Epistle to the Galatians;* Edinburgh: T & T Clark, reprint 1959; 358).

16. On this, see Richardson, *Israel in the Apostolic Church.*

17. But it may be objected, "Why would Paul, in addressing the largely Gentile church at Corinth, refer to the Jews of Moses' day as 'our fathers' (1 Cor. 10:1)? Because for Paul Gentile believers were descendants of Abraham (Gal. 3); hence, they were spiritually related to Jewish forebears. But again, the identification is analogical rather than direct.

18. For more on this, see the useful contribution by L. I. Levine in *The Anchor Bible Dictionary*: Volume 3 H–J (ed. David Noel Freedman; New York: Doubleday, 1992), 839–44.

19. For more details on developments between A.D. 70 and 135, see E. Schürer, *The history of the Jewish people in the age of Jesus Christ* (rev. & ed. by G. Vermes, F. Millar, M. Black; Edinburgh: T & T Clark, 1973), 1:534–57.

20. It has been thought by some that the exile of Jews in 722 B.C. and 586 B.C. fulfilled the Deuteronomistic threat of exile, a threat which remained in force until the coming of Jesus, an event which marked the beginning of new Israel (= the church) and the fulfillment of various prophecies of Isaiah, Jeremiah, and Ezekiel. If this is so, why did Jesus speak of a future restoration for Israel (a term used, in a passage we shall explore next chapter, to refer to eth-

nic Israel or some portion thereof)? If the church is restored Israel, how could Peter (Acts 3:19–21) and Paul (Rom. 11:25–29) look to a future restoration that is ethnically Jewish?

21. *Night* (New York: Bantam Books, 1960), 32.

Chapter 5

1. Pate and Haines, *Doomsday Delusions*, 20–21, 112–33.

2. Ibid., 11.

3. See especially Paul Marshall's *Their Blood Cries Out: The Worldwide Tragedy of Modern Christians Who Are Dying for Their Faith* (with Lela Gilbert; Dallas: Word, 1997); on a related note, see also "U.S. Cites Foreign Foes of Christianity: China, Saudi Arabia Top State Department List," *Washington Post*, July 23, 1997, A18. For the role of religion in recent wars and conflicts, see *Religion, the Missing Dimension of Statecraft* (eds. Douglas Johnston and Cynthia Sampson; Oxford: Oxford University Press, 1994).

4. "Signs of the End?" *The Birmingham News*, May 26, 1996, 1A.

5. In 1992 there were twenty–three major quakes ("major" = above 7.0 on the Richter scale); in 1993 the number fell to sixteen, then to fourteen in 1994; in 1995 the number went up to twenty-two (ibid.).

6. "Chances of Big Bay Area Quake in Next 30 Years is 70%, Study Says," *Los Angeles Times* (Internet edition), October 15, 1999.

7. There were 350 in 1931, more than 4,000 in 1999.

8. In the early 1990s hopes were raised that a new class of drugs, the protease inhibitors, would offer AIDS sufferers effective treatment on a large scale. Unfortunately, by the late 1990s reports began to indicate that drug-resistant strains of HIV were appearing on a wider scale ("Drug-Resistant HIV Becomes More Widespread," *Wall Street Journal*, February 5, 1999, B5).

9. *Wall Street Journal Almanac 1998*, p. 758. Over half of these are in sub-Saharan Africa (ibid.).

10. On this, see *World Health Organisation Fact Sheet* N164, June 1997. Also, "Global Surveillance and Control of Hepatitis C," Report of a WHO Consultation organized with the Viral Hepatitis Prevention Board, *Journal of Viral Hepatitis* 6/1 (1999): 35–48.

11. For an excellent yet relatively brief treatment of this issue, see Laurie Garrett, "The Return of Infectious Disease," *Foreign Affairs* 75/1 (1996): 66–79.

12. "Drug Makers Go All Out to Squash 'Superbugs,' " *Wall Street Journal*, June 25, 1996, B1; see also "Pneumonic Plague Does Not Respect International Borders," *Wall Street Journal*, October 3, 1994; and "US Prepares to tackle 'super–killer' germ," *The Times of London* (Internet edition), June 10, 1997.

13. This is not to suggest that medicine alone is responsible for this progress. World population grew at a rate of one percent per year from A.D. 1000–1750. The mortality rate was high, the fertility rate marginally higher. Improvements in transport and communications began to mitigate the effects of local crop failures, and advances in sanitation and health began to bring down the mortality rate (*Encylopedia Britannica* CD, 1997 Edition, s.v. "Population. Trends in World Population"). For perspective, see Theodore Dalrymple, "Taking Good Health for Granted," *Wall Street Journal*, March 31, 1999, A22; also "Disease by Disease: A look at some of the advances scientists expect to make against specific ailments in the decades ahead," *Wall Street Journal*, R4,9, October 18, 1999.

14. To take but one example, in the United States in 1950 there were about eighty cases of whooping cough per 100,000 people; in 1995 that number had shrunk to about two per 100,000 (*Wall Street Journal Almanac 1998*).

15. HIV is transmitted through tainted blood, as is HCV. Recent scientific breakthroughs in blood screening mean that few people contract the illnesses through blood transfusions. For the most part, HIV is transmitted in the United States through homosexual activity, shared needle use among intravenous drug users, and heterosexual sex involving bisexual partners. In Africa promiscuous heterosexual sex is responsible for most infections. The infection could be largely eradicated through abstinence and monogamous sexual relationships.

16. *Encyclopedia Britannica* CD, 1997 Edition, s.v. "Black Death."

17. Paul R. Ehrlich, *The Stork and the Plow: the Equity Answer to the Human Dilemma* (New York: Putnam, 1995).

18. For more on the subject, see Peter Garnsey, *Famine and Food Supply in the Graeco–Roman World: Responses to Risk and Crisis* (Cambridge: Cambridge University Press, 1988).

19. *Encyclopedia Britannica* CD, 1997 Edition, s.v. "Major Historical Famines."

20. "The UN vs. Christianity?" *World* (Internet edition), August 1, 1998; also "The tin-cup tyranny," *World* (Internet edition), December 6, 1997.

21. Joel was probably referring either to a forthcoming Assyrian or Babylonian invasion (see Stuart, *Hosea–Jonah*, 249–50).

22. Suetonius *Claudius*, 46.

23. "Global Warming Not to Blame for Melting of Huge Ice Sheet," *New York Times* (Internet edition), October 16, 1999; see also "World Disasters Report 1999," by the International Federation of Red Cross and Red Crescent Societies.

24. See "Responding to the Potential Threat of a Near-Earth-Object Impact," American Institute of Aeronautics and Astronautics Position Paper, 1995.

25. E.g., J. Dwight Pentecost, *Will Man Survive? Prophecy You Can Understand* (Chicago: Moody, 1971), 133.

26. For a handy guide to wars in history, see George C. Kohn, *Dictionary of Wars* (Garden City: Anchor/Doubleday, 1986).

27. Based on *Encyclopedia Britannica* CD, 1997 Edition, s.v. "Non-proliferation of Nuclear Weapons, Treaty on the."

28. "Russia, China aid Iran's missile program," *Washington Times* (Internet edition), September 10, 1997; "China a major influence in expanding the nuclear club," *Washington Times* (Internet edition), May 29, 1998.

29. "Britain at centre of Iran bomb web," *Sunday Times of London* (Internet edition), January 19, 1998; "CIA analyst says U.S. winked at cheating," *Washington Times* (Internet edition), June 12, 1998.

30. The use of chemical and biological weapons was banned in the 1925 Geneva Protocol; their development, production, and stockpiling were outlawed by the 1972 Biological Weapons Convention, which also called for the destruction of previously existing weapons (*Encyclopedia Britannica* CD, 1997 edition, s.v. "The Technology of War: Biological Warfare"). Chemical weapons have been used rarely since World War I, while biological weapons have never been used in war (*Encyclopedia Britannica* CD, 1997 Edition, s.v. "The Technology of War: Modern Weapons and Weapon Systems: chemical and biological weapons: Chemical

warfare: history of use"). However, evidence suggests that biological agents were used in human experiments by Iraqi President Saddam Hussein ("Saddam tested anthrax on human guinea pigs," *Sunday Times of London* [Internet edition], January 19, 1998).

31. For a rich source of information on these, see George A. Mather and Larry A. Nichols, *Dictionary of Cults, Sects, Religions and the Occult* (Grand Rapids: Zondervan, 1993).

32. Kyle chronicles the history of many of these figures in *The Last Days Are Here Again.*

33. E.g., Hal Lindsey, *Planet Earth—2000 A.D.* (Palos Verdes: Western Front, Ltd., 1994), 30–44.

34. See, for example, the balanced judgment of Carl F. H. Henry, *The Christian Mindset in a Secular Society: Promoting Evangelical Renewal & National Righteousness* (Portland: Multnomah, 1984); also his later work, *Twilight of a Great Civilization: The Drift Toward Neo-Paganism* (Westchester: Crossway Books, 1988).

Chapter 6

1. Many scholars think Acts, and probably Luke, were written after the destruction of Jerusalem in A.D. 70. However, I see no compelling reason to think Luke-Acts was written so late. Indeed, two lines of argument point in the opposite direction. The first of these is Luke's well-known interest in Jerusalem. His story begins there (Luke 1:5ff.), several comments in Luke's central section remind the reader that Jesus is on the way there (9:51; 13:22; 18:31), it is the place of Jesus' passion, death, and resurrection (Luke 19–24) and the place from which the story of the church continues (Acts 1). Given his interest in Jerusalem, it would be more than a little puzzling were he not to mention its destruction if he knew of it. This is especially so given another important Lucan theme: Jesus as prophet. He is called a prophet (Luke 4:24; 7:16; 9:8, 19; 13:32–33; 24:19) and many of his actions are prophetic in character (e.g., the raising of the widow's son, 7:11–16, a parallel to the story of Elijah and the widow, 1 Kings 17:17ff.). Many of Jesus' observations about the future are fulfilled in the course of the narrative (for a detailed look at this, see B. C. Frein, "Narrative Predictions, Old Testament Prophecies and Luke's Sense of Fulfilment," *New Testament Studies* 40 [1994]: 22–37). If Luke knew that Jesus' predictions about the temple's destruction had been fulfilled, it would have furthered his argument that Jesus was from God to record them. Nonetheless, the point to be made in this section stands whether the date is early (pre-A.D. 70) or late (post-A.D. 70).

2. For an excellent book dealing with how the Gospels were first published and circulated, and the general circulation they would have enjoyed, see *The Gospels for All Christians: Rethinking the Gospel Audiences* (ed. Richard Bauckham; Grand Rapids: Eerdmans, 1998).

3. Biblical scholars have increasingly recognized the extent to which Luke seems to emphasize a future for Israel. For example, the theme is explored by Eric Franklin, *Christ the Lord: A Study in the Purpose and Theology of Luke–Acts* (London: SPCK, 1975), 77–115 and A. W. Wainwright, "Luke and the Restoration of the Kingdom to Israel," *Expository Times* 89 (1977–78): 76–79.

4. The Greek verb is ἀποκαθίστημι (= ἀποκαταίστημι).

5. E.g., *Antiquities* 11 §2.

6. In its only other appearance in Luke–Acts, the word refers to the healing of the man with the withered hand (Luke 6:10; the hand is "restored"). Elsewhere in the New Testament the verb refers to the effects of a miraculous healing at Matthew 12:13, Mark 3:5 (these parallel the Lucan account), and Mark 8:25. In two places it is used with reference to the antic-

ipated ministry of the prophet Elijah: He will come and "restore" all things (Mark 9:12; Matt. 17:11).

7. On any other view one is hard-pressed to explain Jesus' failure to correct the disciples' misunderstanding and the recurrence of the theme at Acts 3:19–21.

8. *The Narrative Unity of Luke–Acts: A Literary Interpretation.* Volume 2: *The Acts of the Apostles* (Minneapolis: Fortress, 1990), 15.

9. On the relationship of "seasons of refreshing" (v. 20) to "times of restoration" (v. 21), compare H. A. W. Meyer (*Critical and Exegetical Handbook to the Acts of the Apostles* [4th ed., New York: Funk and Wagnells, 1883; 81–84] and C. K. Barrett (*A Critical and Exegetical Commentary on the Acts of the Apostles* [2 vols., International Critical Commentary; Edinburgh: T & T Clark, 1994; 205–07) to Albrecht Oepke (*Theological Dictionary of the New Testament,* 1:390) and Ernst Haenchen (*The Acts of the Apostles,* Philadelphia: Westminster, 1971; 208).

10. Meyer, *The Acts of the Apostles,* 81–82; Haenchen, *The Acts of the Apostles,* 208.

11. The social, political, and religious elite of the city do not go out to welcome Jesus as would have been customary for them to do at the approach of a king in the ancient world (they are present in Jerusalem as can been seen from 19:47). When Luke's account of Jesus' entry is viewed against the background of Graeco-Roman celebratory welcomes, it becomes obvious that Jerusalem's "response" to Jesus amounts to an appalling insult. This, in turn, forms the rationale for Jesus' subsequent pronouncement of impending judgment (19:41–44). For a fuller exploration of this theme, see Brent Kinman, *Jesus' Entry into Jerusalem: In the Context of Lukan Theology and the Politics of His Day* (Arbeiten zur Geschichte des antiken Judentums und Urchristentums 28; Leiden: Brill, 1995); also "Parousia, Jesus' 'A–triumphal' Entry, and the Fate of Jerusalem (Luke 19:28–44)," *Journal of Biblical Literature* 118/2 (1999): 279–94.

12. Jerusalem will not see Jesus until it repents—the very thing that Peter preached to the crowds at Acts 3:19–21!

13. Luke 21 is devoted to Jesus' teaching about the destruction of the temple and the signs preceding his return. In particular, Luke 21:20–24 envisions great hardship for the Jews and the people of Jerusalem. Ultimately, "they will fall by the edge of the sword, and will be led captive into all the nations" (v. 24). To what historical event did Jesus refer, and how did his words suggest a future for the nation?

The promised destruction of the temple occurred with the Roman victory of A.D. 70. At that time those in Jerusalem were killed and led captive to the nations—a Diaspora that lasted almost two thousand years.

However, two features of the passage hint at a future for Israel. The argument for this is a little complex, so I beg the reader's indulgence. First, the promised "trampling" of Jerusalem would last only "until the times of the Gentiles be fulfilled" (21:24b). What are the "times of the Gentiles"? The "trampling" of Jerusalem is a picture of foreign domination. It was initiated by the Roman victory in A.D. 70. The language of verse 24 seems to suggest that once these "times are fulfilled" Jewish sovereignty over the city will return. How is this return of Jewish sovereignty suggested? The suggestion is made through the grammatical construction that Luke used.

1. Jerusalem *will be trampled under foot* (indicative mood verb [a verb in the indicative mood means the action presented as real or certain form the point of view of the writer or speaker, see Wallace, *Greek Grammar Beyond the Basics,* 448]) until (*achri*)

2. The times of the Gentiles *be fulfilled* (subjunctive mood verb [A verb in the subjunctive mood means the action is presented as uncertain but probable fo the point of view of the writer or speaker, see Wallace, 448).

This construction implies that the situation or condition described by the first verb—the one in the indicative mood—lasts only until the situation or condition mentioned by the second verb—the one in the subjunctive mood—occurs. In other words, the conjunction "until" (*achri*) here implies that once the action of the second verb occurs, a reversal takes place. In the case of verse 24, the "trampling" ends once "the times of the Gentiles are fulfilled," after which a return to the predestruction situation will occur. Likewise, according to Luke 21:24, once the "times of the Gentiles" be fulfilled, Gentile domination will end. This understanding of the passage is consonant with Luke's earlier (and only other) use of the "until" plus subjuctive mood verb construction. In Luke 1:20, the angel Gabriel said that as judgment on his unbelief, Zacharias would be made dumb. Futher, his inablility to speak would continue "until . . . . these things take place." In the course of Luke's narrative, once John is born and named (i.e., "these things" take place) Zacharias is again able to speak (cf. Luke 1:64–79); that is, a return to the pre-judgment situation occurs. In his fine book Hans K. La Rondelle notes that the word ἄχρι need not imply the reversal just described (*The Israel of God in Prophecy: Principles of Prophetic Interpretation;* Berrien Springs: Andrews University Press, 1982; 167). However, his explanation will not do in the present context, for here we have the clear precedent of Luke 1:20 to guide our interpretation. The grammatical construction of verse 24, with its implicit reversal of the situation, hints at a future for Israel.

A second element of the account to suggest a future for Israel relates to the phrase "led captive into all the nations" (Luke 21:24). This phrase alludes to Deuteronomy 28:64. That section of Deuteronomy contains the curses the nation would face if it should turn away from the Lord. It is followed by a section which speaks of the end of the curses and the restoration of the nation (Deut. 30:1–5). If the Lucan passage first echoes the language of judgment found in Deuteronomy, then places a limit on the outpouring of judgment ("the fulfillment of the times of the Gentiles"), it could be inferred that the end of the judgment in Luke is the same as that found in Deuteronomy 30:1–5—that is, the restoration of the nation after captivity. If the language of the account does not *clearly* point to a future for national Israel, it certainly *allows* for one. See also, for example, my "Debtor's Prison and the Future of Israel (Luke 12:57–59)," *Journal of the Evangelical Theological Society* 42/3 (1999): 411–25.

14. Alongside our investigation into the meaning of "Israel" (chapter 4), context confirms that ethnic Israel is here in view (see Thomas R. Schreiner, *Romans* [Baker Exegetical Commentary on the New Testament 6; Grand Rapids: Baker, 1998], 614–15).

15. The word appears fourteen times in Paul's letters. Ten of those times it is used as a preposition with a genitive case noun or pronoun (Rom. 1:13; 5:13; 2 Cor. 3:14; 10:13, 14; Gal. 4:2; Phil. 1:5, 6) and, consequently, these uses are not relevant to the present discussion. In four passages the word appears as a conjunction before a verb in the subjunctive mood (1 Cor. 11:26; 15:25; Gal. 3:19 and the verse under consideration). In 1 Corinthians 11:26 we read that the Lord's Supper serves to proclaim the Lord's death "until he returns." After he comes, the supper will no longer function in that way. Similarly, in 1 Corinthians 15:25 Christ will reign "until he has put all his enemies under his feet" (NIV). When this is complete, he himself will subject himself to God (v. 28). Finally, in Galatians 3:19 Paul said that the law came as mediator "until the seed should come." Christ is that seed and hence the

mediator is no longer needed (Gal. 3:25; as Paul said plainly in another place, "[We] are not under Law" [Rom. 6:14, 15].

16. Schreiner, *Romans*, 617.

17. C. E. B. Cranfield, *A Critical and Exegetical Commentary on the Epistle to the Romans* (International Critical Commentary; 2 vols.; Edinburgh: T & T Clark, 1979), 574.

18. For a good discussion of this, see Bruce W. Longenecker, "Different Answers to Different Issues: Israel, the Gentiles and Salvation History in Romans 9–11," *Journal for the Study of the New Testament* 36 (1989): 96–98; see also Cranfield, *Romans*, 576–77.

19. Some think the present Jewish state emerged not from the will of God but through the efforts of dedicated Zionists. There is some truth to this—and yet, it could almost as easily be argued that the restoration of Jerusalem under Nehemiah was motivated by King Artaxerxes's desire to help his cupbearer Nehemiah or because he wanted a loyal vassal to act as buffer between himself and potential rivals west of Palestine (Neh. 2:1–8). Whatever the motives might have been, in the end God's will was accomplished.

20. Remember, much of Romans 9 deals with examples of God sovereignly choosing people; if he did so in the past, he can certainly do so in the future!

21. See George Eldon Ladd, *A Commentary on the Revelation of John* (Grand Rapids: Eerdmans, 1972), 115–17; also the surveys of interpretive options in David E. Aune, *Revelation 6–16* (Word Biblical Commentary 52b; Nashville: Thomas Nelson, 1998), 440–45 and G. K. Beale, *The Book of Revelation* (New International Greek Testament Commentary; Grand Rapids: Eerdmans, 1999), 416–23.

22. On the discontinuity between Paul and the law, see Frank Thielman, *The Law and the New Testament: The Question of Continuity* (New York: Herder and Herder, 1999).

23. Finally, while Israel may have a crucial role in the future in relationship to Jesus' return, it is but one element in his return. Even if one takes the position that there will be a millennial kingdom immediately following his return in which all the ancient promises to Israel are realized, this still accounts for little (i.e., one thousand years) of a future that is eternal (an infinite number of years). So while Israel might have an important role in the future, it is in any event a limited role.

Chapter 7

1. For a survey and explanation of the different ways Revelation is interpreted, see *Four Views on the Book of Revelation* (ed. C. Marvin Pate; Grand Rapids: Zondervan, 1998). Each of the four views discussed in Pate's book is adhered to by a significant number of evangelical scholars; hence, no one view can lay claim to being the orthodox one. I take the view that in many places Revelation points to a future tribulation.

2. Revelation 1–3 deals with events contemporaneous with the apostle John's ministry, because these chapters contain letters to seven churches near Patmos, the place of his exile. In Revelation 4 John was transported to heaven and given a vision of the heavenly throne room, a vision which continues through Revelation 5. At Revelation 6:1 the scene of the narrative shifts from heaven's throne-room to earth. The change of scene signals a significant change of theme as well. The shift is marked by the lamb breaking the first of the seals of "the book," and it is with this event that the final chapter of history begins. The breaking of the seals brings disasters unprecedented in scope upon the earth and its inhabitants. After the sixth seal is broken, those on the earth try to hide, saying, "The great day of their wrath has come" (Rev. 6:17; also 7:14). The tense of the Greek verb translated "has come" in Revelation

6:17 suggests that "the great day of wrath," presumably initiated by the breaking of the first seal, has already arrived (the verb ἦλθεν is in the aorist tense; the context of the action described suggests that it should be translated as perfect [as do the NKJV, NASB, RSV, and NIV]). Robert Mounce notes that "in listing the various groups that seek refuge in that great day of wrath, it is not John's intention to cover the entire range of human society but to emphasize that those who might normally have reason to feel secure will be utterly undone." (*The Book of Revelation*; New International Commentary on the New Testament; rev. ed.; Grand Rapids: Eerdmans, 1998; 152).

3. One might infer from the phrase "last days" that a rather brief period of time is in view. However, this interpretation cannot be sustained when we remember that the writer of Hebrews referred to the several years between Jesus' life and the time of the composition of Hebrews as "these last days" (Heb. 1:2).

4. In Revelation 13:1ff. John described "the beast" (το θηριον). The beast is clearly satanic in that (1) it gets power from the dragon (i.e., Satan; v. 2); (2) it speaks and inspires others to speak blasphemies against God (vv. 5–6); (3) it wars against the saints (v. 7). Many commentators identify the beast as the Antichrist (e.g., John F. Walvoord, *The Revelation of Jesus Christ* [Chicago: Moody, 1966], 197ff.; Ladd, *Revelation*, 176ff). Are they correct?

Distinct from and prior to any discussion of who the beast might be is the question of what he is. Is the beast an individual person or something else? One view is that the beast represents the Roman Empire of John's day in that the use of Daniel by the author of Revelation favors understanding the beast as something other than an individual. How so? The use of the term *beast* is not unique to Revelation; Daniel used it to refer to various powers in the ancient world. For example, in Daniel 7 we are told of "four great beasts" who arise. With the benefit of hindsight we recognize that the first "beast" symbolizes the Babylonian Empire, the second the Media-Persian Empire, the third the Greek Empire, and the fourth the Roman Empire (these identifications are not beyond dispute; many scholars identify the empires as Babylon, Media, Persia, and Greece). Since we know that Revelation borrows heavily from Daniel and we further know that the beasts in Daniel symbolize empires, it is likely that the beast in Revelation 13 symbolizes an empire. Furthermore, in Revelation 13:1 the beast is said to have "ten horns and seven heads." If these "horns" and "heads" refer to governments or heads of state which lend support to the beast, it is not easy to think of the beast itself as an individual "having" governments or heads of states. Additionally, almost all the actions undertaken by the beast in Revelation 13 (e.g., making war on the saints, v. 7, and closely monitoring commerce, v. 17) could be done by a government rather than an individual. For more on this, consult Beale, *Revelation*.

What arguments exist to support the view that the beast is an individual? First, if we return to the imagery of Daniel, we discover that having a beast refer to an empire does not preclude a beast also referring to an individual. For example, the male goat in Daniel 8 is probably a reference to the empire of Alexander the Great, with Alexander himself alluded to as "the large horn" of the male goat (vv. 8, 21). In such visions individuals as well as empires can be referred to in veiled language. Second, certain features in the immediate context of Revelation 13 favor taking the beast as an individual. In Revelation 13:11 we read of the emergence of another beast (θηριον) which seems to be an individual: he performs miracles (the word for "signs" [σημεια] is also used by John on occasion to refer to the attesting miracles performed by Jesus [see John 2:11, 23; 3:2; 4:48, 54, etc.]) and he deceives people ("those who dwell on it [the earth]"). Furthermore, in Greek grammar the word *beast* is neuter as to gender (το θηριον). But when the question is asked in Revelation 13:4, "Who is like the beast?," the Greek word for "who?" is not neuter (τι) but masculine (τις). This tends to support the view that a person rather than a thing is in view, even though the word *beast* is, strictly speaking, grammatically neuter. This observation also holds true for Revelation 13:8, where the beast who is worshiped by all who dwell on the earth is referred to as "him" (αὐτον), a masculine rather than neuter Greek pronoun. It seems best to conclude, with Beale, that while the beast is an empire he is also personified by an individual—and vice versa (*The Book of Revelation*, 681ff.).

5. The word *Antichrist* (ἀντιχριστος) is used five times in the New Testament, all in the writings of John (1 John 2:18, 22; 4:3; 2 John 2:7). The standard dictionary of New Testament Greek notes, "The word is not found outside Christian circles" (*A Greek–English Lexicon of the New Testament and Other Early Christian Literature* [2nd ed.; Chicago: University of Chicago Press, 1957, 1979], s.v. "ἀντιχριστος," 76), so we may surmise that it was invented by early Christians. If we break the word down into its component parts, we see that it consists of the preposition ἀντι and the noun χριστος. The preposition is typically translated either as "in place of " or "for" (*A Greek–English Lexicon of the New Testament and Other Early Christian Literature*, s.v. "ἀντι," 73). In the context of the passages in which the word appears, it is clear that this Antichrist (or spirit of Antichrist) stands in opposition to the true Christ, Jesus of Nazareth. Thus, the Antichrist is a false messiah who comes in place of the true One.

6. James Everett Frame notes, "The two things [apostasy and Antichrist] are not identical, although they are apparently associated both essentially and chronologically," (*A Critical and Exegetical Commentary on the Epistles of St. Paul to the Thessalonians* [International Critical Commentary; New York: Charles Scribner's Sons, 1912], 252); Bruce agrees (*1 & 2 Thessalonians* [Word Biblical Commentary 45; Waco: Word, 1982], 167). On the connections between Matthew 24:15ff. and 2 Thessalonians 2:3ff., see G. Henry Waterman, "The Sources of Paul's Teaching on the 2nd Coming of Christ in 1 and 2 Thessalonians," *Journal of the Evangelical Theological Society* 18 (1975): 105–13.

7. As to the aspirations of the United Nations, its secretary general, Kofi Annan, recently averred that the UN should not hesitate to project military forces into sovereign nations when it deemed such an act necessary ("Two Concepts of Sovereignty," *The Economist*, 18 September, 1999). For a realistic assessment of the U.N., see the penetrating critique by Abba Eban, "The U.N. Idea Revisited," *Foreign Affairs* 74/5 (1995): 39–55, who notes the original visionaries "were inspired by a utopian vision" (ibid., 39). He does not, however, argue there is no future role for the U.N. For a different and decidedly more optimistic vision of its future, see Paul Kennedy and Bruce Russett, "Reforming the United Nations," *Foreign Affairs* 74/5 (1995): 56–71; they state, "The founders of the United Nations system were utter realists" (ibid., 56).

8. Indeed, the notion that church and state ought to be separate was rarely if ever held in the ancient world.

9. This Matthew passage, in turn, probably refers to the coming of the Roman leader Titus to Jerusalem in A.D. 70—an event which resulted in the destruction and desolation of the temple (see Appendix D). Titus was clearly a political figure, endowed with political and military authority.

10. Professor Beale has argued that Revelation 13 presents the kingdom of Satan in deliberate juxtaposition to the kingdom of Christ. Christ died, rose, and was given universal

authority. Similarly, the beast in Revelation 13 is slain, rises, and is given universal authority. The difference between them is that in the end, although Satan tries to mimic Jesus, Jesus defeats him completely. While emphasizing that Revelation 13 originally applied to Satan and corrupt political and religious entities (e.g., Rome and false religions, especially emperor worship), Beale does allow that there might be a future, more individualized application of the passage: "This analysis leaves open the possibility of an Antichrist who comes at the end of history and incarnates the devil in a greater way than anyone ever before" (*Revelation*, 691; his discussion of Revelation 13 is most enlightening; see pp. 680–730).

11. In its day the Roman Empire exerted its considerable power throughout the ancient world. After its demise in the fifth century A.D. no comparable empire emerged to replace it and, in fact, none has arisen since.

12. Christians can argue the benefits and liabilities of international political, military, and economic coalitions, but they should not be drawn into arguing that the existence of such coalitions and agreements necessarily constitutes fulfillment of biblical prophecy about the end.

13. It is true that certain political leaders have been able to maintain some level of public support in spite of legal difficulties. For example, in November 1923 Adolf Hitler engaged in an attempt to overthrow the Bavarian government—an attempt that was forcibly rebuffed and led to his conviction for treason and a subsequent term in prison; he was nevertheless elected to rule Germany and was eventually accepted by a great many Germans as the upholder of national virtue. In the United States in the early 1970s President Richard Nixon enjoyed the support of a substantial proportion of the citizenry in spite of the fact that credible evidence existed that he had engaged in the cover-up of crimes. In the 1990s President Bill Clinton had nearly unprecedented public approval despite widespread recognition that he had committed felonies while in office.

14. In this case, the Greek genitive should be understood as a "Genitive of Product" (See Wallace, *Greek Grammar Beyond the Basics*, 106–07).

15. The phrases "man of lawlessness" and "the son of destruction" (2 Thess. 2:3) may reflect Jewish idiom and mean "the man characterized by lawlessness" and "the man destined for destruction" (Bruce, *1 & 2 Thessalonians*, 167).

16. Paul does not use the Greek article here (ὁ) with "god," hence the phrase ἀποδεικνύντα ἑαυτὸν ὅτι ἔστιν θεός can easily be translated, "proclaiming himself to be a god" (v. 4).

17. *1 & 2 Thessalonians*, 168.

18. For example, in Romans 15:19 Paul referred to his own preaching ministry as having been confirmed by "signs and wonders, in the power of the Spirit" (ἐν δυναμει σημειον και τερατον). Similarly, he reminded the Corinthians that in his ministry at Corinth "the things that mark an apostle—signs (σημεια), wonders (τερας) and miracles (δυναμις)—were done among you with great perseverance" (2 Cor. 12:12 NIV).

19. Paul's description of the man of lawlessness seems to parallel John's description of "the beast" in Revelation 13. The beast of Revelation 13:1–8 is an individual who, like Paul's man of lawlessness, is energized by "the dragon" (= Satan) and is worshiped (Rev. 13:4). He makes war with the saints and blasphemes God (Rev. 13:5–7).

20. For more on this episode, see Schürer, *The History of the Jewish People in the Age of Jesus Christ*, 1:152–56.

21. For an excellent treatment of this, see E. Mary Smallwood, *The Jews under Roman Rule: From Pompey to Diocletian. A Study in Political Relations* (2nd ed.; Leiden: Brill, 1981), 21–27.

22. On this, see, in particular, the Jewish writers Josephus and Philo. Their language is similar to Paul's: Josephus said that Gaius seemingly thought himself a god (θεον ἑαυτον δοκειν, *Jewish War* 2 §184), while Philo noted that Gaius was not only saying but also thinking that he was a god (οἰομενος ἐναι θεος, *Embassy to Gaius* §162).

23. See *The Cambridge Ancient History*: Volume X. *The Augustan Empire 44 B.C.–A.D. 70* (Cambridge: Cambridge University Press, 1934/1985), 662f.

24. On this theme, see the still valuable contribution of Lily Ross Taylor, *The Divinity of the Roman Emperor* (American Philological Association Monograph Series 1; Middleton, Conn.: American Philological Association, 1931).

25. For years prior to this the Jews had compromised with imperial expectations by offering sacrifices to God on behalf of the emperor. This was a far cry from what Caligula wanted: his own statue in the temple and sacrifices offered to him (see Josephus, *Jewish War* 2 §195ff.).

26. On the date of 2 Thessalonians, see D. A. Carson, Douglas J. Moo, and Leon Morris, *An Introduction to the New Testament* (Grand Rapids: Zondervan, 1992), 347–48.

27. For a more detailed description of events, see Smallwood, *The Jews under Roman Rule*, 316–27.

28. For the link between his "coming" (παρουσια) and the second coming, see 1 Thessalonians 2:19; 3:13; 4:15; 1 Corinthians 15:23; Matthew 24:3, 27. On the meaning of "appearance," (ἐπιφανεια) note the comment of Frame: "In the N.T. ἐπιφανεια appears elsewhere only in the Pastorals, where the Christian παρουσια is supplanted by the Hellenistic ἐπιφανεια; in the LXX . . . , it is used of the manifestation of God from the sky" (*Epistles of St. Paul to the Thessalonians*, 266–67).

29. Although as we noted earlier, this could have been said of Caligula.

30. See Josephus, *Jewish War* 6 § 237ff. It is recognized that Josephus was hardly an impartial observer (see Steve Mason's *Josephus and the New Testament* [Peabody: Hendrickson, 1992], 35–82).

31. It is not helpful to look at Paul's use of "temple" without the modifier "of God," because it appears in isolation only twice, and in each instance is used metaphorically (1 Cor. 6:19; Eph. 2:21). Outside Paul the phrase "the temple of God" is used four times in the New Testament (Matt. 26:61; Rev. 3:12; 11:1, 19).

32. For a brief survey on the use and development of the concept, see Robert G. Zimmer, "The Temple of God," *Journal of the Evangelical Theology Society* 18 (1975): 41–46.

33. By early Gospel writers I refer to Matthew, Mark, and Luke. Most commentators think John was written later, ca. A.D. 90s (see Carson, Moo, and Morris, *An Introduction to the New Testament*, 166–68). It is true that according to John, Jesus referred to his body as a temple (John 2:13–22), but this would hardly explain Paul's remarks in 2 Thessalonians 2:4.

34. See especially the work of Leen Ritmyer, who locates the ancient Holy of Holies in the middle of the rock in the Dome of the Rock ("The Ark of the Covenant: Where It Stood in Solomon's Temple," *Biblical Archaeology Review* 22 [1996]).

35. These assurances regarding the temple are often understood as fulfillment of Daniel 9:27, where "the coming prince" makes a treaty with Jews and then breaks it. Since the breaking of the treaty in that passage results in the interruption of sacrifices at the temple, we may surmise that the treaty deals, at least in part, with temple worship.

36. After all, in the Old Testament the "tent of meeting" served as a portable temple before the erection of a permanent one.

37. When Paul spoke of the coming "day of the Lord" in 2 Thessalonians 2:2, he had in mind not a single twenty-four-hour period but an extended time frame in which certain events associated with the end occur (for more on the Old Testament background of "the day of the Lord," see chapter 2). It is the time during which God's wrath is poured out on unrepentant humanity, culminating in the salvation of his people and the destruction of his (and their) enemies. According to Paul, this time cannot begin apart from "the apostasy" and "the man of lawlessness."

38. In some first-century literature, ἀποστασις signifies political rebellion (e.g., Josephus, *Vita* § 43). For the view that Paul had in mind here a widespread political rebellion, see F. F. Bruce, *1 & 2 Thessalonians*, 167ff. As to the charges made against Paul, see the excellent book by Frank Thielman, *Paul & the Law: A Contextual Approach* (Downers Grove: InterVarsity, 1994).

39. For more on this, see Frame, *Epistles of St. Paul to the Thessalonians*, 251ff.

40. Paul used the Greek article ἡ here with ἀποστασια; hence, Paul might have had a particular "apostasy" in mind. For more on how the article should be understood, see Wallace, *Greek Grammar Beyond the Basics*, 206–54.

41. Paul is by no means alone in making the case for Jesus' deity. For example, according to John 1:1–3, Jesus (= "the word," see v. 14) is the divine agent of creation (for a brilliant exposition of this and the Greek grammar involved in the passage, see Wallace, *Greek Grammar Beyond the Basics*, 266-70), something true only of God according to the Old Testament. The night before his death Jesus asked that he might share in God's "glory" again as he had before creation (John 17:5)—a remarkable request given that Yahweh says in Isaiah 42:8 he would not share his "glory" with any other! Further, the enemies of Jesus thought he claimed to be God (see John 5:17–18;8:48-59; 10:22–31), and Thomas the disciple called him "God" after the resurrection (John 20:26-28). In Luke 8:22–56 (a passage paralleled in Matthew and Mark) Jesus' deity is suggested by his absolute authority over what is seen (the storm on the lake, Jairus's dead daughter) and what is unseen (the legion of demons, the hemorrage of the woman); over what is "natural" (death and illness) and over the "supernatural" (the unusually violent storm and the demonically strengthened man). Finally, Hebrews 1:6 quotes Psalm 104:4, where angels are enjoined to worship God, but in Hebrews the readers are invited to worship the Son of God—Jesus! The deity of Jesus is not peculiarly Pauline; it runs throughout the New Testament. As to the nature of Jesus' death, Paul said it was "for us" (Rom. 5:8). This can be understood as "for our benefit" or "in our place" (see also Rom. 3:24; 1 John 2:2; Gal. 1:4; 2:20; 1 Pet. 2:24; 3:18). At times each meaning seems to be implied. For more on the subject, see Leon Morris, *The Apostolic Preaching of the Cross* (3rd rev. ed.; Grand Rapids: Eerdmans, 1965).

42. For the texts of various creeds, see the helpful collection in Grudem's *Systematic Theology*, "Appendix 1: Historic Confessions of Faith," 1168–1207.

43. See Kenneth Scott Latourette, *A History of Christianity Volume 1: Beginnings to* A.D. *1500* (originally published by HarperSanFrancisco, 1975; rev. ed.; reprint Peabody: Prince Press, 1997), 112–235.

44. *Theological Dictionary of the New Testament* 2:364-72.

45. Ibid., 369.

46. This may, in turn, be related to the description we have in Revelation 5:14 of heaven as a place where people laud the lamb of God, saying "You are worthy to take the scroll and to open its seals, because you were slain, and with your blood you purchased men for God from every tribe and language and people and nation [ἔθνος]" (Rev. 5:9 NIV).

47. "Status of Global Mission, 1999, in context of 20th and 21st centuries," Global Evangelization Movement Website (*www.gen–werc.org*). See also Patrick Johnstone, *Operation World. The Day-by-Day Guide to Praying for the World* (Grand Rapids: Zondervan, 1993).

48. "Status of Global Mission, 1999, in context of 20th and 21st centuries," Global Evangelization Movement Website (*www.gen–werc.org*).

49. Ibid.

50. In our modern Western society—a society that places enormously high value on tolerance—Christians are sometimes resented for attempting to "impose their values" on non-Christians. Oddly, in the modern world this charge does not refer to forced conversions at the point of a sword or at the barrel of a gun, but instead, to Christians' practice of explaining their faith to non-Christians and encouraging them to convert. This effort to convert non-Christians is often based on compassion for them and, above all, on Jesus' command to proclaim the good news to those who don't yet believe (Matt. 28:18–20). Christians cannot at once be obedient to Jesus and cowed by culture; they must proclaim the gospel, even if it means they are stigmatized as "extremist," "intolerant," "religious imperialist," and the like. We should strive to share our faith in appropriate, winsome, and culturally sensitive ways—but if a culture objects to the mere notion of hearing the gospel, then like the early Christians "we must obey God rather than men" (Acts 5:29). In so doing we will assist in preparing the world for the time of Jesus' coming.

51. On the other hand, it may be that there is enough ambiguity in history to allow that some or all of these "certain signs" have been fulfilled, thus keeping alive the hope that Jesus could come at any moment. One could make a plausible—not to say convincing—argument that the Roman emperor Titus fulfilled the promise of temple desolation, that there was enough doctrinal apostasy in the early church to regard the promise of its coming as fulfilled, that the church has successfully evangelized the world, and that sufficient numbers of Jews have repented to fulfill Acts 3:19–21. I do not find this convincing, but admittedly we are severely limited in our knowledge of church history.

52. As I neared completion of this book, I discovered that Charles Hodge had reached nearly the same conclusions regarding events which must precede Jesus' return (see *Systematic Theology*, 3:792).

53. Some regard Ezekiel 37–39 as supplying firm evidence that Israel must be in the land before the end times; the evidence from Ezekiel is not convincing. (see Daniel I. Block, "Gog and Magog in Ezekiel's Eschatological Vision," in *The reader must understand. Eschatology in Bible and Theology* [eds. K. E. Brower and M. W. Elliott; Liecester: Apollos/InterVarsity, 1997], 85–116).

Chapter 8

1. For more on its history, see the dated but still useful summary in George Eldon Ladd's *The Blessed Hope: A Biblical Study of the Second Advent and the Rapture* (Grand Rapids: Eerdmans, 1956), 19–60; also Craig A. Blaising and Darrell L. Bock, *Progressive Dispensationalism* (Wheaton: Bridgepoint/Victor, 1993), 9–56.

2. For the pretribulation position, see especially J. Dwight Pentecost, *Things to Come* (Grand Rapids: Zondervan, 1958); John F. Walvoord, *The Rapture Question* (rev. and enlarged ed.; Grand Rapids: Zondervan, 1979) and his *End Times: Understanding Today's World Events in Biblical Prophecy* (Swindoll Leadership Library; Nashville: Word, 1998). For a posttribulation perspective, see Ladd, *The Blessed Hope*; Robert H. Gundry, *The Church at the Tribulation: A Biblical Examination of Posttribulationalism* (Grand Rapids: Academie/ Zondervan, 1973) and the latter's more recent *First the Antichrist: A Book for Lay Christians Approaching the Third Millennium and Inquiring Whether Jesus Will Come to Take the Church out of the World before the Tribulation* (Grand Rapids: Baker, 1997).

3. Walvoord comes very near to advancing the idea that Posttribulationalism is tantamount to heresy. He writes:

> The situation described in 2 Thessalonians 2 indicates that the teaching that the church would go through the Tribulation was already being advanced by certain teachers whom Paul opposed in this passage. It is sometimes assumed that in the early apostolic period only pure and accurate doctrine was taught. Nothing could be farther from the truth. . . . It seems quite clear that most of the heresies that later emerged in the second and third centuries had their small beginnings in the apostolic church. Most students of history agree that there was Posttribulationalism in the second century. Here in 2 Thessalonians 2, however, it becomes evident that there were already those who taught that the church would go through the tribulation, or as it is here described, the day of the Lord. It is most important to observe that Paul labeled this a false doctrine and urged the Thessalonians not to be deceived by this teaching (*The Rapture Question*, 238).

I have never heard this apparently harsh sentiment echoed by pretribulationalist friends or colleagues (see also Walvoord's *End Times,* 22).

4. In Paul Marshall's *Their Blood Cries Out*, xv.

5. Demy and Ice, *Prophecy Watch*, 100; also 101–108.

6. Walvoord, *The Rapture Question*, 172.

7. Walvoord, *End Times*, 197.

8. Walvoord, *The Rapture Question*, 246.

9. Carson, Moo, and Morris, *Introduction to the New Testament*, 347.

10. That being "asleep" can refer to death is clear from other New Testament passages that use the idiom (e.g., Acts 7:60; 1 Cor. 11:30).

11. Walvoord, *The Rapture Question*, 198–99.

12. The verb is in the aorist tense.

13. For example, Caesar Augustus was regularly welcomed on his travels, both within and outside Rome (Dio Cassius 51, 20, 2–4; Suetonius *Augustus* 53, 1). The emperor Caligula was fêted despite the fact that he was accompanying the body of Tiberius for burial (Suetonius *Caligula* 4,1). Similarly, Emperor Nero received grandiose welcomes in his travels (Suetonius *Nero* 25, 1–3). Trajan, too, was splendidly welcomed (Pliny *Panegyricus* 22, 1–5).

14. A more detailed discussion of this can be found in my "Parousia, Jesus' 'A–triumphal' Entry, and the Fate of Jerusalem (Luke 19:28–48)," 280–84.

15. Robert Gundry, *The Church and the Tribulation*, 103–105.

16. For more details relating to this argument, see Robert H. Gundry, "The Hellenization of Dominical Tradition and Christianization of Jewish Tradition in the Eschatology of 1–2 Thessalonians," *New Testament Studies* 33 (1987): 161–67. He also comments that the pic-

ture of a festive meeting with the Lord would have enhanced "the consolation he [Paul] seeks to bring the grief-stricken Thessalonians" (167).

17. Walvoord, *The Rapture Question*, 247–48.

18. Stanley Toussaint, *Behold the King: A Study of Matthew* (Portland: Multnomah, 1980), 280.

19. For more on this, see Ladd, *The Blessed Hope*, 105–20.

20. It is sometimes observed that the phrase implies Jesus wanted disciples to be entirely kept from the devil, so that when the phrase is applied to the church in Revelation 3:10 it too is promised to be kept from the time of tribulation, i.e., by the pretribulation rapture. But as noted, in the preceding comment (v. 15) Jesus explicitly asked that believers not be taken out of the world.

21. Beale, *Revelation*, 291.

22. Ibid., 292.

23. Elsewhere in Revelation we are told that the Antichrist seeks to compel worship from all people by requiring a "mark" for them "to buy and to sell" (Rev. 13:17). Many on earth get the mark; believers refuse it. But it may be that not every unbeliever gets the mark. If there are no unbelievers alive after Jesus returns.

24. In *The Pre-Wrath Rapture of the Church: A New Understanding of the Rapture, the Tribulation, and the Second Coming* (Nashville: Thomas Nelson, 1990), Marvin Rosenthal suggests the rapture takes place after a period of tribulation—hence it is in some respects posttribulational—but prior to the climactic events at the end of the tribulation depicted in Revelation 8:1, where the full fury of God's wrath is poured out on the earth. I am sympathetic to parts of his presentation, but I am not at all confident in his interpretation of Revelation 8:1 or of his insistence that God's wrath is purely an end-times phenomenon.

25. Matthew and Mark are identical at this point; Luke differs from them (compare Matt. 24:30–31, Mark 13:26–27, and Luke 21:27–28).

26. Gundry suggests that Paul's comments here may reflect the kind of teaching found in John 11:25–26, where Jesus hinted at the resurrection and translation of believers ("The Hellenization of Dominical Tradition," 164–66).

27. Revelation 19:11ff. depicts Jesus as a conquering king when he returns with "the armies of heaven" (v. 14). This last phrase probably refers to believers who accompany Jesus at his return (they are dressed in "fine linen," as is the bride of Christ in v. 8). This may be John's way of acknowledging—like Paul and Matthew before him—that Jesus makes his return with his people (as in 1 Thess. 4:17; Matt. 24:30–31; see also Col. 3:4).

28. Walvoord, *The Rapture Question*, 173.

29. For a fuller survey of opinions about the timing of the rapture, see Gleason L. Archer, Jr., Paul D. Feinberg, B. Douglas J. Moo and Richard R. Reiter, *Three Views on the Rapture: Pre, Mid, or Post-Tribulational?* (Previously titled *The Rapture*, Counterpoints Series; Grand Rapids: Zondervan, 1984/1996).

30. As noted in chapter 3, "firstfruits" were just that: the first fruits of a harvest, collected early in the season and indicative to some degree of the harvest to follow. Thus, the phrase implies that Jesus' resurrection was but the first—merely the down payment, so to speak—of a series. That a great number of people should eventually be resurrected corresponds to Old Testament teaching (Isa. 26:19; Dan. 12:1–3); it also agrees with Paul's teaching in other places (e.g., 1 Thess. 4:13–18). In verse 22 Paul observed that just as all people eventually

die by virtue of their humanity (their association with Adam), all people will eventually be raised on account of Jesus.

31. E.g., J. N. D. Kelly, *The Pastoral Epistles* (Black's New Testament Commentary xiv; Peabody: Hendrickson; reprinted from London: Black, 1960), 179–80.

32. On this theme in pre-Christian and post-Christian Jewish writings, see T. Francis Glasson, "The Temporary Messianic Kingdom and the Kingdom of God," *Journal of Theological Studies* n.s. 41 (1990): 517–25.

33. 4 Ezra is dated to the late first century A.D., but may well preserve teaching of a somewhat earlier time. So also 2 Baruch 40:3.

34. I do not take Psalm 2 to be an example of predictive prophecy (see chapter 1); hence, I think its words applied originally to David and his royal successors, not solely to the coming Messiah.

35. Amillennialism, the view that Jesus' return is simultaneous with the end and that no literal one-thousand-year reign of Christ is to be expected in the future, has a long and very respectable theological pedigree. In its favor are the following: Revelation 20:1–6 can be understood as referring to Christ's present reign from heaven and his victory over the devil at the cross; Scripture teaches only one resurrection (not the two presupposed by premillennialists); it is difficult to imagine why God would have resurrected believers living among sinners during a literal millennial reign (what purpose could be served by this?); once Jesus returns, how could some people persist in sin and ultimately follow the devil in rebelling against his rule (Rev. 20:7ff.)?; Much of the language about life in the millennium corresponds to talk about the new heavens and earth—perhaps the two are in fact one (adapted from Grudem, *Systematic Theology*, 1115–16).

36. E.g., Anthony Hoekema, *The Bible and the Future*, 227.

37. For a survey of views of the millennium, see Robert J. Clouse, *The Meaning of the Millennium* (Downers Grove: Intervarsity, 1977).

Chapter 9

1. Did the Gospel writers reliably transmit Jesus' message? On this, see Craig Blomberg, *The Historical Reliability of the Gospels* (Downers Grove: InterVarsity, 1987) and Robert H. Stein, *Gospels and Tradition: Studies on Redaction Criticism of the Synoptic Gospels* (Grand Rapids: Baker, 1991), 147–87. I take it that Jesus' message is reliably transmitted in the Gospels.

2. This is not to suggest that devout and religious people were excluded, for they were not (Luke 1:5; 2:36; 8:40; Acts 6:7).

3. "Psalm 49: A Personal Eschatology," in *"The Reader Must Understand": Eschatology in Bible and Theology* (eds. K. E. Brower and M. W. Elliott; Liecester: Intervarsity/Apollos, 1997), 76.

4. Jesus was delivered from its power through the Resurrection (Acts 2:27, 31 quoting Ps. 16:8ff.). Yet Scripture distinguishes between the hopeless condition of the wicked in Sheol and the hopeful expectation of the righteous, who look to future deliverance (e.g., Ps. 49:13–15; also Rev. 6:9–11).

5. Though the fate of angels is not our concern here, Scripture indicates that Satan and the demons, i.e., corrupt and fallen angels, are held in a sort of spiritual prison, the "abyss," before their ultimate punishment in hell (in all but one of its nine occurrences in the New Testament, the word *abyss* is associated with Satan and demons; Luke 8:31; Rev. 9:1, 2, 11;

11:7; 17:8; 20:1, 3). Second Peter 2:4 hints at the same thing, noting that God imprisoned certain evil spirits to await future judgment. Scripture also suggests that good angels may be "judged" by believers (1 Cor. 6:3).

6. It would perhaps be more accurate to say that spiritual regeneration is the dividing line between those who spend forever with God and those who do not. By "spiritual regeneration" I refer to God's impartation of new spiritual life to those he has chosen to be his own by means of his Spirit. Indeed, Paul said possession of the Spirit is the *sine qua non* of a relationship with God (Rom. 8:9). In the New Testament this regeneration is invariably accompanied by faith, so much so that Jesus and his followers urged people to believe in order to receive forgiveness and new life (e.g., John 3:16; Acts 16:31). To those readers familiar with theological debate, my comments here are related to the doctrine of salvation, particularly the debates between Calvinists, Arminians, and others. For more discussion, see Grudem and his bibliography (*Systematic Theology*, 657–720).

7. For an excellent discussion of this thorny passage, see Schreiner, *Romans,* 104–45.

8. The common linkage between *geenna* and a first-century garbage dump in the Valley of Hinnom is called into question by Peter Head, "The Duration of Divine Judgment in the New Testament," in *"The Reader Must Understand,"* 223.

9. See, for example, E. Earle Ellis, "New Testament Teaching on Hell," in *"The Reader Must Understand,"* 199–219 and the sources he cites, especially Edward Fudge, *The Fire that Consumes* (Fallbrook, Calif.:Verdict, 1982).

10. For more on this, see Hodge, *Systematic Theology*, 3:844–55; Grudem, *Systematic Theology*, 1140–53.

11. For more on the fate on nonbelievers, see Gabriel Fackre, Ronald H. Nash and John Sanders, *What About Those Who Have Never Heard? Three Views on the Destiny of the Unevangelized* (Downers Grove, InterVarsity, 1995); also *Four Views on Hell* (ed. William Crockett; Counterpoints Series; Grand Rapids: Zondervan, 1996).

12. God will judge his people some day. It is not clear precisely when this will occur. Some think it will happen before the millennium. In favor of this view are the following: (1) Believers are said to reign with Christ in the millennium (Rev. 20:4–7). This might presuppose their prior evaluation by Christ to determine their fitness to share his reign (if the parable of Luke 19:11–27 applies). Since the great white throne judgment of Revelation 20:11–15 takes place after the millennium, there must be another, earlier time at which *believers* are judged. (2) There is no mention of believers at the white throne judgment; perhaps this is because it is for nonbelievers only (the two events are distinct). (3) Similarly, that the judgment seat of Christ involves *believers* is made clear in a handful of passages. In 2 Corinthians 5:9–10 Paul said "We have as our ambition . . . to be pleasing to Him [the Lord]." He followed up this remark with the explanation, "For we must all appear before the judgment seat of Christ." Thus, the "we" who aim to please the Lord, a phrase that must apply to believers rather than non-believers, are the "we" who are evaluated by him. Paul mentioned only believers in connection with the judgment seat of Christ; hence, it is not a time when all people are judged; it is distinct from the great white throne judgment.

On the other hand, the view that believers and nonbelievers are evaluated in tandem is favored by these facts: (1) Where future judgment is mentioned, it typically involves both the righteous and the wicked (Matt. 13:24–43; Luke 19:11–27; John 5:26–29; Acts 10:42; Rom. 2:5–8; Rev. 11:18). (2) The linkage between believers reigning with Christ in the millennium and their evaluation at the judgment seat of Christ is never explicitly made; indeed, the number of those who reign with him may be limited to those martyred during the tribulation (Rev. 20:4). (3) The great white throne judgment may involve believers, for John's comment that "if anyone's name was not found written in the book of life, he was thrown into the lake of fire" (Rev. 20:15) leaves open the possibility that many people evaluated do have their names written in the book of life.

I think the judgments will occur together, but because Scripture does not address the issue extensively or often, we cannot be dogmatic about conclusions reached. In any event, doubts about the timing of judgment is overshadowed by the certainty that it *will* occur.

13. In context Paul's words here refer primarily to future evaluation of Christian teachers, yet the principle stated envisions a wider application.

14. I have been unable to locate the precise location of the quotation. It is attributed to *The Weight of Glory* in class notes on eschatology written by S. Craig Glickman at Dallas Theological Seminary.

15. For a good introductory survey of the parables, see Klyne Snodgrass, "Parable," in *Dictionary of Jesus and the Gospels* (eds. Joel B. Green, Scot McKnight; consulting ed. I. Howard Marshall; Downers Grove: InterVarsity, 1992), 591–601.

16. Peter also speaks of the "burning up" of the earth, but context indicates this "burning up" has a purgative, not annihilating, effect (2 Pet. 3:10–13). For more on this topic, see Gale Z. Heide, "What is new about the new heaven and the new earth? A theology of creation from Revelation 21 and 2 Peter 3," *Journal of the Evangelical Theological Society* 40/1 (1997): 37–56.

17. In fact, it is his overwhelming presence which makes the present heaven "heaven."

18. Robert Gundry argues that the "city" is equivalent to its people ("The New Jerusalem: People as Place, not Place for People," *Novum Testamentum* 29/3 (1987): 254–64.

19. C. S. Lewis, *The Great Divorce* (a Touchstone Book; New York: Simon & Schuster, 1996; originally published by Macmillan, 1946), 67–68.

20. For a lonely contemplation of life forever with God, see Brent Curtis and John Elridge, *The Sacred Romans, Drawing Closer to the Heart of God* (Nashville: Thomas Nelson, 1997), Chapter 12.

Appendix B

1. Most liberal-critical scholars think Daniel was written in the second century B.C.; most conservative-critical scholars think it was written much earlier, around the sixth century B.C. The argument about the fulfillment of Daniel's seventy weeks made in this chapter is not affected by the date of Daniel's composition, though I believe it was written early.

2. The nation was commanded by God to give the land a rest—to let it lie fallow—every seventh year; they did not do so.

3. The Old Testament scholar James Montgomery called Daniel 9:24–27 "the dismal swamp of O.T. criticism" (*A Critical and Exegetical Commentary on the Book of Daniel*; International Critical Commentary; Edinburgh: T & T Clark, 1927; p. 400). There is no consensus as to its interpretation, and the absolute correctness of any interpretation is put in doubt by the fact that the style of Hebrew used is difficult and there are several variations in the text itself as reflected by manuscripts and early translations. Most interpreters do agree on two points: (1) the "years" referred to are "weeks of years," and (2) the values of the years must be constant (i.e., some can't be "literal" while others are "figurative"). Various chronologies have been set forth, but to my knowledge the one that best satisfies (1) and (2) above is Hoe-

hner's (*Chronological Aspects of the Life of Christ* [Grand Rapids: Zondervan, 1977]). For an excellent, if somewhat dated, survey of positions, see *The Book of Daniel: with Introduction and Notes* by S. R. Driver (Cambridge: University Press, 1936), 143–50 (I would not agree with his conclusions, but his statement of the problem is well done).

4. Hoehner, *Chronological Aspects*, 119–28.

5. Biblical years were sometimes reckoned as having 360 days (for the detailed argument on this, see Hoehner, *Chronological Aspects*, 133–39).

6. The following is taken from Hoehner's *Chronological Aspects*, 139: 444 B.C. to A.D. 33 = 476 years (if the years are 365 days long) = 483 years (if the years are 360 days long).

7. Dating Jesus' life is a fairly complex issue, but the A.D. 33 date for his death is strongly suggested by the fact that his ministry lasted about three years (see Hoehner, *Chronological Aspects*, 55–63) and began shortly after that of John the Baptist, which began in A.D. 29 (Luke 3:1; Tiberius Caesar was made undisputed Caesar in A.D. 14).

Appendix C

1. Greg Beale, *Revelation*, 108–70. At various points I take issue with Beale. I hasten to add that he has, in my opinion, produced the finest modern commentary on Revelation, one that has greatly enhanced my understanding of and appreciation for the last book of the Bible. His commentary is recommended reading.

2. The phrase does not appear in all Greek texts of Daniel 2:45, but it may well be original in that the Hebrew phrase translated *dei genesthai* in Daniel 2:28–29 (מה די להוא) is also found in Daniel 2:45.

3. Beale, *Revelation*, 181–82.

4. *Revelation 1–5* (Word Biblical Commentary 52a; Dallas: Word), xciii.

5. The letters to churches are generally recognized as having direct relevance to specific congregations in the first century; the vision of Jesus' return is recognized as still future. Much of the debate, then, about how Revelation should be interpreted centers on Revelation 6:1–19:10 and whether events described there have already occurred. On this question, Beale concludes that Revelation is an elaborate but largely symbolic description of the inauguration of God's kingdom and its progress in the world. He labels his view "a Redemptive-Historical Form of Modified Idealism" (*Revelation*, 48). For him "no specific prophesied historical events are discerned in the book, except for the final coming of Christ to deliver and judge and to establish the final form of the kingdom in a consummated new creation—though there are a few exceptions to this rule" (ibid.). He further concludes that because the book must have had "significant relevance" for first-century Christians, a futurist interpretation— one that sees chapters 6–22 as still unfulfilled—is not tenable (ibid., 47).

Part of the problem here is defining "significant relevance." By this Beale seems to mean that if most of the events described in Revelation were not destined to be fulfilled in the near future, then the first-century audience would neither have comprehended nor been edified by reading the book. But why must the book have been, to use Beale's phrase, significantly relevant to John's first-century readers? After all, much of the Old Testament is prophetic in nature. It points to future events—events that its authors and original audiences might not have fully understood. Moreover, many passages from the book of Daniel, whose language and imagery is frequently borrowed by Revelation, would have been incomprehensible to Daniel's first readers. For example, if Daniel wrote in the fifth century B.C., would his earliest readers have realized that his prophecy of a "small horn" in Daniel 8:9 referred to

Antiochus Epiphanes IV, a political figure who was not even born until the third/second century B.C.? Not likely. And yet, from that observation we do not conclude that Daniel could not have been pointing to Antiochus in Daniel 8. A further point needs to be made here: "Relevance" is a slippery term. As a Christian I find the promise of a future judgment and resurrection to be highly relevant to the way I behave now, even though the judgment/resurrection is extended into the future. Paul exhorted the Corinthians to right living on the basis of his teaching about a coming resurrection at the return of Jesus—something that did not happen in their lifetimes (1 Cor. 15:58). Similarly, could Christians living in the sixth century A.D. not have read Revelation and, though not understanding it in all its particulars, been strengthened by its teaching that God, Jesus, and their people would ultimately be vindicated?

Some of Revelation is future (19:11–22:5); the possibility that Revelation 6:1–19:10 might refer to future events cannot be ruled out on the grounds that all John wrote must have had "significant relevance" for his original audience (and indeed, Beale does not rule out entirely the possibility of a future application for some of John's visions). Furthermore, even if we believe these chapters refer primarily to past events or are general descriptions of church history, it is possible that a future, specific, and complete fulfillment awaits. For example, in Revelation 13:15–17 we learn that:

> He [a second beast] was given power to give breath to the image of the first beast, so that it could speak and cause all who refused to worship the image to be killed. He also forced everyone, small and great, rich and poor, free and slave, to receive a mark on his right hand or on his forehead, so that no one could buy or sell unless he had the mark, which is the name of the beast or the number of his name (NIV).

To give further attention to the passage for a moment, concerning the "image of the beast," Professor Charles sees in this a reference to the ancient belief in the magical powers of statues. This belief was occasionally used by the Roman authorities to further belief in the divinity of the emperor and the imperial cult (R. H. Charles, *A Critical and Exegetical Commentary on the Revelation of St. John, with introduction, notes, and indices* [International Critical Commentary; New York: Charles Scribner's Sons, 1920], 361). He points to the Roman official Pliny's letter to the emperor Trajan in the early second century A.D. which stated that under threat of capital punishment some people denied being Christians and to establish this they "worshipped your statue and the images of the gods" (Pliny *Letters* x, 96). The emperor commended Trajan for his handling of the cases involving Christians, adding that "when a person denies himself to be a Christian and shall give proof that he is not (that is, by adoring our gods) he shall be pardoned on the ground of repentance" (Pliny *Letters* x, 97).

As to "the mark of the beast," the great classical scholar Adolf Deissmann long ago observed that the mark (*charagma*) of the beast alluded "to the custom, now known to us from the papyri, of imprinting on deeds of sale and similar documents a stamp which contained the name and regnal year of the Emperor" (*Light from the Ancient East: The New Testament Illustrated by Recently Discovered Texts of the Graeco–Roman World* [trans. Lionel R. M. Strachan; Peabody: Hendrickson, 1995; reprinted from the 1927 edition originally published by George H. Doran Co., New York], 341). But what about the mark on the brow and right hand of the person? (Rev. 13:16). Is there any ancient example of this? In all likelihood the mark is figurative; it is a deliberate parody of John's comment in Revelation 7:3 that God's servants will get a mark on their foreheads. John seems to be saying that Satan tries to mimic

God by identifying his servants in the same way God did. We do not find a literal, historical fulfillment of the prophecy in the past; it is not clear that we should expect to find one in the future.

When it comes to the identity of the beast itself (Rev. 13:1ff.), most commentators think the beast is the Roman Empire as represented in the person of the emperor (H. B. Swete, *The Apocalypse of St. John* [London: Macmillan, 1906], 160–66; Charles, *Revelation*, 344–46; Robert H. Mounce, *The Book of Revelation,* 244; David Aune, *Revelation 6–16* [Word Biblical Commentary 52b; Nashville: Thomas Nelson, 1998], 732–36; Beale, *Revelation*, 717). However, Professor Beckwith wrote long ago:

> Conclusive as is the evidence that the heads of the Beast are the Roman emperors in the office as Satan's agents in the war against God's children, it is however clear that this application of the symbolism does not cover the whole significance of the Beast. Activities and attributes are assigned to him which cannot be predicated of any Roman emperor in his ordinary human personality, as is also a career falling after the destruction of the Roman empire. . . . But as one who, like the head wounded unto death and restored . . . and who is to marshal all the armies of the world against the spiritual hosts led out of heaven by the Messiah, 19:11–19, the Beast will then be more than man, he will join with his human personality a mighty demonic power. In that manifestation he will form the last great human leader of the enemies of God (Isbon T. Beckwith, *The Apocalypse of John. Studies in introduction with a critical and exegetical commentary* [New York: Macmillan, 1919], 397. See also Ladd, *Revelation*, 176–77).

The description of the beast of Revelation 13 would have originally applied to the Roman Empire and its leaders, but that would not necessarily have exhausted its meaning; it might also serve as a type or model of a "beast" yet to come. This is especially so when we remember that the beast of Revelation 13 is eventually cast into the lake of fire by Jesus at his return (Rev. 19:19–21)—a fate very remarkably similar to the one awaiting "the man of lawlessness" who will be slain by the Lord Jesus at his coming (2 Thess. 2:8 NIV).

6. Beale, *Revelation*, 52.

Appendix D

1. *Matthew,* Expositor's Bible Commentary: Volume 8 (Grand Rapids: Zondervan, 1984), 491. For a good scholarly bibliography on the section, see Donald A. Hagner, *Matthew 14–28* (Word Biblical Commentary 33b; Dallas: Word, 1995), 682–83; also 685–86; 692; 696–97; 703–04; 708. For the most technical English language analyses of the materials, see G. R. Beasley-Murray, *Jesus and the Last Days: The Interpretation of the Olivet Discourse* (Peabody: Hendrickson, 1993) and David Wenham, *The Rediscovery of Jesus' Eschatological Discourse* (in Gospel Perspectives: Volume 4; Sheffield: JSOT, 1984).

2. Carson, *Matthew*, 491–95. For a more recent survey, see David L. Turner, "The Structure and Sequence of Matthew 24:1–41: Interaction with Evangelical Treatments," *Grace Theological Journal* 10 (1989): 3–27.

3. As Hagner notes, "The conceptual unity of the parousia and the end of the ages is indicated by the single Greek article governing both" (*Matthew 14–28*, 688). For more on the Greek grammar involved in the phrase τί τὸ σημεῖον τῆς σῆς παρουσίας καὶ συντελείας τοῦ αἰῶνος, see Wallace, *Greek Grammar Beyond the Basics*, 270–90.

4. Some writers combine the two by suggesting the events of A.D. 70 are a model for events in a later tribulation, both of which are, to some extent, in view in the passage. I do not find their arguments persuasive.

5. Gundry seems to prefer this meaning (*Matthew*, 482).

6. One could reply to this objection by saying that a careful reading of Matthew's *context* shows that Jesus must be referring to events after A.D. 70. In Matthew 24:4–13 Jesus listed events and circumstances that do not signal the end; however, in verse 14 he described something that does point to the end: "And this gospel of the kingdom shall be preached in the whole world for a witness to all the nations, and then the end shall come." We could then infer that the appearance of the "abomination of desolation" in verse 15 occurs only after the gospel has been preached everywhere (cf. Matt. 28:18–20; Acts 1:8).

7. On this, see Richard A. Horsley, "Popular Messianic Movements around the Time of Jesus," *Catholic Biblical Quarterly* 46 (1984): esp. 480–83.

8. If the term is restricted to referring to events around A.D. 70, then we are again faced with the question, "Was Jesus right to say he would come 'immediately' after the tribulation?" But it may be that the Greek word translated "immediately" (*eutheōs*) in Matthew 24:29 has greater flexibility in meaning than we might at first suppose. When we hear the word *immediately* we often take it to mean "without delay" or "occurring in the next moment." But *eutheōs* can have a somewhat broader range of meaning. To be sure, it often does mean "in the next moment" as in Matthew 8:3; 14:31; and 20:34. But in several other places it likely means something like "next" or "the next thing you know," without the denotation of chronological immediacy.

For example, in the parable of the soils Jesus spoke of certain seeds as springing up "immediately" (Matt. 13:5). And yet a certain process must be in view—one that involves a delay in time (it takes a while for seed to sprout). Similarly, after Jesus had fed five thousand men and the excess food was collected, he and the disciples "immediately" got into a boat (Matt. 14:22). Does this mean there were no good-byes or thank-yous or questions from the crowd? Not necessarily; it probably means that the next significant moment for the narrative was Jesus' ordering the disciples into the boat. In Matthew 25:14–30 Jesus told the parable of the talents. After the master distributed the talents to his servants, he "immediately" went on his journey (v. 15; some versions put the word *immediately* into v. 16). Again, does this suggest that there was no good-bye, no final meal, no last embrace? No, it means instead that the next significant event in the narrative was the departure of the master. When we take these uses of *eutheōs* into account in thinking about Matthew 24:29, we can see that after the destruction of Jerusalem (an event asked about in v. 3 and answered in vv. 15–28), the next (i.e., *eutheōs*) significant event (significant in the sense of being related to the question about Jesus' return asked in v. 3) is the coming of the Son of Man (vv. 29–31). This understanding of Matthew 24:29 may be reinforced by the fact that in place of Matthew's "immediately" the parallel passage in Luke speaks of "the times of the Gentiles" (Luke 21:24)—an extended time of Jewish tribulation. For more on this, see George C. Fuller, "The Olivet Discourse: an Apocalyptic Timetable," *Westminster Theological Journal* 28 (1966): 157–63.

9. In contrast to Matthew, Luke 21:5–28—the major apocalyptic discourse of the third Gospel—is more easily understood. Matthew 24:4–28 approximates Luke 21:5–24 and Matthew 24:29–31 parallels Luke 21:25–28. The two passages are complementary.

INDEX OF ANCIENT SOURCES